Praise for Heartbroken

"With lyrical prose and startling honesty, Laura Pratt writes about a familiar condition. Who among us has not been heartbroken? But despite the common thread running through this memoir, I've never read anything like it. There is such rare beauty in the candid generosity of Pratt's words as she invites us to indulge our broken hearts, then take the pieces and build something new with the knowledge she has shared. Many will feel seen and comforted by this beautiful work of emotional art."
—Marissa Stapley, *New York Times* bestselling author of *Lucky*

"In *Heartbroken*, Laura Pratt probes the bruise of romantic despair with intellect, levity and courage. The book that results is as mesmerising, gut-wrenching and agonisingly poignant as the subject of heartbreak itself."
    —Leah McLaren, author of *Where You End and I Begin*

"Beautifully lyrical, astonishingly honest and sparkling with humour and insight, *Heartbroken* changed the way I think about love and loss. In it, Laura Pratt gathers poets, philosophers, songwriters and scientists across the ages to help her explore and map the heart's deepest valleys. It is an achingly generous, riveting tale filled with solace and grace."
                —Kim Pittaway, co-author of *Toufah: The Woman Who Inspired an African #MeToo Movement*

"Make no mistake, Pratt, like Elizabeth Smart, will break your heart with her raw-to-the-bone confessional. But this writing is 'smart' in another way, teasing out the literary history, psychology, and physiology of heartbreak, and the lessons learned from her chosen 'high frequency life.'"

—Harry Thurston, author of
Lost River: The Waters of Remembrance

"Laura Pratt is a marvelous writer. If you're reeling from a fresh heartbreak—or still mystified by the impact of an ancient one—*Heartbroken* will help you heal it. This is an astonishingly generous and profoundly intelligent book filled with arresting insights. It lets you in on the author's own exquisite heartache and reckoning with it, while allowing you to more deeply understand your own relationship with loves lost. I devoured it."

—Haley McGee, author of *The Ex-Boyfriend Yard Sale*

Heartbroken

Heartbroken

Field Notes on a Constant Condition

Laura Pratt

Random House Canada

Library and Archives Canada Cataloguing in Publication
Title: Heartbroken : field notes on a constant condition / Laura Pratt.
Names: Pratt, Laura, 1967- author.
Identifiers: Canadiana (print) 20220255857 | Canadiana (ebook) 2022025589X | ISBN 9781039005761 (softcover) | ISBN 9781039005778 (EPUB)
Subjects: LCSH: Pratt, Laura, 1967- | LCSH: Separation (Psychology) | LCSH: Grief. | LCSH: Dating (Social customs)
Classification: LCC BF575.G7 P73 2023 | DDC 155.9/3—dc23

Text design: Lisa Jager
Cover design: Lisa Jager
Image credits: Kai Wai Wong / Getty Images, Crazy nook / Adobe Stock Images

Printed in Canada

10 9 8 7 6 5 4 3 2 1

Penguin
Random House
RANDOM HOUSE CANADA

To you, if you've also been broken.

Contents

Prologue
The End

"It's over," he said, and pitched himself out of the car, even though I'd barely come to a stop outside Union Station. I can't imagine he kissed me. But I can't imagine he didn't. He always kissed me. And then he was gone like he meant it, tearing across Front Street, all rage and long limbs.

In eight minutes, his train to Montreal would lurch away from the platform and my world would cleave into two. Unless I could hold it together.

I swung the minivan around a corner into an underground parking lot across from the train station. It was midday on a Toronto Tuesday and the place was packed. Seven minutes and not a spot in sight. I abandoned the vehicle at a crazy angle and ran up the ramp without breathing and into the January sunlight and across the road and through the heavy doors. The ticket lobby was vast and limestone-slick, glinting bronze under light pouring in from the Roman bath windows at either end of its hundred-foot vaulted ceiling. It was enormous and swimming with souls, each trailing their own carry-ons and crises.

We were there too, imprinted from the hundreds of passages we'd made to each other's cities for all those ecstatic biweekly sojourns, the legacy of our pyrotechnic chemistry still messing with the lights. For six years I'd occupied this space in a state of anticipation and joy; now it was the opposite.

He had a two-minute lead on me. The possibility that I might've lost him already prickled my synapses, but I snuffed it out. I tore through the Great Hall, skating along its Tennessee marble toward the wide staircase that led down to the trains. He was at the bottom, his duffle bag across his taut shoulders, his posture concrete. I called out to him. He turned. His eyes were mean. Reflected in them, I could see the email he'd found that morning on my computer, a too-effusive note of gratitude to a former male colleague for bolstering me during a rough patch that had sparked his jealousy.

My eyes overflowed as I careened down the stairs, panting and saying, "I'm sorry!" again and again. He just looked at me, his winter coat rising and falling with his breath. I began to cry. People's heads jerked up and they stole glimpses of us. We were a developing scene beside the ticket counter.

He didn't budge. My stomach clenched in disbelief. He had flown, so I would fight. I would shame him with my drama, a public display that insisted on compassion. But his wrist was steel when I touched it.

How I had loved that skin. I remembered the first moment I caught sight of it, a tease through his open collar as he approached in a hotel parking lot at our very start. I remembered thinking: *I can't wait to be with that.* Now there were five minutes left, tops.

He turned and hustled down the next set of stairs to the sub-basement, a holding pen for passengers organized according to their destinations. I followed, sobbing, to the queue for his train, which ended outside the women's washroom. "Don't go!" My ragged horribleness, all snot and misery, was a shame. The people around us—checking their phones, living their lives—adjusted their energy to accommodate ours. There wasn't a soul in that cavernous underground cell who wasn't tuned in to our performance. We were a farce.

He looked at me, his eyes narrowed. "No more," he said in a voice conscious of all that humanity. "I'm done." I knew that tone. Sam could accelerate rapidly and we'd sped before. But now he was on fire. Something about *this time* was making the roots of my hair ache.

Trains rumbled above.

I pushed in to fill up all the space beside him. I pleaded with him with my voice and my eyes. I said, "I'm so sorry!" in great, heaving gulps. But I meant: *Save me. I am slipping under the waves. You are my life raft. Do not let me sink to the bottom of the ocean.* My hair was plastered to my face with my tears; he stepped away from my pull. "Please don't go!" I said. All the eyes in that sub-basement flicked to me. The curious, the entertained, the sorry.

"I am leaving now and this is goodbye," he hissed. He was beautiful, his features at their peak in his rage. Ironically, his smile lines were their most pronounced when he was pissed.

"Will this be the last time I see you?" I asked. It was a tectonic question. A final slam against his resistance. Having to say so out loud would shock him. Surely.

He told me, "Yes. It will be the last time you see me."

He used to give me the scuba-diving signal we'd learned in Cuba that lets your partner know you're watching out for them. *See me?* he would indicate across prickly public spaces. *I've got you.* His gaze now was vacant. He'd withdrawn his investment.

The crowd leaned in for my response to his terrible declaration and I did not disappoint. I reached for his face and wept, never not looking at him. And then I paused a shuddering moment in that cold, final place and took him in. Just in case.

That he allowed all this theatre terrified me. I felt, inside that drama, inside that station, worse than I had ever felt. *How could he be leaving? How could we be ending? How could one person lose an entire other person, a person who was so essential?* The vastness of the questions floored me, flattened me to the tiles outside the women's washroom.

Boarding began, and the underground procession whose ranks included a furious man who was a container of all our life together, all the moments that were ours alone, readied to board a train. Two minutes.

"Please," I wailed. But the line's momentum pulled him with it and he was swept up in the rolling luggage. "Don't go!" I choked from beside the women's washroom, from the saddest patch of the black universe. But he did.

And so I sank down down, into the waves, no longer attached to him or anything. I could be swept into terrifying anywhere now that nothing secured me to this earthly plane. I was at everything's mercy, churning away from what gave me my shape. I was unmoored.

I don't remember if he looked back. But I can't imagine he wouldn't have. He always looked back.

This was where heartbreak began.

I

Heartbreak

Like disappointment and decline, heartbreak is universal. All of our histories are littered with it, in forms and degrees. If you're alive on this earth, you know heartbreak—or will. Death and loss have much to answer for. Everything that lives, dies. Everything we have, we can lose. Friendships, parents, love. When I was twelve and just beginning to notice patterns, I wrote *Nothing human is constant* on my binders in ballpoint—early inklings of my central script.

Romantic heartbreak—the brand typically intended by the word—distinguishes itself from other sorrows with its roots, which are in rejection and dismissal. Here is the conscious exit of another human who has free will to do otherwise. Here is the loss not only of a primary partner and best friend but of self-worth. Of care and concern and support and comfort. Of reassurance and structure and ease. Here is the loss of peace.

And so this is romantic heartbreak's grim message: you are not precious, and must process this sentence on your untethered own. Worse, you have to do it in a world whose horror-struck populace will undermine and misunderstand your heartbreak from the minute you start talking about it. It's not okay to admit you feel incomplete without a partner, even though, for most of human history, we've organized ourselves in pairs. If depression is an illness, a passive misfortune, heartbreak is a violation of societal expectation, a failure to do for yourself what people are supposed to be able to do for themselves.

The public disdain is terrible but also dangerous, because it trivializes this massive human experience that kills a piece of a person forever. In his 2011 account of his baby's death in the *New Yorker*, Aleksandar Hemon describes the permanence of his grief like this: "Her indelible absence is now an organ in our bodies, whose sole function is a continuous secretion of sorrow." Same thing with romantic heartbreak. *Indelible. Continuous.* People imagine its resolution at their peril. You can get by and even conceal your wound from casual observers, but the only hope for the purported (according to a survey by YouGov, a British market research and data analytics firm) 85 percent of the female and 73 percent of the male population who have suffered heartbreak is the opposite—not trivializing but acknowledging it. Wrapping their arms around its misery and trying to understand it.

Heartbreak is a turbulent passage—a time of loss and mourning and agonizing reflection. People's encounters with it are as different as people. There is fixation and suicide;

there is emerging acceptance and enlightened outlook. And there is madness enough to fire a factory. When Edvard Munch's lover left him, he said: "I had the misfortune to suffer passionate love . . . and for several years I was close to insanity." Heartbreak invokes grief and ego and obsession. Music and place and time. And memory—heartbreak is so much about memory.

Sam and I had been together a little more than six years, a long-distance relationship that had seen me living with my four children in Toronto and him living with his half-dozen guitars in Montreal. Ours had been a fairly typical relationship, but it was made romantic and exceptional by our physical separation and sensitive personalities. That it blew up wasn't a surprise. We kept our temperature up the whole of our time together; the pot was bound to boil over.

After Sam's train departed that Tuesday afternoon, I retrieved my van and drove home inside a psychic tunnel. When I got there, I hunted for a guitar pick. Sam, whose fingers always leapt along an imaginary fretboard, shed picks like pennies. He was Chris Robinson, hanging together with E strings, leaving scraps of his music everywhere.

I found a pick right away in the lint trap of my dryer—a plastic, pear-shaped reason to believe—and pushed it into my pocket. My fingers loved it, in lieu of him, and when I stroked it, it was like I was touching Sam's most precious quality. Later, after telling my children—aged seventeen, fifteen, thirteen and eleven—about what happened and watching sorrow swamp their faces, I fell into the imprint he'd left in my bed and put the pick under his pillow. I pressed my palm into its flat green comfort and floated out to sea, inhaling six years of him off the pillowcase.

The next morning and every one after, I plucked the pick up from my bed and drove it deep in my pocket. And the next night and every one after, I took it out of my pocket and placed it back under my pillow. When I went to the gym to outrun myself, I would place the pick in the bottom of my running shoe. When I showered, I rested it on the side of the tub.

One middle of the night after Sam left, I couldn't find the pick beneath any pillow. I sprang out of bed and turned on the light and yanked off the duvet. It wasn't there. I crawled around my box spring, compelling my fingers to make contact with this plastic talisman in the carpet, despairing at the symbolism if it was lost.

It was nowhere, and I was ruined. I restored the darkness to my room, this site of his last showing, and collapsed back into bed, now utterly alone. I was a bobbing dinghy on the curving horizon, awaiting the gust of wind that would complete my obliteration. I knew my children might wake and hear their mummy howling through the upstairs winter darkness, stealing all the security from their world. But I was powerless, turning and turning in the widening gyre. From outside my window, the moon looked in on the disaster. And I felt bad for having lost something else.

And then I heaved myself out of bed and turned on the light and flipped the mattress against the wall with the strength people discover in crisis—a mother lifting a car off her child, a passerby rescuing an adventurer from under the ice. And on its edge inside the bed frame's steel perimeter, I found the guitar pick.

It was a sign, I was certain. That some revelation was at hand. That he'd be back. That there would be another train, this one returning him from Montreal. I replaced my mattress and crawled back where Sam used to be, my fingers clutching the darling plastic piece of him.

The moon, still watching from my window, finally saw me sleep.

When you experience psychological shock, adrenalin floods your bloodstream and your hippocampus flies into fast, thoughtless action. Nature protects you in the aftermath of an explosion, filling your brain with cotton batting even as your lungs are hemorrhaging and your organs emptying into the air. Here is a third option to trauma's fight-or-flight ultimatum: freeze.

That means the black bear may be tearing into your flesh, the rapist may be crushing your bones, but you're a block of cement. Maybe you're even smiling, to minimize trauma's reach down your throat, because humans are strange that way. Splitting is a psychological mechanism that defends the brain against intolerable situations, a mad dash for the safe harbour of self-deception, where endorphin waves so satisfyingly crash.

My friends and family, watching my grocery shopping and how I got my kids to school, couldn't have imagined the emotion that roared behind my rote exterior then, how my insides were on fire. My cool outside concealed that I suffered the way Sappho did when she begged Aphrodite "to come to me again and release me from this want past bearing." But I was split in two.

On the first of February, four days after Sam left, I sent him an email. I had breathed in the interval. I had slept and fed my children. I had dressed and driven. And that was everything. I had never taken my thoughts from him.

"It is quiet now," I said. "Tonight, this minute, this hour, ever since you left. My life is incredibly quiet."

It was his birthday, which upped our melodrama. "I wish we could have been together," I wrote. "I wish we could have spent the day hacking through the jungle we built around ourselves." I actually thought this would be an attractive idea to him. I wanted to believe a tender part of him would pipe up from the pit with: *Whatever it takes, let's work it out.* I was so desperate for relief.

It was different from what I'd said the last time I wasn't there for his special day. But two years earlier, when he'd turned forty-two, our separation had been a matter of practicalities—it had been my weekend with the kids—not because the world had cracked down the middle. "Happy birthday, my sweet man," I'd emailed then, light as a feather. "I am so sorry I can't be there with you. One day there'll be no more birthdays apart."

But now Sam was forty-four and had fled and I was telling him I missed him eight times in a tumbling note I didn't proofread before pressing Send, to exploit its drama before everything returned to what it had been. I didn't believe it yet, that he was gone. The idea was too big to be true. Another fight was all. A bad one, like in the summer when I'd punched his arm on the highway, where we'd had to drive from the cottage to spare the kids our drama (though I could no longer remember what set it off). But just a fight. He'd be back. I told someone I'd been doing some writing for in Montreal that I would be off-line for a bit, but would be available again soon.

I was confused. Sad but also angry. When I looked back across the last several months of our relationship, I could see him withdrawing grumpily and couldn't imagine the reason for it. "You pulled further and further away," I accused. "You were so often mad. You'd pick me up from the train station mad and then be mad at me if I fell asleep in the movies or wanted to stay in for the night. Everything became fraught. There was ammunition all around us.

"Of course I think about you constantly," I told him, sounding like a Victorian character. "As I know you do me."

But beneath the bravado was this brewing panic. What if we *were* done? What about the waitress at La Belle Province who always liked my hair and the chairlift at Mont-Tremblant and the fact that we knew every little thing about each other? What about the worlds we'd created and occupied so completely? What would become of all *that*? The private jokes and secret triggers and *all the memory*. Where would that get absorbed?

I decided it had simply changed forms, this thing we cultivated for six years, this ball we kept aloft. I thought about energy, which scientists insist hunkers inside all things. Objects at rest. Trees. Bacteria, the weather, even emptiness, all are energy. Dr. Richard Feynman, who won the Nobel

Prize in Physics for his contributions to quantum electrodynamics, once said that "the energy in a cubic metre of space is enough to boil all the oceans of the world."

And so love is surely energy too. Love is surely the highest form of energy, vibrating at the highest frequency in its ping-pong passage through virtual quantum particles, which exist only theoretically and so can't be seen. Love is surely the biggest thing we can't see, this precious current streaming between two people, their interacting vitalities creating a new vitality, theirs alone. Surely there are more than 100 billion of these unique energies out there, one for every soul who's ever lived, one for every love affair that's ever been, even if it is no more. Surely they buzz around outside our ken, lifting the leaves, driving the rain, igniting the fireflies.

The endurance of love's energy is one of heartbreak's most tremendous gifts.

Before Barney Clark, a Seattle dentist with end-stage heart failure, went in to have his heart replaced by a machine in a Utah hospital in 1982, his wife reportedly asked the doctors, "Will he still be able to love me?" Such is the assumed relationship between love and the heart, the organ that's more metaphor than any other. The heart is the seat of emotion, the scarlet stamp of Valentine's Day, the bloody shorthand for all our passion. Dr. Sandeep Jauhar, an American cardiologist and author of *Heart: A History*, is good with that. He thinks it's time doctors and philosophers meet in the middle on matters of this circulatory centrepiece. When our hearts snap with fear or rupture with grief, our emotional lives jump the divide, crossing into our physical lives. Devastated, the nerves command the blood vessels to constrict, and the heart races in response. Blood pressure skyrockets, breath quickens, pain roars.

That's what happened to a bunch of people on Japan's biggest island after the Chūetsu earthquake struck in 2004, killing sixty-eight and injuring almost five thousand. When researchers checked a month after the tremors, they found a twenty-four-fold increase in a condition called takotsubo cardiomyopathy among survivors, especially folks who lived near the epicentre. The *takotsubo* references the round-bottomed Japanese pot whose profile the typically V-shaped left ventricle, your heart's chief pumper, adopts when your emotions get shaken up. In a 2019 TED Talk, Jauhar projected photos of normal and grieving hearts; the swollen latter were bulbs of pain. More than 90 percent of the syndrome's victims are female, between fifty-eight and seventy-five years old, sometimes misdiagnosed with cardiac arrest. Women reeling from heartbreak are given clot-preventing antiplatelets and sent home.

But such siloed thinking's on the way out, says Jauhar. "What many doctors have concluded is what I, too, have learned in my nearly two decades as a heart specialist: the emotional heart intersects with its biological counterpart in surprising and mysterious ways." While the affliction most know as "broken heart syndrome" typically resolves itself within a few weeks, there's no question of extreme cases. Any enlightened physician could tell you as much: heartbreak can kill you, drowning your heart in a deluge of stress hormones.

Studies uncover healthy patients on the brink of cardiac failure because they've been slammed by bad news. The hormonal flood, shrug the doctors, overwhelms the organ's ability to keep pumping. Various researchers have published papers on people's risk of dying after losing a spouse, including a 2014 study in the *Journal of Public Health* that found that, within the first three months of their spouse's death, people were 66 percent more likely to die. "More die of heartbreak than anything else," author Saul Bellow said in his 1987 book *More Die of Heartbreak*.

One need only look to the monkeys, whose serious emotions make them likely stand-ins for humans. When primates are separated from loved ones, say multiple studies, their cortisol levels spike and their nerve endings droop, proving the importance of social bonds to our species' endurance. The pain this super-stress combo inflicts on the lonely animals ensures the perpetuation of our existence. You're more likely to survive if somebody loves you.

And even if you do outlive heartbreak, there's no escaping its corporal consequences. American social psychologist Naomi Eisenberger is one of the scientists who discovered that the part of your brain that lights up when you're physically hurt is the same part that lights up when you suffer so-called "social pain" from rejection, exclusion or loss.

But heartbreak's assault to the spirit is its deepest wound. Its mass fills you, crowding everything else from your consciousness. When you're heartbroken, it's your identity. To what degree it consumes you depends upon a lot of things.

Luck. Circumstance. Resilience. You can never *really* recover from heartbreak—a critical truth. But you can reach an understanding of it.

"The best thing for being sad is to learn something," T.H. White wrote in *The Once and Future King*. "That is the only thing that never fails. You may grow old and trembling in your anatomies, you may lie awake at night listening to the disorder in your veins, you may miss your only love. . . . There is only one thing for it then—to learn."

Heartbreak has much to teach us. To have smaller expectations. To endure the unendurable. To live with loss. "Heartbreak asks us not to look for an alternative path, because there is no alternative path," wrote poet David Whyte. "It is an introduction to what we love and have loved, an inescapable and often beautiful question, something and someone that has been with us all along, asking us to be ready to let go of the way we are holding things, and preparation perhaps for the last letting go of all." Another gift: how heartbreak hardens us for other disasters.

Before that wintry ending, I hadn't known heartbreak. I'd had a youthful marriage that lasted half a year, but its demise had seemed natural, the mature descent to the juvenile incline. The ending of a fourteen-year relationship that produced four kids was harder—but it was still more bend than break. Our children's existence guaranteed enough of ours, together, to avoid the snap that comes at the end of things. And then came Sam, and, later, proof that heartbreak isn't about one person's personality, irrespective of a partner, but a pairing.

Our romance was astonishing for lots of reasons, but especially for the access it allowed each of us to the other. Our love ran deep, like the caves we scuba dived in Cuba, and both ways. No one had ever loved me—or let me love him—like Sam. I always felt profoundly connected to him. And to myself, in his company, which was an exceptional thing. I fell in love twice inside this connection, with him and with me. He encouraged the parts of me I loved best: creativity, gratitude, joy. When I was with him, I lifted out of my maternal frame of soberness and duty and submission, into a space where I could just be, alongside this exciting companion who delivered me into a world of music and cool, assertion and swagger. With Sam, I was a version of myself that appealed to me. I liked to think he'd say the same of me and how my cultured, domestic life enriched his solitude. We each reinvented the other, which is a terrific act of love. When he left, I lost him *and* that version of me, so the loss was double. And there's no question that the potency of our romance upped the potency of our loss. "There is only one thing left for us," Héloïse told Abelard penitently at the forced demise of a legendary love story they felt was an offence to God. "That in our utter ruin the pain to come will be no less than the love that has gone before."

When his love had been gone eleven silent days, I wrote Sam again. It was midnight on a February Friday, and my birthday this time. I was at McDonald's, where I'd come to get out of the house so as to spare my children another encounter with their raggedy mother. My head was too full of blood to make room for the tragedy of their immersion in this.

In this note, I told him I missed him ten times. I told him I was sorry, too, for sins specified and not. And I asked for another chance. "I am broken in two over here in Toronto," I said. "I feel abandoned by you, rejected. Not fought for. Please don't snuff us out."

I wept when I wrote these words, which looked so flat on the screen. Beside my laptop I had a stack of paper napkins and a Diet Coke. No food. I hadn't eaten since Sam left. I was slumped in a yellow vinyl corner booth, against the window that looked out at the intersection where I'd once watched cars crash, seen a guy fly into the air. Now it was me who skidded along the pavement, a smash of bones and flesh.

But on this birthday night I was focused on this letter, which would save me, which *had to* save me. I had gone too long without his voice and his company and his care. I was in trouble.

I called him "my dear sweet only love." I said, "I wish I could unzip your chest and clear out all the resentment and zip it up once there's only love left." I quoted lines from songs that were ours—emotional turf. I acknowledged that I'd noticed he'd grown unhappy in recent months. And I charged headlong into the email he'd found that Tuesday morning. The intimacy had both wounded Sam and sparked a jealous fuse. It was on the strength of this discovery that he'd angrily declared his exodus.

I copped to the crime in this note and, as I had in the train station, begged forgiveness. I called it "highly inappropriate" and said I was "sincerely sorry" for how he must have felt reading my words. But I didn't spend a lot of time on it. I was shocked that Sam had gone through my email alone in the house that morning, and embarrassed by this personal, guilty find. Also, I knew he'd absconded for more than that, that we were bigger than this petty wrongdoing. The disconnect made the world feel out of proportion. "You left me so easily!" I keened.

I could not say if anyone in that cold midnight restaurant noticed me bent over this assignment. I was oblivious in my corner, a terrifying dementor, bawling, her long, dreadful fingers tapping such misery into a keyboard. I emptied the whole of our story across the Formica, the Saturday night hockey pitchers and the curving mountain drives and the times I'd wept with joy in his bed. The ancient private jokes we'd delighted in retelling. Our shared love of absurdity and laughter. Our TV shows and our families and the rituals that propped up my life. The sweet armfuls of *us* we'd each been carrying around for more than six years.

The email was 6,367 words long. I could have flown to Montreal in the time it took to read it. I was supposed to be there anyway, celebrating our birthday weekend with all that city's enchantment in my mouth, inside my dear mountain's embrace. But I'd had to let that plane ticket lapse. When I'd written the airline seeking compassion, they'd responded apologetically, but said heartbreak did not qualify for a refund.

"I am heading out into this lonely birthday without you," I said at the close of my letter, when I'd sat in the yellow vinyl booth for more than an hour, almost two, sobbing into all those paper napkins, channelling despair and my amazement at his non-stop silence through my fingers.

"It is so cold, baby," I wrote. "My heart is so heavy. Please honour our sweet, deep emotion with another look."

And then I pressed Send and snapped my laptop shut. I gathered up my sodden napkins and stumbled into the indifferent universe, hoping enough time had elapsed to spare my children my disconsolate apparition, now one year older.

Sam wrote back to me a day later—to preserve my birthday, he said—to say he was done with us. He was sorry, he said, but sure. We hadn't been any good since the cottage in the summer, since the fight in the car when I'd hammered his arm. He wrote that he was sad to be a constant source of disappointment to me for not moving to Toronto, that each day he stayed in Montreal felt like failure to him.

And that he'd miss me, he wrote that, which elated me. His final gesture.

What happened next on that extraordinary day after I turned forty-seven was I went to ash. The last scrap of my juicy soul was consumed in a blast of supercharged heat and sent fluttering onto a grey mineral hill of who I used to be. It was an early deposit in the cinders of my heartbreak, part of the dense foundation that would collapse under its own gravity as a thousand strata accumulated on its back.

For seventeen days in the summer of 2018, a mother orca carried her dead infant in the icy crest of the Salish Sea, nosing the calf, Tali, whose life was half an hour long, above the surface in a thousand-mile tour of Pacific grief. Watching from the intersection of science, spirituality and theology, the world understood heartbreak's inevitability. The magpies who bury their dead under twigs. The trembling dog who sobs in the shelter when his best bud abandons him. The peccaries who sleep next to their deceased friends. They are proof of heartbreak's most fundamental underpinnings. They are comfort for any sad human who's navigated the same emotional waters.

The Cambridge Declaration on Consciousness in non-human animals had confirmed the biological fundament of heartbreak six summers earlier. In this groundbreaking publication, scientists trampled an easy alibi with the assertion of something astonishing: animals experience moment-to-moment consciousness, just like us. Their brain and body functions hum and surge on neurobiological and hormonal readouts. They register grief. They experience heartbreak.

The news, which confirms our common suffering, which increases support for the burden, is strangely reassuring. There is always succour in knowing we're the same as others. If I can break, so can you. It helps make you compassionate and speeds the race to intimacy with the humanity you encounter in its wake. The Buddhists have a word for that. *Bodhichitta* offers enlightenment as a package deal: for the victim, yes, but also for anyone she encounters. We achieve bodhichitta when we've been cracked open by life—heartbreak's a fast track— and connect with others while our guts are exposed. Stunned by our anguish, goes the philosophy, we realize others have suffered the same. For many of us, our impulse shifts with this—and we run back into the burning building. "Instead of transcending the suffering of all creatures, we move toward the turbulence and doubt," writes American Buddhist nun Pema

Chödrön. In a state of bodhichitta, we are one, deeply connected by our common humanity. Another of heartbreak's gifts.

He was still gone on Valentine's Day. He had not said another word to slacken the ropes of his email from five days before. He had not texted me or written me or phoned me. He had not mounted the creaking steps of my porch, a surprise visitor from Montreal ferried by remorse and regret.

I woke up crying. It was dark and bitterly cold. The temperature had not topped freezing for four weeks. It was way too early to get up, but I was in free fall and had nowhere to land. Everything familiar and reliable that had given me scaffolding and shape and permanence had been snatched away. There was only my dog, Presli, in this black universe and I soaked her fur with my sadness.

And then I found fragile purchase. All my plasma, paint-peeling from my insides like a chemical attack, galvanized around an idea. I would phone him. *I would ask him to come back.* Why I hadn't thought of that was insane, and the insanity delighted me. Maybe it would be all it would take. To hear my voice. *Of course it would!* It *was* Valentine's Day. And he was the love of my life.

The plan bought me the strength to creak from my bed into the first aching minutes of the day. I made my children heart-shaped breakfasts and nestled stuffed-animal Valentines beside their plates—something to hug when Mummy slipped into the darkness. Then, I waited. As much as I could, I surrendered my attention to the merciful distraction of the Olympics on the television, dispatching for two weeks from the frozen coast of the Black Sea. I watched aerial skiing and free skating and women hurling themselves headfirst down a frozen track, hoping for the best. Every passing minute was electrified with anticipation for the night ahead. It could be that my voice flew a little in this energized stretch, that a single-string *pling* returned to my suffocated symphony. I thought: *Maybe our story will have picked up again before tomorrow, before the torture of another thrashing overnight.* The idea made me shiver.

In my mind, I played out the conversation. I practised what I would say. *I miss you. I am sorry it came to this. Please let's try again.* I planned restraint and dignity. Plain speaking. I imagined his silence, but also the crack of his capitulation— surely his pride had just been waiting for this release. My soul soared at the notion.

Valentine's night came at last, with all the home-bound lovers and their paper bouquets. I walked to the bar at the bottom of my street. The mid-winter darkness was cold and I shivered inside my coat, too big now for my shrinking frame. "Rarely in life do we meet someone who takes our breath away with their purity and kindness," Sam wrote me on our first Valentine's Day. "I love you more and more. Be excited about the future and spending it together." I met my friend Monika, whose supportive company I'd selected judiciously. Over a litre of house white and a couple of hours, she told me, *Of course he'll come back—how could he not?* and I guzzled her reassurance. I was water molecules on the jittery boil.

"I've got to go," I told her, when my water bubbles started popping. I felt like it was time. I hurried out of the bar and into the huge black night. It was even colder than it had been, but I was bound this time for transformation, and that helped.

I'd decided to phone him from my car, which was parked half a block up. I couldn't possibly tackle this conversation inside the public airspace of my house, and it was too cold to do it outside. I got in and drove to the park where Sam and I had played hide-and-seek with the kids when they were little. I recited my script and thought of him way out there in Montreal, smoking a joint and messing around with his guitar—Friday night things. Not expecting me.

I was terrified. My fear of a conversation with this newly estranged man who'd called me "pumpkin pie" two weeks earlier was enormous. Big enough to overpower the easy reflex of our six-year ritual of nightly calls. *What if he was furious? What if he was mean?*

But God oh God it also thrilled me, the possibility of talking with Sam again. I had missed his dear soul so much.

I dialed his number and waited. *Ring, ring, ring,* my phone went. In the space between the burblings hung my well-being, my safety, my continuance. *Ring. Ring. Ring.* My windshield fogged, though not with my breathing, because I was not. And then the phone clicked, and Sam's recorded voice came on.

He had chosen not to pick up. Outside, I heard a noise like a body slapping pavement from a tall-building fall.

I hung up and let another scenario flood my brain. I imagined Sam way out there in Montreal setting down his guitar, stilling the chords that made the air in his apartment so rich. I imagined him looking at his bleating phone. I imagined him ignoring me. Me, who had loved him so well and for so long. Me, who was the other half of him.

"The opposite of love isn't hate," Elie Wiesel wrote. "It's indifference."

I called back. The ringing again. The recording again. I hung up and then I called him three more times. Four. Seven. Twelve. Each time the endless burbling, like blood in the throat. Each time the click. More bodies slapping pavement.

I was in shock. I thought of him pacing his apartment's length, willing me to end the torture, to give up already. But I didn't. I filled the minivan with my tears and I did not stop. I dialed his number over and over, heard his recorded voice activate, cheerfully, again and again. Not broken the way mine was when I decided, *this time*, to leave a message.

There wasn't enough oxygen in the world to feed the breathless petition I sent down the phone line to this man who had been my cherished love. In great gulps I pleaded for him to release me, remember me, reanimate me. *I am nothing,* I sobbed. *Dirt. Dead.* I cried until I had made an ocean and his machine had exceeded its capacity to contain my pain.

And then my phone buzzed and it was him. A text.

"Stop calling me," it said. "Talk to your mother or your friends. We are not together anymore."

When passersby stepped across the bodies to peer into the wailing van, they couldn't see me for the swells of tears breaking against the windows.

"Heartbreak," says poet David Whyte, "begins the moment we are asked to let go but cannot." Among those things we're asked to let go of: plans, rituals, security, expectation. History. A future.

Hope.

Letting go of those things with regard to Sam was an extraordinary idea. Like space travel or solving disease. He was knit into my skin. This was where the guitar picks came in. The inscriptions in all the books he gave me. "Happy Birthday to someone so dear to my heart," he'd written inside the first—Dylan's *Chronicles*, one of his favourites. "May all your days be filled with song."

These are the artifacts suffused with a love story that take on super powers when it's cut short. In the baroque Kulmer palace in the upper town of historical Zagreb, Croatia, the Museum of Broken Relationships acknowledges them. This gallery houses objects discarded for their whiff of shuttered romance, a universal collection whose accommodation is extended as a salvational alternative to emotional collapse. Coffee cans and drawings and lingerie. A Linksys router from San Francisco with the note: "We tried. Not compatible." There's even a gift shop on the way out where the afflicted can pick up "Turn over a New Leaf" bookmarks.

Equally theatrical is the museum's digital version, where people upload photos of their material reminders of lost love along with stories describing them. There's an axe a jilted ex used to chop his lover's furniture to kindling when she left him, a twenty-seven-year-old crust from the wound of a first love in Mürzzuschlag, Austria, and an espresso machine from a twenty-year relationship in Paris with a note saying: "For a long time he loved the coffee I made for him using the espresso machine he gave me. For a long time he loved me. And then, one day, he no longer loved the coffee I made for him using the espresso machine he gave me. And then, one day, he no longer loved me."

In 2016, a spinoff branch of the museum started up in Hollywood—a likely locale for such preoccupation—and in the summer of 2019 a temporary collection came to Toronto. "Our societies oblige us with marriages, funerals, and even graduation farewells, but deny us any formal recognition of the demise of a relationship," the sign outside the collection read. Later, it quoted Roland Barthes in *A Lover's Discourse*: "Every passion, ultimately, has its spectator ... [there is] no amorous oblation without a final theatre."

My final theatre had been robbed of all the quiet pleasures. Loving my lunch, remembering a movie, filling with music. These were extravagances I could no longer sustain in the days and weeks after Sam broke my heart. Now the whole of my being was occupied with mourning. Figuring, remembering, thinking, revisiting, untangling, replaying. Waiting for my phone to fill up with him. I could barely drive or walk or stay upright. My head was crowded and melting.

I worked to remind Sam of me regularly. Feverishly even. I emailed him letters written from sobbing coffee shops, I sent him texts, I mailed him cards sprayed with Un Jardin sur le Nil so it would travel up his nostrils and into the avenues of his brain that we'd carved together. I phoned him and left shattered messages on his machine, reading from notes in my car, always looking for the words that would convince him of my worth. Sometimes I videotaped myself so he could see my pretty face and the way his rejection had made it bony and sad.

"Oh, my sweet darling one," I said in a mid-March email when I'd been six weeks on my own. "I am in such pain. Please find a way back to me."

I still hadn't eaten. I'd lost twenty-five pounds and I told him as much. I also told him to remember our love. "I wake up every morning and just cry and cry," I said. "Don't extinguish us."

I wrote to Sam, who didn't write back, because the universe required it. Allowing this love to wash into the water cycle would be entropic. If *we* were not worthy of lasting acknowledgement, nothing was, and the world might as well wheel into the mystic. That was how I saw it, though not consciously. Keeping us alive with overtures—emails, texts, some posted letters—I assumed he received (his part of the exchange) was simply a responsibility I folded into my ego, a precious thing with whose tending I'd been unexpectedly charged.

But this conviction is part of heartbreak: the stoking of the fire gone out is as integral as the mourning of its heat. The universe would know our story because I would insist upon it. Anything else felt like a travesty. Surely Sam felt my stoking across the five hundred kilometres that had separated us from the start. "I am beside you," he used to say to me from Montreal when I lay in bed in Toronto. But that was before he stopped saying anything at all. I told him often that I interpreted his failure to write back and ask me to stop my campaign as reason to hope. If he didn't kick shut the door, I'd say, I would imagine a crack. It wasn't manipulation—it was a plea for release.

There was no kick and the crack consumed me.

Throughout my penance, I stayed alive and perceived the sun's passage across the sky. And that was all. I could not listen to music. I could not be alone. I could not sit in my house surrounded by silence and tortured by yearning. I could not be with people, crowded by their exuberance. I packed up my children for uncharacteristic excursions to Ping-Pong parlours and arcades and board-game cafés—anything to occupy them so I might climb into myself and wallow in the swill there.

One unbearable Sunday, I cried on the highway on the way to a suburban trampoline gym when the radio played a song called "Let Her Go," whose refrain says our love for someone only reveals itself when that person leaves. After I parked, I told my children to make their own way in and I stayed in the car to imagine Sam hearing the same lyrics and having to pull over until he could stop sobbing. The idea filled me with such complicated sadness.

On Friday nights, I would go to art classes where I would splash my sketches with tears and send my friends texts that said I was afraid I might die. Once, I visited an art gallery where visitors wrote wishes on strips of paper and hung them from the ceiling. I wrote mine with great care and attached it to one of the fishing lines, where it was instantly lost among hundreds of dangling desires. *I miss you so much, Sam,* my strip howled. *Please come back.*

I watched the fluttering paper forest for a long, long time, conjuring a scene where he would come into the gallery and find my note and know the message was mine and that he had to heed it.

It was still early days, but I soon knew the trick: to figure out heartbreak's value. It's such a booming, transformational rite of being alive, if you believe the experience means something, and yet it feels like a waste of time because you seem to end up with nothing. There's actually lots to work with here, depending how supernatural you're prepared to get. Heartbreak's universality and exceptionality make it such a curiosity that every discipline takes a run at it—physiology, Eastern spirituality, poetry, metaphysical conjecture and on.

The reports they return reveal a surprisingly sacred state, a state that lifts a person from the morass of existential mediocrity into the extraordinary, that broadens their breadth. In her memoir *Untamed*, Glennon Doyle wrote, "Every great spiritual teacher tells us the same story about humans and pain: Don't avoid it. You need it to evolve, to become."

The evolution's uncomfortable, but imagine how dull life would be inside the narrow bandwidth of never knowing loss, of never opening the rooms in your brain for contemplating its worth. How much more interesting it is to have a range of life experience that extends from joy at a train station to crushing despair on the very same tracks. This expanded ribbon of incarnate experience? Surely the greatest of heartbreak's gifts.

2

Love

Sam and I met in a bar, the most conventional of places. It was the mid-November Saturday night before the Santa Claus parade and it was freezing. I took public transit and wore the same fat parka the mailmen pack themselves in to do their rounds in Alaska. The bar was a long-time Toronto standard, where jazz musicians like Moe Koffman and Buddy Guy played. My girlfriend and I had come to see an old classmate, Dan, whose band was on stage that night. Sam was there from Montreal to celebrate a Toronto friend's birthday.

The place was big and crawling with characters. We had heard it was a cougar pickup joint, and confirmed it at first sight. Above the caterwauling, Dan's band covered Dire Straits and Tom Petty. Alexandra and I watched the blowsy dancers go for it from our table near the stage. I wore black and silver and drank white wine. My straightened hair was so long I could almost sit on it. I was forty years old—some distance from the cougars—and on the town. I'd had no relationship since the big one broke up—fourteen years and four kids in—two summers before. Dating was an extraordinary idea to me.

It was well into the night when the waitress brought over two green cocktails and pointed to a table over my shoulder. I knew who had sent the drinks without having to follow her finger. We had noticed this lovely stranger as he loped past our station in his jeans and brown leather earlier. "Look at him," Alexandra had said. "He's for you."

When I saw him apparently leaving after that, bisecting the dance floor en route to the door, I registered disappointment. The wine had warmed me and I had been so long on my own. But then he came back and joined his friend at their table. His dark hair sprang from under his toque when he pulled it off, and he sat down with his long legs spread wide. I'd felt his buzzing presence behind me ever since. And now the cocktails.

I asked the waitress for a pen. I was charmed by the gesture, which seemed so Cary Grant, and wrote something on a napkin I hoped was funny and smart. Then I gave the note to the server and asked her to please take it to the table that had treated us. Grace Kelly would've turned around and raised her glass, but I didn't dare make eye contact. I kept my gaze forward and hoped he had one more gesture in him. He did.

"Hi there," the lovely stranger said when he walked over to meet me a few minutes later, his very first words to me.

"Hi," I said. And our story began.

We talked about our cities and our jobs. He was tall and had a beautiful face, seawater eyes and every bone a statement. We exchanged names and ages and when I told him he looked too young to be thirty-seven, he showed me his driver's licence to prove it. I laughed at the Coke-bottle glasses he wore in his photo, then regretted it when I saw him deflate. We found out we were both Aquarians, born a week apart. Truthful, just and curious. Affectionate and imaginative. Unpredictable and detached.

Then he asked me to dance and we put our arms around each other and swayed like we were in grade eight. We danced slowly, even when the songs were fast, an unruffled anomaly inside a frenzied scene. With each turn, I'd catch my friends' looks and smiles. Then I'd close my eyes and wish for more songs.

But it was the band's last set and the bar's last call and time to break it up. My musical buddy came down from the stage and I made introductions. Sam, the lovely stranger, was a club guitarist too, and they chatted about playing while the lights came up. Beside them on the dance floor in this north Toronto tavern, I felt like a firefly, crackling with an anticipation I couldn't place.

Mercifully, Sam's friend suggested we go for coffee. It was a ridiculous idea for those wee hours but the perfect antidote to all the helium in my brain. The four of us piled into someone's car and headed to an all-night diner called Mars. Sam sat in the front seat and I sat behind him. His fingers reached back and found mine and we held hands, he and I, two strangers after all, the entire ride. And we did it again on the flight to my house to drop me off. We'd mobilize that memory for the rest of our relationship as chemical proof of our attraction.

At the end of my driveway just this side of the sunrise, we got out of the car and Sam walked me along the broken concrete pathway to my front porch. It was so cold out. Inside the house, my children were sleeping. Above us, the moon was in its glowing first quarter. The sky was cloudless, and if we'd looked up, we might have seen the brilliant debris from Comet Tempel–Tuttle vaporizing in the Leonides as we crossed its thirty-three-year path around the sun. Gifts from the angels, said ancient people.

But we only looked at each other. When he kissed me— such a novelty for this lonely single mom—all these stars rained down.

Love is the soul of heartbreak. Its summits are the towering counterpoints to heartbreak's pitiless trenches. If you couldn't climb so high, you wouldn't plunge so low. Love exists to affirm heartbreak's power. The one is as invigorating and life-affirming as the other is lethal.

When you are in love, every part of your person is stained. "Love is a multifarious neurobiological marvel that comprises countless neurotransmitters and hormones," said a 2007 editorial in *Psychiatry*. Its spreading wound is exquisitely tuned to every sensation. In its embrace, every breeze is a kiss, every blue sky a glowing personal gift, every slight a devastation. Love is a thousand golden threads in our lives' tapestry, the shimmering bands that criss-cross the cloth.

Cloaked across our shoulders, love lightens every step, brightens every thought, saturates every sense.

No wonder humankind has weighed in on the subject with such fervour, scientists picking through the hormones, philosophers untangling the spirit, poets sending to the heavens more laments than they can contain. And still we're at a loss. "Everything to do with love is a mystery," seventeenth-century French poet Jean de La Fontaine wrote, as quoted by Jean-Claude Kaufmann in *The Curious History of Love*. "Exhausting this science is not something that can be done in a day."

For most of human history, love was for children and whatever god was in vogue and that was it. Romantic love was an absurd idea. Men and women's collaborations in the days of prehistoric promiscuity were practical: procreation, safety, the most efficient use of resources. That meant lots of cave kids who didn't know their fathers. Then our evolutionary script wrote us into life-threatening scenes that called out for the protective powers of coupling. Love, says American anthropologist Helen Fisher in her much-referenced treatise *Why We Love: The Nature and Chemistry of Romantic Love*, emerged as the by-product of females needing males to pitch in with the kids. To accommodate, the brain extended the primal infant attachment system to include mates, a biological development that rewarded men for their constancy with the same biochemical gratification that bonded mothers to their babies. Romantic love's earliest stirrings.

By the days of ancient Greek civilization (around the eighth century BCE), love got more sophisticated. In Greek mythology, the ancient god of sexual love and desire delivered as much pain as pleasure. Eros, whose father might have been Chaos or Zeus, was Aphrodite's boy. Like his mother, the sovereign of ardour and beauty, Eros was interested in love. He shot arrows at people to impregnate them with it. But he was impetuous and had famously bad aim, so the relationships he ignited were sometimes dubious.

Once, Apollo made fun of Eros's archery skills, so Eros loaded his bow and shot the big god with a golden arrow that made him fall in love with the nymph Daphne, who had pledged eternal virginity. Then Eros shot Daphne with a lead arrow that injected her with everlasting hatred for Apollo. Apollo pursued Daphne feverishly after that, and she ran and ran. Eros, keen to sharpen Apollo's torment (though Daphne's he left untended), helped him catch up with his repulsed target. Just as he did, Daphne pleaded with her father, the river god Pleneus, to change her shape; he turned her into a laurel tree. Apollo was crestfallen and declared his love eternal. "Always my hair will have you, my lyres will have you, my quivers will have you, laurel tree." He made her leaves evergreen so she'd be immortal. Artists love this story, and have long filled their studios with proof. It could be that Klimt's gold-burnished *The Kiss* depicts the moment of Daphne's transformation.

In the Middle Ages, people's thinking on love expanded again, and tentative conversations began about a love that was virtuous and natural, and that ran in two directions, not just one way to God, says Laura Ashe, a historian of English medieval literature, history and culture at Oxford's Worcester

College. By Eleanor of Aquitaine's time, she and her Court of Love cohorts were discussing the scandalous idea that love could exist inside marriage. (They concluded it couldn't.) Historians agree that this court, in which French noblewomen bantered about impotence and jealousy and virtue, fanned the flames of courtly love, an emerging concept that saw knights swooning melodramatically over unattainably married ladies.

Later, Shakespeare painted his enamoured characters in lunatic hues, always emphasizing the indiscriminateness of love's affliction. In *As You Like It*, Rosalind says, "Love is merely a madness, and, I tell you, deserves as well a dark house and a whip as madmen do: and the reason why they are not so punished and cured is that the lunacy is so ordinary that the whippers are in love too."

Twentieth-century Uruguayan writer Mario Benedetti made the crazy connection plain with a fable about anthropomorphized human emotions playing hide-and-seek at the beginning of time. Madness counted to a million and then, one by one, found everyone—Beauty, Passion, Envy, even Doubt, sitting on a fence. But for all her pains, she could not find Love. She scoured the universe for this elusive player and was about to give up when she saw the branches of a rose bush rustling. Madness poked a fork into the plant and blinded Love, who was hiding there. Her part in the accident devastated Madness and she vowed to spend the rest of her days as Love's guide in recompense. Madness and Love haven't been apart since.

"It's cold here," I wrote Sam on November 22, five days after we met in the stars. "Snow arrived, as predicted. But I've got this furnace I've been carrying around with me the last couple of days, stoking it into the wee morning hours with a telephone cradled on my shoulder. So I'm warm enough. You'll see."

We'd been in touch the very next night, exchanging tentative emails about the Santa Claus parade and the traffic getting out of Toronto that we'd read and reread before sending. The next day Sam asked if he could call me and we started trading our stories in epic nighttime conversations that straddled a provincial border, crackling fibre optics linking Canada's biggest cities. We spoke for hours every night, stopping at two in the morning. But only because we had to sleep. He would phone when he got home from teaching his last guitar class at ten thirty, and I'd listen to him take off his boots and put away his sheet music and imagine his intimate life so far away.

He told me about his west-end neighbourhood in Montreal and I told him about my west-end neighbourhood in Toronto. We talked about food and music. Television and travel. Work and winter. He said he was charmed by me. In my family room five hundred kilometres away, I floated to the ceiling.

We decided to see each other again, a week after the first time. We'd meet in Kingston, the midpoint city between us. He made us a reservation at a Comfort Inn right off the highway and I installed my kids with their father. I told everybody I was spending Saturday night with an old friend, not a long-haired guitar player from Montreal who had stirred up all my senses.

I made a CD of moody songs and packed it in the car with a ghetto blaster, two colours of wine and an overnight bag I filled a day in advance. I packed a nightgown too— such a secret garment to share with a man I'd known only a few hours.

Temperatures had plummeted below freezing on Saturday, but the sun was high and bright when I headed off that afternoon. I wore black sunglasses with my red ski jacket. Snug-fitting jeans that I tucked into long leather boots. I could be anybody with this new man; I chose smouldering. I spent the highway drive inside my head, spinning a fantasy, remembering his features, conjuring the night ahead. The whole way to Kingston, my minivan never touched the ground.

Sam was there when I pulled into the grey parking lot in front of the low-slung garrison of hotel rooms. I got out and waited while he walked toward me, one hand on my open trunk, my face split in a smile. It was the first time we'd seen each other in daylight. He approached in slow motion, jeans and brown leather, his face split too. So I had not imagined him.

I went up on my toes when he reached my car and put his arms around me. My head fit into the crook of his neck so well. Anyone pulling off the highway just then would have heard two pilot lights igniting.

Sam carried my bag to our room around the back of the hotel and put our wine bottles outside the door to the parking lot. Nature's refrigerator, he said, and I laughed. I laughed again when he called hotel bedspreads bacterial breeding grounds and stripped the patterned blight off the mattress of the only bed in the room and stuffed it in the corner. I told him I did that too.

Then I busied myself with the CD player, my heart thudding in my ears. "*Help me out,*" the Killers implored when I got it started. Sam poured white wine into the two plastic cups that came with the room. And then, our preamble spent, we perched on the bare bed and toasted the moment. We talked about our drives and our families. He listened and asked questions and told stories. He made me laugh and feel amazing. It was still just afternoon, but I was already wishing for more songs. "*If you can, hold on,*" the Killers said. We did after that, for such a long time.

Night fell quickly outside our sliding door, which fogged every time Sam opened it to refill our cups. At some point he produced a joint that we smoked in the hotel's chain-link parking lot, and then stumbled back to the room and the wine and the bed in great whoops of joy. We howled to imagine marketing pitches for our highway hovel across the screeching off-ramp from a McDonald's, delighting in each other's revealed taste for pushing storylines into camp. When we realized we shared an appreciation for B-grade 1970s TV, all was lost. How thrilling to recognize your own zaniness in someone else. To fall back against the mattress and laugh for an hour with him, your leg against his.

And then we stopped laughing and began kissing and everything got swept up into the magnetic air streams that blew through that limestone hotel room that night. We were drunk and high and euphoric. And so, so amazed to have found each other, kindred Aquarians who had lived their entire lives without one even knowing about the other.

Later, after we'd been transformed, we went to the chicken restaurant across the courtyard and blinked at its electric brightness. Nothing was the same after that.

"How wonderful to go to the fields when one's heart is consumed by love! The goose cries out, the goose that snatched the bait and was trapped. Your love distracted me and I could not keep it. I will fold the nets, but what can I tell Mother when I return each day without birds? I will say I failed to set my nets, because the nets of your love have trapped me." That this snatch of enraptured exposition was written in Egyptian hieroglyphics more than three thousand years ago (and quoted much later by Diane Ackerman in her book *A Natural History of Love*) confirms the guarantee of love's first pleasures. The Danish call this period *forelsket*. The Filipinos call it *kilig*. The scientists call it *limerence*.

In limerence, a person enters what American psychologist Dorothy Tennov declared "an involuntary personal state" of passionate preoccupation with someone else. The phenomenon, which takes place in the exhilarated days of early romance, is spurred by a cascade of hormones and neurotransmitters that send the brain into a tizzy over the object of its desire.

Tennov's assignment of biochemical status to romance's earliest days slams the magic down to earth, but also legitimizes the way it consumes us. So ecstatically does the psyche thrum in this state that any other input is redundant. Love addles the limerent's focus for the likes of food, sleep and work. All her cerebral exertions are for dreaming. Limerence, said Tennov, is "the greatest joy, the height of euphoria, walking on air."

Other, less romantic researchers regard the condition as an alternative to real love, a lovesickness so powerful it subsumes the real thing. Intense and unstable, go the claims. An unhealthy obsession with another human. An addiction, even, that precludes enduring commitment. American psychology professor Albert Wakin calls limerence a combination of obsessive-compulsive disorder and addiction that afflicts 5 percent of us. He wants it added to the DSM.

But Tennov had no such understanding of the stuff. When she introduced the concept to the world in her 1979 book *Love and Limerence: The Experience of Being in Love*, she called limerence an entirely natural stage in the course of falling in love. "This 'thing' I aimed to study," she wrote, "was a normal condition, not a pathological state."

In the late 1990s, American neuroscientist Helen Fisher and her colleague Lucy Brown set out to discover what happens in our brain during this intoxicating phase. They recruited participants who'd aced the Passionate Love Scale, a measure researchers devised in 1986 to demystify the "state of intense longing for union with another." Then they put these passionate subjects inside an fMRI machine and asked them to fantasize about their romantic interest. When they did, the patch of brain that craves pleasure glowed red: limerence's physiological roots.

Not everyone can ignite this fire. In his 2014 book *Principia Amoris: The New Science of Love*, researcher John Gottman explains that it takes a particular pheromonic cocktail to start a limerent spark. A person has to smell right and taste right and feel right. But once lit, says Tennov, limerence can smoulder for weeks or decades. It most typically sputters out at about eighteen months.

In any case, says Fisher, you should light limerence up while you're in it; this kind of enchantment is not to be squandered.

We took a trip to New Orleans five weeks after we met. Sam researched our options and booked us a room in a boutique hotel on Tchoupitoulas Street, on the edge of the French Quarter, for the week after Christmas.

We arrived at our accommodations without our luggage, which the airline had lost. Sam made lots of calls to retrieve it, perched on the bed, fuming down the phone. I hovered behind him, loving his self-possession, basking in his care. Eventually, we had to go buy clothes. I modelled for him outside the Gap change room, his gaze filling every crack of me. Our luggage didn't materialize for three days. When it did, Sam pranced, naked, to his bag in our room's entranceway and wrapped his arms around it. I hooted at the sight and raced to take a photo. What a lovely, loony man I had discovered in this, the winter I was forty.

The view outside our smoke-free room, which had been a steal, was of a wall on the other side of a gravelly enclosure. Once, when Sam was leaning out the window to have a cigarette, he spied a glass heart pendant in the stones below and fished it up and gave it to me.

We spent our days exploring the city, wandering among the psychics and voodoo dolls. We went to Café Du Monde and Sam bought me beignets. We sat on vinyl kitchen chairs inside the open-air restaurant and talked about whatever flew into our heads, devouring our novelty with the fried dough. He told me about his Dutch heritage and all the trips he'd made to Europe. I told him about interviewing an astronaut and asking what visiting outer space had changed for her and her saying *everything*. The band played "What a Wonderful World" while we ate. When we stood up, we were covered in powder.

At night, we sampled restaurants and then tumbled into Bourbon Street to drink hurricanes and Big Ass Beer inside a crush of tourists and horse-drawn carriages. We stopped to watch live music often. We'd sit close at little tables and rest our hands on each other's legs. At Maison Bourbon, we introduced ourselves to the bandleader and at the break we bought his CD. At another club, I approached the guitarist and told him I was with a guy who was a bit of a guitar god, if I had to say, and he invited Sam to sit in on a few songs. I could tell he was thrilled when he went up onto the stage and let the guy hang a guitar around his neck. He watched the other player's hands and picked up the music right away. He looked beautiful, his face bright and intent, his fingers flying. When he came back to our table, he was buzzing. Loving Sam was always set to music.

We discovered a Mexican restaurant in the French Market where they made guacamole at the table. We drank margaritas there, our sticky fingers meeting between our glasses, and then went to a hookah bar and sucked vanilla-flavoured smoke through a hose. Never again, we declared, on our lurching walk back to the hotel.

Sam wanted to go to Preservation Hall, the crucible of this musician's love for New Orleans. His father had filled his childhood with Dixieland jazz and he was sentimental about the style. We sat on the wooden floor right in front of the ancient musicians, so close we could feel the string bass's drawl with our feet. Sam requested "Just a Closer Walk with Thee" for his dad and when they played this emotional hymn, he cried.

One sweltering afternoon we took the Streetcar Named Desire and walked through the Garden District like lovers. When we went into a store to buy water, the papers were filled with stories about Benazir Bhutto's assassination in Pakistan. We came back out into the sunshine and walked in solemn conversation for such a long time, past the second-hand shops and among the Frisbees in the park. Each memory was a little stone, which I gathered up and cherished. The beginnings of our rock pile, all the moments that were only ours. "Wild leaves," Patti Smith called them, in her tribute to Robert Mapplethorpe. "Every leaf a moment," she said. "Every word that's spoken / Every word decreed / Every spell that's broken / Every golden deed."

Sam took me to see St. Louis Cemetery No. 1, New Orleans's oldest gravesite, and we negotiated our sweaty selves through the above-ground tombs that house the city's notable dead. We visited the 1881 vault of Marie Laveau, where tourists scribble Xs on the whitewashed mausoleum in hopes the voodoo princess will grant their wishes. Afterward, we went down to North Rampart Street and he told me his secrets. He spilled all his youth and sadness across the hot sidewalk as we walked the long urban blocks. I felt humbled by his confidence. And something else too—though love in a month seemed extravagant.

One night at dinner at the Gumbo Shop, eating jambalaya under its ceiling fans, Sam told me he liked to collect books on the cities he visited. I dashed across the street when he went to the washroom and bought him a big New Orleans hardcover from a store with a window sign saying *Laissez les bons temps rouler*. I handed it to him after I breathlessly reappeared and he just beamed.

Another night, we got dressed up like tourists for a dinnertime cruise of the Mississippi on the steamboat *Natchez*. We had our picture taken in front of the giant red paddlewheel and then boarded the boat for an unhurried two hours up and down the river. It was cheesy as anything and we spent the whole trip in gales. Sam perfected an imitation of our host's microphoned drone about the quality of the buffet and I shook with laughter at our table. More stones for our collection.

One afternoon in the middle of our vacation, Sam and I were waiting in the line outside Acme Oyster House and his phone rang. I knew it was someone prickly by the way his body pulled away from mine to take the call. He talked for so long I had to go into the restaurant on my own when a table came up, and I sat there in its neon-checkered interior for a bit before Sam appeared. He told me it was his ex-girlfriend, which I'd guessed, and I ate my hush puppies under this sad cloud. After lunch, he stopped me on Decatur Street on our way to get pralines. "We are together now," he said, taking my hand. "I'm with you."

Scientists recognize three phases of romantic love: attraction, lust and attachment. Each is characterized by its own set of brain-launched hormones whose surge maps could be overlaid across maps of love.

The first stage, attraction, involves the brain pathways that control "reward" behaviour. Here, romantic potential prods neurons to release a bath of adrenalin. The heart speeds, the palms sweat, the senses heighten. Adrenal glands go into overdrive, tiny miners' picks hammering away. Feverish norepinephrine spikes exhilaration and energy while smothering a need for food and sleep; epinephrine delivers the same rush that agitates firefighters and parachutists.

Then the taps turn on the dopamine—the desire hormone, born in a nest of sizzling neurons near the brain's middle floor—which blisses you out. Here's the prize sent down the chute when we do things that feel good. Hetero women get a hit when they look at a man's face; hetero men when they smell a menstruating woman. The hormone's a critical part of mammalian happiness; without it, we're without joy. Rats with blocked dopamine receptors starve themselves to death in front of their dinner.

The adrenalin-and-dopamine combo, along with phenethylamine, a nervous system stimulant that surges in proximity to someone desirable, mimics a cocaine high. You bomb around on negligible fuel, optimistic and bold, senses in overdrive. And when it hits your bloodstream, it blocks the passage for fear, social judgment and critical assessment. *Attraction: all systems go.*

Lust, phase two, is all about sex. Our evolutionary imperative to reproduce is a tunnel-vision motivator in relationship forming, sweeping us onto the floor, pushing us against other bodies. This is when the sex hormones board vessels in all our plasmic rivers. Testosterone—the adrenal glands' gift of libido—soars when we're in lust, enhancing dopamine's rush. The marquee female sex hormone, estradiol, and its spectrum of reproductive utilities also spike in this phase. Women with lots of it give off a scent men like in their noses.

At last comes love's most evolved iteration, attached love, the graceful third stage of romantic contentment. In *The Art of Loving*, Erich Fromm distinguishes between attached love and everything else as the difference between saying "I need you because I love you" and "I love you because I need you." The former—the script of the fortunate soul who's surfaced from lust and limerence into the real thing—is the gold ring.

Sam told me he loved me in the hallway outside an office I was working at one afternoon in our first winter. It was close to the highway, and he'd driven me there on his way back to Montreal. I don't think he expected to say it, but our aching farewell had filled the corridor with the most persuasive energy. "I love you, too," I told him after. And then the whole world bloomed.

We went back to Kingston a few more times, moving to a hotel with a pool whose closest restaurant served pizza, not chicken. But mostly we stayed in our room during these getaways, a congress of fingers and lips and limbs in beds stripped of their covers. We were tireless in those days and our hunger for each other was enormous. We would kiss for hours, telling each other everything in passionate, wordless conversation.

But there were also words. "Baby, I can't say how much it means to spend these days together," Sam wrote early on. "How much it means to have you as my girl. It is so special to share in your memories. These feelings run so deep." Also: "You have made my life full with the beautiful person you are."

Eventually, we adopted a pattern of visiting each other's cities every second week, alternating the accommodation and the traveller with a week of relative solitude in between (more relative for me with my children than for Sam).

Stays in my city were a dose of domesticity. A yard to mow and a dog to feed and a house where my kids were sometimes a presence. We'd drink wine in the hot tub and drive my mini-van to concerts at Massey Hall. First, he stayed in the basement bedroom on his Toronto visits, a fraught decision I arrived at after much twisting guilt over how this modern spectacle would damage my children. I would creep down to see him after they'd gone to sleep and we'd crack the earth open under that guest bed and make the room a field of poppies.

Then Sam began sleeping with me in my bedroom. The graduation to upstairs seemed natural. The kids liked him and he liked them back. No one ever imposed themselves on anybody else. He never played father, with them or me. He was always their friend. He bought them a guitar and taught chords in the family room to whichever kid he could snag in the Friday afternoon gap before they left for their dad's. He chatted with them about music, played riffs from musicians they liked. Jason Mraz and Coldplay. He watched skateboard tricks and gifted artifacts such as video game consoles and a vintage Jimi Hendrix concert poster he'd picked up in Amsterdam.

My children were young when Sam and I were in our early days together, between five and twelve, and they connected with Sam's energy, which was also young. He was a good listener and they'd tell him things they were thinking about. They found the same pleasure in the bawdy, and their inside jokes, which sent them into hysterics, accumulated. "Spending time with the children was very special to me and I think they are all really sweet," my boyfriend wrote after staying a week with us in our second year. "It means so much to me sharing the 'everyday' with the girl I love."

Stays in his city were kid-free bacchanals. PlayStation and Led Zeppelin. *Jeopardy!* and Santana. A little iron balcony with a spider plant where we'd go to smoke and regard the changing seasons in his neighbours' trees. Lebanese food on his couch with his cat, Tigger. Happy hours in his parents' verdant backyard. Saturday breakfasts at La Belle Province— bacon and eggs, no beans, extra fruit. And all those nights in his bedroom with the artificial Christmas tree and the lava lamp. We slept pressed against each other, so we never had far to travel.

How splendid it was to fall in love with not just a person but a place. An experience, a family, a whole new storyline for your show. I knew from its opening shots how blessed I was to be cast. I would, for this act of my life, have love in every scene.

Everyone knows love is magic. How else could Paris adore Helen of Troy before even meeting her? How else could a potion convince Tristan of Isolde? But Sigmund Freud had a more pragmatic understanding. He called love *eros*, a force related to productivity, opposed by the ego and driven by a passion to create and preserve life. And Carl Jung said love was an expression of the human's desire for psychic wholeness. He assigned it a feminine designation, and pitted it against the concept of *logos*, and the masculine principle of rationality. The combination, as he described in his later writing on alchemy, was a Western yin and yang.

Psychoanalyst Fromm agreed that this idea of *mortal separateness* was "the problem of human existence," and that love was the only cure. But mastering love, he said, is as much a challenge as mastering medicine or carpentry. For one, you've got to nail the tenets of care, responsibility, respect and knowledge. For another, you've got to dedicate yourself utterly. "The mastery of the art must be a matter of ultimate concern; there must be nothing else in the world more important than the art."

Once love is mastered, wrote prominent French sociologist Jean-Claude Kaufmann in his book *The Curious History of Love*, a couple "builds a strange little world for two." Our world, Sam's and mine, was the coziest thing I'd ever known and we moseyed through its early weeks and months in such bliss.

He was so *interested* in me. His attention—the inquiries after my day and my children, the memory of the things that mattered—buoyed me. Author Toni Morrison famously said that all a child needs to know is whether your eyes light up when they enter the room. An ancient reflex that can't be stifled. "When we are loved," said Tzvetan Todorov in *Life in Common: An Essay in General Anthropology*, "we feel that we exist." We know *naz*, Urdu for the validation you get for being someone's beloved focus. Sam filled me with *naz*.

"Sometimes on this journey through the years we meet people who humble us with their generosity and spirit," he wrote me once, with characteristic sincerity. "You have made a place in my heart that will never fade."

Loving Sam was such a pleasure. He let me into him deeply and we swam through each other freely. I always said Sam had no ego, that he would never feel lesser for someone else's success. He had an empathy that exalted you, made you beautiful. And I loved myself when we were together as much as I loved him. In April, I wrote from Holland, where I'd gone to work on a story for a travel magazine. I called him *mijn lieve kleine bruine eend*—"my dear little brown duck"—and told him "five months of you pool on the surface of my skin like lemonade." We craved each other on this trip, and limerence was in high flight. Our decadent, time-zone-challenged overseas calls—phone sex to start my day and conclude his—had stoked our ardour. I wrote him about it in swooning emails while he was sleeping and I was in castles and houseboats six hours away.

"With you, my sweet love, I have exercised muscles I never knew I had. I have surfed along the crest of your every breath. You have crawled into my soul and taken up residence. I am changed and enlightened and broadened. I know kindness now. I know compassion. And I know real love, offered in profound and sincere abundance by a tall and angular poet." It didn't seem excessive then; I meant every flooded word.

A long-distance romance hadn't been in either of our sights. The goodbyes, which were its most poignant hallmark, were always tragic. *Dor*, the Romanians call it—a jagged longing for someone you love. When he'd take the train out of Toronto on a Sunday afternoon, he'd leave me notes to find when I returned from the station. "Baby, remember," he said in one. "I love you. So many memories still to be made. You have touched me with who you are more than words can say. I am here for you wherever I am in this world." Once, he bought a tray of lasagna from the gourmet store down my block and left my eldest daughter meticulous instructions on how to prepare it so I'd have dinner ready after dropping him off. When I'd take the train out of Dorval, he'd wait on the platform while I found my seat and then press his palm up to mine on my window. When my car would pull away, he'd put his hand on his heart and I'd watch his long, sad face until I couldn't see him anymore. "I miss you already," I'd text from my seat, and think of his seawater eyes.

"If love's a sweet passion, why does it torment?" Henry Purcell wondered in *Fairy Queen*, an opera that used *A Midsummer Night's Dream* as its libretto. It's the persistence of the desire, said Plato, the endless pursuit of someone else, that torments. He tells the story in his *Symposium* of Zeus splitting two-headed and double-limbed humans down the middle, and consigning them to lifetimes searching for their other half.

Four hundred years later, Ovid was just as severe. "Love is a kind of war, and no assignment for cowards," he wrote in *The Art of Love*. "Where those banners fly, heroes are always on guard. Soft, those barracks? They know long marches, terrible weather, night and winter and storm, grief and excessive fatigue. Often the rain pelts down from the drenching cloudbursts of heaven, often you lie on the ground, wrapped in a mantle of cold."

But the hellos were scorching explosions in airports and train stations, tremendous *retrouvailles* after almost two weeks of humming absence. These slow builds were excruciating in the first week, but thrilling in the second. Sam said often how lucky we were to have this stretch of vibrating anticipation. Regular relationships, he'd say, rarely reached these heights. Consolation for our divided reality. "The flip side of our endless goodbyes was the extreme ecstasy of our hellos," I reminded him in my McDonald's letter. "Show me a six-years-plus-old couple still as hot for each other as us and I'll show you an anomaly."

The first sight of him was always Christmas. He'd throw his bag in the back seat and finally, after so long, be beside me again. We'd play the Stones and drive past the lake and into my neighbourhood, talking about everything and on fire. We'd fall into my bed the minute we hit my house and, after, go out for cheeseburgers, and it was always sunny.

The weekday deserts between these oases were relieved by nightly ten-thirty phone calls. They were rewards for long dry spells, and we'd text "See you at the party" to each other over our workdays. He'd tell me about his students and music. I'd tell him about my kids and writing. We'd eat late dinners together and watch TV, exquisitely synchronized episodes of Letterman and *The Wire*, *Rome* and *The Sopranos*.

Each on our own couch in our own city, our phone hands-free on our own coffee table. Then we'd tell each other where we wished our hands were in crescendoing conversations that ended climactically.

In the early months, I read Sam a children's book about a twelve-year-old loner in the clammy malaise of late childhood who meets a misfit girl named Sistine Bailey in the woods. In a story that invokes William Blake, the boy tells the girl about the tiger he found behind the Kentucky Star Motel. And when she says, "Where?" instead of "Are you crazy?" he knows he picked the right person to tell. I liked this detail, because it reminded me of the certainty I felt for Sam. "In what distant deeps or skies / Burnt the fire of thine eyes?" I read to my new love in those formative evenings, and felt as if I was high, such beauty in my mouth.

When it was time to go to bed, Sam would stay with me while I turned off lights and locked doors, whispering up the creaking staircase so I wouldn't wake my children. I'd get into bed with him still in my ear. "Remember," he would say at the end of our calls. "I am right beside you." He loved me and I missed that so much after he went away.

3

Immersion

The first time he came to Toronto, Sam asked to see my running route and I drove him along its curving path through my
neighbourhood, hugging five kilometres of sidewalk and
answering his questions. I beamed the whole trip at his show
of interest in what my life looked like when we were apart. I
was charmed by him, too.

The first part of a relationship, when it's limerent, is a
blast. Here is where you both get to show off about the great
parts of your lives, to invite the other guy into your world and
persuade them of its specialness, your chest so puffed you
barely fit into your team jersey. There's nothing like the chemical immersion that takes place in these early days, as you let
the things you're learning about each other inform your falling in love, as you share your private delights with someone
who's rapidly becoming one themselves. Welcoming each
other into your places is a big piece of that; by making room

for someone else in your space, you allow the set pieces that'll backdrop the new narrative. *Here is my favourite bakery. Here are my parents. Here are my children.* To taste someone's cannoli or see the house they wish they could live in or share their streetcar route is as good as a census for learning who they are. The early part of a relationship is for immersion—and it's a hell of a thing.

My first weekend in Montreal, we ate steamed hot dogs with cabbage and Sam showed me the pool where he'd spent his teenage mornings swimming laps. We walked around its concrete borders toe to heel, and talked about his butterfly stroke. He'd been a big swimmer, Olympics bound, and I knew he was sharing a sacred place. After, we bought a paper bag of bagels from St-Viateur, where Duddy Kravitz could've been ahead of us in line, and ambled along Sainte-Catherine, past the Simons and Sephora. We drove up *the mountain*, the sedimentary divide between the affluent and English Westmount, and Outremont, the francophone "other side," and got out at the lookout so Sam could play hometown impresario and spread his arms wide above the view. For dinner, we went to an *apportez-votre-vin* in the Plateau and plonked our Malbec on the table like we owned the place. So *this* was Montreal.

On the Sunday, before I left for home, Sam gave me a coffee-table book on his city with an inscription inside: "Baby, I so look forward to showing you more and more of my Montreal. It is so special having you here."

Sam showed me his Montreal for six years, and at the end it was ours. Our routes and stops and favourites. There was his apartment, of course, all Hendrix and hedonism. *Home*. Outside was the café and park and underground lot where he rented a space to park his car. We'd get into it on Saturday mornings and drive to the diner on Saint-Jacques for bacon and eggs, no beans, extra fruit. To Les Amazones, the strip club where I'd let Sam's provocation provoke mine. And across the parking lot to PJ's for beer and hockey on Saturday nights, but only when both our towns were on the bill. There was the dollar cinema, where the guy would bolt between the ticket booth and the candy stand like he was two different people. And there was the train station, with all that potential.

A city without moderation, Montreal adored lots. Sex, for one, which crept across the terraces like a fog, the secret message in the ambient French that always had my ear. Music, for another, which you first heard above the train this side of Dorval and kept hearing for as long as you stayed. Carlos Santana and Steven Tyler and Neil Young. A dozen house bands doing their thing in every outskirt tavern. Sam himself, if you were lucky, his guitar across his body as fast as it occurred to him, which it always did.

Then there were the seasons, of which she had just two. "In Montreal spring is like an autopsy," wrote Leonard Cohen. "Everyone wants to see the inside of the frozen mammoth. Girls rip off their sleeves and the flesh is sweet and white, like wood under green bark. From the streets a sexual manifesto rises like an inflating tire. 'The Winter has not killed us again!'"

Sam and I would celebrate with canoe rides in the Lachine Canal and Sunday happy hours on his parents' deck. We'd ramble up Mount Royal through backlit white spruce, pointing out the prettiest houses to each other, always the same ones, as if we needed reminding. Sometimes we'd park beside Lac aux Castors and walk among the wild parsley and bloodroot of this urban playground, laid out by the same architect who designed Central Park, Frederick Law Olmsted, whose friend eulogized his 1893 death thus: "An artist, he paints with lakes and wooded slopes; with lawns and banks and forest covered hills; with mountain sides and ocean views." We would pause regularly to appreciate his artistry on this Cretaceous centrepiece, to admire divine vistas from igneous rock pews.

When Montreal wasn't warm, it was cold. The city succumbed to this annual transformation without a sound, rolling up its jazz and stilling its tam-tams like it happened every year. Montreal got snow before Toronto, and it would always be a shock to arrive and find it stacked on November balconies and church spires and the recycling bins in the alley below Sam's apartment. In the morning, we'd emerge onto his street in this new light that threw our shadows long up sudden snowdrifts that would turn out to be mounds of car, their owners philosophical, donning layers and digging out their wheels, day after day.

I loved my immersion in this city in those early days every bit as much as I loved my immersion in Sam.

In California in the Summer of Love, a social psychology graduate student at UC Berkeley named Arthur Aron laid a kiss on fellow student Elaine Spaulding in front of Dwinelle Hall, a seven-storey bastion of classics and Slavic languages, and then they fell in love. At the time, like every other social psychology graduate student, Aron was looking for a topic people didn't think could be studied scientifically—so he might study it scientifically. When he sought research on this experience he was having with Spaulding, he found none, so he said, "Here's my topic," and the pair set out to uncover the roots of romantic love, including whether instant intimacy could be created between two strangers. They devised questions strategically to stimulate a sense of closeness and then watched strangers in a lab work through them—superficial ("Who would be your ideal dinner guest?") to deep dive ("What would you save from a fire?"), identifying the ones that encouraged mutual appreciation and the most personal data revelation. They settled on thirty-six open-ended, provocative questions, which, when posed by pairs of strangers sequentially, inspired in them highly positive feelings for each other.

Since then, the research has flared and spread around the science realm. In 2015, Mandy Len Catron wrote an essay for the *New York Times* about her experience with the experiment, called "To Fall in Love with Anyone, Do This," shooting it into viral territory. That near strangers could cultivate romantic feelings in one another simply by following a path of inquiry was an appealing proposition for literary exploration, and the author eventually developed the essay into a book and inflamed a burst of social curiosity over the idea.

The trick to the experiment, Aron has said, lies in two truths: that being asked questions stirs in someone a sense that they're cared for, and that the exercise offers rich opportunities for sharing. Participants feel seen and in sync with each other. And much further along the intimacy scale than they might otherwise be in "a process that can typically take weeks or months," wrote Catron.

Still, there's something delicious about the more drawn-out experience of organic immersion—especially if it takes place in a Great Lake. "I have to show you Grand Bend," I said to my new boyfriend Sam, when I first found the mettle. He, a Quebec boy with scant knowledge of Ontario cottage culture, told me he couldn't wait. He came into Toronto from Montreal late on a Thursday in our first July together, and when we found each other in the basement after the kids had gone to bed, I was on fire, lit up by my dual passions—for Sam and for Grand Bend. We left the next morning after packing the car—with our bags and music, his guitar and my schnauzer, Luther—and leaving the kids with their father. We were at the blistering start of our love affair and about to go to the beach for a week without a care.

This sensual, sunny beach town on western Ontario's Lake Huron—a sunlit wilderness denied water by a strand—was perfect for us. Here was a land of hot sand and pounding surf and intemperance. But here also was a land of grace and nature. A land of quiet and communion, whose lake never lets you down, whose sky contains your whirling thoughts, no matter how high. It was here that I most enjoyed being immersed; taking Sam into the depths with me was such a joy.

My grandparents cottaged in Grand Bend first. My grandfather was a bandleader who used to play with his orchestra at the Lakeview Casino, a sprawling beachfront dance hall that made the postwar summers jump. When it burned down in 1981, the year my grandfather died, they cast his dust into Huron's winds and let it mix with the ashes of this place where he'd led his band.

Grand Bend, just a pebble on Lake Huron's southern shores, was where I learned to grieve and swim and be alone. Two minutes up the highway was the private beach road that I knew in my sinew, across whose sun-splattered width I'd sprinted in so many fevers to beat my brother to the water, over whose repeating hills I'd flown in my Nana's Volkswagen, standing between her knees, along whose edges I'd run with my dog before so many sunsets. All the cottages of my life were studded along it—the ones my parents took for me and my brother those summers our bathing suits were never dry, the teenage cottages, when there was a roller rink on the main strip, all those rentals of my children's childhoods, when I'd thrilled to dip my own dear ones in my great lake. Grand Bend had billeted my life, which I'd unfurled by the summer along its sand. "I will arise and go now, and go to Innisfree," W.B. Yeats wrote of his most precious idyll. "... And I shall have some peace there, for peace comes dropping slow."

For me, peace dropped to Grand Bend's beach, which was a constant surprise, though I'd watched its golden bloom in fifty years of seasonal unveilings. This ribbon, which threaded through all my Augusts, was the measure of my being. When I was twelve, I talked to God on that beach, asked for adolescence. When I was fifty, I asked for mercy. It was the place that knew me best.

The drive was the first pleasure. For two and a half hours, Jackson Browne and Eric Clapton cultivating our in-vehicle soundgarden, we carved through cornfields whose prodigious shows I'd watched every year, past towns whose front porches I'd memorized. And I told him love stories the whole way. *These are the places that made me*, they might have all begun. *This is who I am.*

You knew you were in Grand Bend by the water treatment plant and the broken-down sign saying the movie at the drive-in. Then it was left along the Bluewater Highway, past the Shell station and hardware store and golf course. We always took a tour of the main street before anything else, an annual inventory of its vicissitudes. Down to the bottom, where your eyes got their first hit of Huron, around the loop and back up, breathing in the sunscreen and french fries, assuming the mood. Taking Sam down this sunshiny spectacle, watching his face absorb the sunglasses and ice cream stands, the bloated beach toys strung up between stores, the streaming parade of bikinied bathers, felt like giving him a gift.

I had booked us a cabin in a cluster of cottages off the main street. These were among the low-rent workhorses of this summer town, bare-bones lodgings on the main strip's side streets that university students pooled their money to rent. It was called Wondergrove, and we would prove it so.

We shared our semicircle of tree-tucked cabins with droves of young men, attracted by their price tag and proximity to the town's throbbing main artery, who stuffed themselves into these tiny domiciles with all their contraband liquor. Across the dirt courtyard from where they drank beer and howled with laughter on their deck, we unpacked our things. Inside our brown log cabin we had: an itchy couch, a rustic landscape watercolour, a brown laminate table to dine and roll pot on, a kitchen we never used, a hallway view of where our juvenile neighbours vomited behind their deck, a bedroom. All that mattered was the bedroom.

We never came up for air that first week in Grand Bend. We fucked from morning to night, bathroom and bed, losing track of time, only realizing our hunger after all the restaurants had closed. Night after night we'd walk up to the last-ditch pizza place on the highway and then back to the cottage to smoke a joint and play the Stones and take off our clothes again. We couldn't get enough of each other, drawing out the pleasure like royalty, kissing for days, our mouths never satisfied.

One boiling afternoon, we were in such a rush for conflation we forgot to close the cabin door. We bounced off the wood-panelled hallway till we hit the mattress, moaning when we went for breath, snapping off all the bedsheet's corners. Afterward, when we raced to seal ourselves in, we found all the young men on their deck looking over at our cottage, not howling anymore. Now we had a running joke to tell when we weren't using our mouths for anything else: the triumphant lesson our seasoned sexual prowess provided for the young ones.

We came back the next summer, and this time our neighbours were a toddler and her all-leather parents, who perched a giant skull with red-light eye sockets on their deck railing the first day. That was the year my dog, Luther, was so old and blind. Once, he tumbled off our deck and wandered away. When someone found him, he got sent to the nearby dog pound, and Sam and I went to pick him up. The vet scolded me for Luther's rough condition and said he didn't seem well-loved. I was crying when I returned to the car and Sam went back into the office to defend me. It had been so long since anyone had had my back.

In our second year, Sam started joining me and the kids on our August week, moving through cottages with us, barbecuing sausages and stoking campfires and killing spiders. Bringing our rituals song, his lavish music warm as the sun. Folding into our Grand Bend folklore as though he'd always been a part.

The pros of using cultural immersion as a tool of investigation are considerable. Research both formal and casual demonstrates powerfully the value of enthusiastic participation in another person's world as a means of understanding it. There is simply no better way to appreciate and accumulate qualitative information about someone else's existence than to share experiences with them.

In academic circles, cultural immersion gets a lot of attention as an option for young people keen to learn about another's language or culture. Numerous programs extend the opportunity for students to participate in the daily activities of people that are different from their own. By actively integrating with someone else's life, you gain empathy for them and indulge an opportunity for them to celebrate those parts that thrill them—a pleasure. And the relationship is enhanced for the generosity and intimacy of the gesture. People are transformed through immersive experiences with other individuals, one study, published in the *International Journal of Environmental Research and Public Health* in 2021, reported. By engaging in intentional immersion and guided reflections, they become aware of the need to re-evaluate their perspectives, expectations and assumptions about themselves and others. So everybody emerges from the experience enlightened.

Amsterdam was another site of immersion for Sam and me. Though we didn't get there till the fourth year of our relationship, this city, Sam's favourite, played a part in our story from the start. My familiarization with Sam was always expanded in tandem with my familiarization with this Dutch sweet spot. "Amsterdam is always good for grieving," he used to say, quoting Steve Earle. It was where he would come when his parents died, he told me in our earliest days, his pre-emptive plan to stave off grief with comfort from his darling. The Netherlands was a wonderland to Sam, a site of ancestry and asylum. His parents were Dutch, immigrants to Canada from Vlissingen, a herring hotbed between the Scheldt River and the North Sea where the Royal Netherlands Navy builds its ships. They had crossed the Atlantic in 1961, fresh off their Parisian honeymoon and keen for wide open spaces. When Sam was born nine years later, his mom and dad's love for their homeland was his first inheritance. He wore it in Canada like a scent, Holland on his wrists and behind his ears.

The day Sam and I arrived in Amsterdam, Osama bin Laden died in Pakistan with $745 and two telephone numbers sewn into his clothing. We learned this at the Central Coffee-shop on Prins Hendrikkade, where we'd taken a load off after disembarking the plane and then train, eight hours out of Toronto. Everyone in there was watching the TV behind the back counter and it felt surreal to be part of this moment, so far from home.

We were in Europe at last, a trip we'd been talking about since the Christmas four months before, and were eventually bound for Spain to join his family for an overseas celebration of his parents' fiftieth wedding anniversary. And now there we were, perched on stools at a coffee shop where people dropped in for a pre-rolled NYC Diesel and a steamed chocolate milk. Outside, stylish commuters spilled out of the ornamental Amsterdam Centraal train station, visitors from Brussels and Cologne, hopping through Amsterdam with leather satchels on their backs. "Amsterdam is just as I remember it," I wrote my eight-year-old daughter. "Such an old, historic city. The entire downtown is ringed with canals and bridges. And everybody here rides bicycles! No matter where they're going or what they're wearing. All these elegant people riding off to work on their bicycles, eating or talking on the phone or even reading while riding!"

We stayed at the Hotel d'Amsterdam, a clean and simple five-storey inn on Tweede Helmersstraat with seventeen rooms and curly iron balconies. It was not far from the breakdancing *straatkunstenaar* and herring hawkers of the Leidseplein, the busy square at the southern end of Amsterdam's central canal ring. In the morning, we'd go to a supermarket and buy croissants and chocolate. Then we'd walk. Along the canals with cars parked on their perimeter and loafing tourists on their sunny banks. Past stacked apartments wearing funny hats. Under a sky made Dutch by its criss-cross of tram wires. And everywhere, bicycles.

We spent our first afternoon at the Rijksmuseum, the Renaissance beauty of its Gothic exterior priming the eyes for more inside. This iconic national museum was eight years into a ten-year renovation when we visited, so was fenced in with scaffolding. But its masterpieces were there, including Rembrandt's *Night Watch*, which we paused so long in front of, marvelling at its seventeenth-century light.

On our second night in Amsterdam, Sam took me to his favourite restaurant, an Indonesian standard on Lange Leidsedwarsstraat above an all-hours nightclub. The first thing you saw when you reached the top of the steep interior stairs were the wooden statues on the bar, golden Javanese girls in supplication to the juniper gin bottles on the mirrored shelves behind them. A server in batik sat us at the front under ceiling stains that looked like yellowed continents and we ordered *rijsttafel*, an Indonesian extravaganza that ate up the table with a dozen dishes—fried rice, chicken brochette, banana fritters and on.

Afterward, we caught a tram to the red-light district, where I tried not to embarrass the women in their purple-lit windows by meeting their eyes. We drank beer at a picnic table we shared with German tourists outside the Stones Café. Then we made our way through the crowds, festive hangers-on from Queen's Day, the nation's biggest party a few days before, to the Sex Palace Peep Show. The unassuming storefront of this Amsterdam fixture, flush with its tidy neighbours, was a standout only for its neon "live couples" announcement, which bounced off the canal water. The cabin we squeezed into had a sticky floor and a slot for us to drop two euros for a two-minute look in on a live couple, their robotic coition more fascinating than titillating.

We went shopping on Kalverstraat, the city's retail mecca, the next day, and I felt so electrified to be in this town with someone who kept its map in his head. Amsterdam was warmer now, ten degrees more than when we'd arrived, and we left our jackets at the hotel to walk in the sun past all those tilting houses that stood like soldiers, so close to rivers of water. Sam bought street herring, lifted from a salt barrel and washed with milk, from a stand with the city's triple Xs on its side, and I grimaced with his every swallow. Then we strolled more herringbone-brick sidewalks past more flowerpot door stoops to the Dampkring, the legendary coffee shop on Handboogstraat with a resident stoned cat named Bowie. We drank vanilla milkshakes there and smoked Jack Herer spliffs at a window counter seat that was never not the cat's.

The next afternoon, we left Amsterdam and travelled to Palma de Mallorca and then Barcelona, where we set up in another cozy budget hotel, this one smack in the Gothic Quarter, the old city's *corazón*. We walked to the beach that night along two-hundred-year-old streets lined with palm trees and lamps designed by Antoni Gaudí, and ate chicken paella on a patio sprayed by the ocean. Everybody was out under that Moorish moon—ambling families just thinking about dinner at 10 p.m.—and Sam and I were flying. We took a bus tour the next morning that unloaded its tourists at the Basílica de la Sagrada Família, Barcelona's unfinished masterwork, still shaking off ashes from a fire in the sacristy two weeks before. Later, we walked Las Ramblas, the tourist-packed pedestrian promenade the Spanish poet Federico García Lorca once said was the only street in the world he wished would never end.

After Barcelona we flew to Mijas, a city in Málaga province on Spain's southern coast, to meet up with Sam's family. A typical Andalusian white town, Mijas clings to a hillside 450 metres above the sea. We stayed in Casa Domingo, a bleached mansion carved into forest that Sam's Dutch aunt and uncle had bought to host their international kin. Inside the studio apartment we shared on its ground floor was terracotta and blue Delft tile and a square bed in a white frame. Outside were mandarin and grapefruit trees, a swimming pool and Spanish breezes like twirling flamenco.

In the middle of the week, we piled into the rental car and headed for town to celebrate the trip's highlight, Sam's parents' golden moment. Our group took up the entire terrace of a whitewashed restaurant with a view of a courtyard bathed in Spanish midday light. We ate gazpacho, chorizo and shrimps with garlic, and toasted their half century in three languages. Back at our villa at magic hour, everyone gathered on the sun-gilded balcony and Sam played guitar. He sang "Landslide" and his mother cried. Then his father projected a video of their wedding onto a screen, and everybody laughed and drank wine and commented on the reception guests' hats.

The next day, we drove five hours to the Alhambra, the thirteenth-century palace and fortress of the Moorish monarchs of Granada, whose walls were made of red earth and sacrifice. We parked under an orange tree and spent the day roaming this tremendous site, brilliant with history and cypress. The filigree walls of the Palacios Nazaríes were a geometric marvel in Islamic architecture; they looked like paper cut-outs. At Christmas, Sam gave me framed photos of us posing in their latticed sunwork.

I left for Toronto after that, because my little girl was turning nine and I needed to be there to mark it. Sam would hang on in Europe for twelve more days, taking a trip to Morocco with his sister and then travelling back to her home in Paris with her. He emailed from his aunt's villa after dropping me at the airport. "My love," he wrote. "You are in the air now on your way home and I am right beside you. I love you, sweet one, so, so much. This has been such a wonderful vacation. The bed is way too big without you and I miss having you with me. Though of course you always are. Thank you for being such a great partner. My little poquita, my love."

Before flying back to Canada, Sam returned to Amsterdam for one more dance with his darling. He wrote me from there and told me he'd spent the day retracing our steps. "I thought about how special our time here was," he said. "It's amazing that in just a few days we really did make it our town."

And so the immersion was complete. We had each shared the place we'd loved before we loved each other. And we'd each left our traces in the other guy's spaces, eternally infecting their air.

4

Grief

On the first Friday in April in my first spring alone, it was raining and only six degrees. The kids were with their father, and they were all at the house. I should have been on a train to Montreal for a weekend of joyful inhabitation of my other self. Instead, I was alone at the library, gathering up the work I never got to during the day and pushing into the chilly bluster when the place closed. By the time I reached the subway, I was drenched. I took a shivering train ride downtown to a running store and paid sixty dollars for a green T-shirt, a race chip and my paper number, with safety pins on the corners. Then I went back into the rain.

On Sunday morning I got up early and put on my running clothes for the five-kilometre race around the park by my house. My daughter pinned my number to my shirt and my son loaded my iPod with running music. I strung the chip through a shoelace and the kids bade me luck. They'd meet me at the finish line, they said.

It was bitter and bright when I came onto the porch in my running shoes, and the walk to the car was so quiet. I'd forced myself to do this, a last-minute decision. I'd been operating by the moment since Sam left; everything was hard. I didn't brush my hair or eat or try. I resented demands on my brain, which was consumed with despair. Questions made me irritable; responsibility was incompatible with my state of mind.

I'd decided on the race because I thought of the email I'd send him afterward, the pride I imagined him feeling for my grit. I remembered my first 5K five years earlier, when he'd set his alarm so he could wish me luck at the start.

This year, the streets were empty and so was High Park. I thought that was strange, given the popularity of this urban annual. I worked my way along the winding park road, wondering how close to the start line I could get before the parking spaces filled up. But they never did, and there was no one there when I reached it.

I pulled into a spot and phoned my daughter to look up the date of the race. It had been the day before. *The Saturday.*

After, I wound my way through the rest of the park and came back out onto Bloor Street. I didn't know where I was going or what I would do. Everything felt broken. My race, my email, my grit. My spirit clenched, willing the universe for Saturday again. But it was still Sunday when I pulled onto a side street and turned off the engine.

There, I wept like a jellyfish—no dimensions or restraint. How terrible it was to have failed and to have nowhere to unburden the sorrow. How I ached for him to return to the parts of me he'd fled, the parts that were sucking water that wrong-day morning I was so alone.

If I could have, I would have called Sam at that moment, fumbling for my phone on the passenger seat. And he would have calmed me in a flash, chuckling at my mistake and smoothing out my anxiety. "It'll be okay, baby," he would've said. Like he did for the year my mother had cancer, the year he never left me alone.

But Sam had retreated into silence nine weeks earlier and I was alone now. With my missed park race and Sunday side street. With all the free-falling mornings when I'd remember he was gone, again and again, as Gerard Manley Hopkins knew when he wrote, "I wake and feel the fell of dark, not day."

I'd push on regardless, rousing my children, feigning the lightness their daily launches deserved. I was close enough to mornings that had been weightless—strewn with prattling adoration for Presli the dog, the industry of lunches and mittens—that I could fake them. I could stay inside my skin until I was free of the last child. Then I would bail. Would reduce to just autonomics.

Two months earlier, when the person I adored had called me "love," I had been made of meatier stuff. Now I was carrion. Without him, the world was mean, filled with predators and the potential for things to go wrong.

There's a long tradition of trying to uncover the value of sadness. Darwin's champions, insisting on an explanation for the finer points of their existence, call the emotion not only inevitable but necessary. By expressing our grief, we attract the help we need and prolong our species. Grief is the underbelly of happiness, say the poets. Entertaining melancholy earns us access to joy and deeper perception. To understand the misery of the trees losing their leaves in the fall is to understand the cycle of life that brings flowers in the spring.

By assigning meaning to our pain, we render the suffering useful. Even if its meaning is punishment, as people so often perceive. At least punishment can be redressed—with prayer or sacrifice or disgrace. As religion scholar Elaine Pagels wrote in a *New Yorker* essay about the death of her son, the punishment angle allows grievers "some sliver of agency." If you have none, she told NPR's *Fresh Air* in 2018, "that's almost intolerable."

But she found a different message in the Gospel of Truth, one of the more than fifty sacred Gnostic texts discovered in Egypt in 1945: suffering doesn't improve you, and it has nothing to teach you. But it does have an ennobling feature. "When [you] suffer, there is a potential in that dreadful complex of experiences of grief to open up to other people in a deeper way that can demonstrate our connection with [each other]." She wrote about embracing people at the back of the church after her son's funeral. "Standing there, I had a vision of a vast net of thick ropes, with enormous spaces between the knots. Heinz and I had found no meaning in our son's death. The most that we could do was *create* meaning, by caring for each other and for our daughter. As we walked out of the church that day, I had the sense that those knots were our connections with those we loved, and that nothing else could have held us in this world."

Grief has a complicated history. The Old English term *reave* or *bereafian*—whose ancient definitions include "to be robbed" and "deprived of something valuable"—has become our modern word *bereavement*. In February of 45 CE, the ancient politician Cicero tumbled toga over sandal into it when his daughter, Tullia, died. The great Greek orator suffered Tullia's loss profoundly, and wrote as much in effusive letters to his friend and financial adviser, the knight Atticus. In his correspondence, says Aaron Seider, a classics professor at the College of the Holy Cross in Worcester, Massachusetts, we find the rare personal expression of an emotion that literary sources of the day mostly sidestepped, preferring critical conjecture of other people's melancholy.

In medieval times, grief was still in the closet, and despair, like self-destruction, was a sin, its inward-looking focus an assault to God's magnanimity. But humans, being what they were, defied both. Christine de Pizan wrote of a "great incomparable suffering" in Ballad XV, in the fifteenth century, which not only put into her head "grievous despair," but counselled her to kill herself. "Asleep or awake," she wrote, "every hour finds me in sadness."

Sadness found Shakespeare too, multiple times. In *Henry IV, Part II*, Falstaff describes the king's illness as "from much grief." After Cordelia's death, King Lear mourns his daughter with these last words: "Break, heart; I prithee, break." And in *Much Ado about Nothing*, lovestruck Benedick moans, "Everyone can master a grief but he that has it."

By the time Emily Dickinson was lamenting "a pain—so utter—It swallows substance up—Then covers the Abyss with Trance—So Memory can step Around—across—upon it," widows wore black for two years and mourners saved dead lovers' fingernails. But grief was still a mystery, its impact on people's memory, feelings, thoughts and identity baffling everyone who cared to consider it.

Heartbreak knows grief as a sister; it is its most elemental expression. Academic literature advances a standard that gives grief's reins to mourning widows and widowers, galloping past the other losses. But if heartbreak, with all its moorless, drowning dreadfulness, isn't cause for grief, what is?

The widows and I are equally bereft—rewrite the exclusions.

The days of those first months after he left slipped by in such blackness. I dwelled in a trough, dragging my anguish a metre below the sidewalk. I took my children to school and dance and the dentist ("The Feet," said Dickinson, "mechanical, go round"), but I twisted him through my brain constantly. The effort left my head too congested to work. I couldn't focus or remember or sleep. In the pie chart of thoughts, my pie was mostly for grieving.

After dropping my children at school, I'd drift to libraries and coffee shops, where I'd install myself at cold tables and think about Sam. I'd read old texts and emails and marvel at the proximity of his love. "I miss you," he'd said. Also: "Take care of my girl." And: "I love you baby and we will see it through." Things that made me feel cared for and valuable. At lunch, I'd drift home to make grilled cheese and ravioli and try to decipher the school forms my kids pushed under my eyes. I resented the persistence of their schedules, but our midday routines relieved the roaring despair.

Inside me was a constant rainfall. I cried in my car, and in the public bathrooms at lunch. Like Didion, I'd be swept away by "sudden apprehensions that weaken the knees and blind the eyes and obliterate the dailiness of life." One obliterated afternoon, I was sobbing at the library and caught the attention of a white-haired eastern European man sitting across the common table from me. He conveyed his pity with hand signals and sad eyes. Embarrassed, I struck up stilted conversation and learned he was from Kazakhstan and knew no English at all. He showed me that he was watching YouTube videos on his laptop to learn the language. The man gave me sad eyes again the next day, and then on the third I saw him writing something on his hand from his YouTube lesson. "I want to do this to you," he told me slowly, earnest as anything, pointing at his closed fist. Then he unfurled it so I could read the word on his palm. "Abduct," it said.

The scene alarmed me. But mostly it made me sad that I couldn't share its absurdity with Sam. We'd have gone to town with this weirdo guy. "I so miss talking to you," I wrote him when he had been gone three months. "I read something or hear something and want to share it with you. Reflexively, I make plans for us. I think about what restaurant we should visit, or that we need to get tickets for James Taylor. I get a zing of excitement when I think of our next meeting, the way I always have."

But these zings were nosediving now and I was stepping over the pocks they left in the earth en route to my bedroom, where I retreated—often—to discharge the brave face and unstifle the grief from my throat. I'd lower my leaden body onto the bed and look out my back window at the same framed scene Sam had looked at on his last night there. Spidery tree branches fragmenting a dark sky. *What had he been thinking?* I would wonder. *How much of what would come the next day did he know then?*

I thought about these things a lot. How something ordinary could suddenly turn so exceptional. How I had left him that last morning in my room, stealing away to work at the coffee shop so he could sleep before his train trip, never imagining a thing. That he would rise from bed and sit at my computer and find a reason to end us. *Had he been looking for one? And why?* I thought of my lips on his rough cheek. His sleeping breath—infected with pneumonia, we'd learned on the weekend—in my nostrils. *Was that our last kiss?* The way I'd caught him looking at me the night before, an icy, reflexive glance as his brain cooked an exit plan (*maybe?*). And then how, hours later, he was gone from my bed and my house and my life. *Poof.* Imagine that.

"He manages like somebody carrying a box / that is too heavy," American poet Jack Gilbert wrote of a man navigating grief. Still, says George A. Bonanno, a clinical psychologist at Columbia University who studied grief and published an important study on the subject in *Journal of Personality and Social Psychology* in 2002, most individuals can heave it successfully and return to healthy functioning by the second year after a loss. But grief has a spectrum. On one end are the lucky ones, the resilient types whose experience with grief is springy: a bungee dip down and then back up. A third to two-thirds of bereaved people are resilient grievers, says Bonanno—the biggest fraction. While their pain is acute, it subsides after a few days or weeks and they can return to their life's regular rhythm. Some of this population even emerge from the experience improved, relieved for the closure of a painful period.

Further along the scale are grievers Bonanno slots in the "gradual recovery" category. These folks—about one in ten—suffer intensely, but reliably rise above it in time. While they haul the remnants of their grief forever, they mostly pull themselves together after a year.

At the far end of the spectrum huddle the saddest of sacks. Freud first acknowledged complicated grief in his 1917 paper, which was dedicated in part to separating normal mourning from major depressive disorder. But it wasn't until much later that researchers identified a combination of depression and PTSD in people navigating certain strains of grief. This prompted the development of a new diagnostic category, "prolonged grief disorder," added to the DSM-5 in 2020. Katherine Shear, professor of psychiatry at the School of Social Work and founding director of the Center for Complicated Grief at Columbia University, told the *Washington Post* in 2021 that this new category addressed "a small but significant group of people" for whom grief doesn't resolve. "It is ongoing, pervasive, intense and debilitating."

Today, says an article from the same year in *Focus*, a journal published by the American Psychiatric Association, "prolonged grief disorder" presents in about 10 percent of the bereaved population. And while the DSM-5 lists it as a "proposed disorder requiring further study," it has an official berth in the eleventh edition of the WHO's International Classification of Diseases, defined there as grief that "lasts well beyond what most others would consider acceptable."

The melancholics who suffer this mix of trauma-like and depressive symptoms manifest in an inability to accept the loss, a preoccupation with the missing person, confusion about their role in life and a diminishment of hope for the future. Complicated grief, of which prolonged grief is the most common form, can be debilitating and include recurrent pangs of painful emotions. The most compelling of those is *yearning*: an unremitting desire for a person's return—the hallmark feature of complicated grief and, in all that time since Sam went away, my jam.

When four months had passed, I wrote Sam again. "I am hurting so much," I keened. "Please talk to me. Please stop ignoring me. I am in so much pain. Please no more. Please reach out to me. I am here. Please give us another chance. Please talk to me. Please no more pain. Please no more pain." But his silence grew louder with every effort to loosen it.

The mornings were the worst. I would wake up into darkness, immediately depleted. My brain's natural impulse to leap for the day could find no traction. I would thrash about in my bed, tangling my angst, so hungry for internal calm. But my soul would just fall and fall, the roller coaster's first big drop never levelling off.

The days were the worst. Making sad, sticky oatmeal for my children's breakfast, my feet so heavy on the kitchen floor.

Then pushing through the hours in my furrows, dreadful in the rain, desperate in the sun. I barely worked and barely ate. I couldn't be alone or with people. Music was a minefield; any song might bust open all my organs, send them spiralling into the air.

The evenings were the worst. I'd yearn for bedtime so I could steal away to the mercy of sleep. Until then, I'd take my phone into the basement and call tireless friends to ask *what happened* again and again. To pick through the scene for clues I'd overlooked that spoke of his imminent return.

The nighttimes were the worst. Even in his *Famous Guitars* T-shirt with my hand on his pick. My headboard-hung dream catcher, which Sam bought me in the hotel gift shop after Cuba, had stopped working. It filtered dreams that abandoned me in hovering states of wishfulness. I had the same one repeatedly: a hyper, fizzing reverie where we'd reunited and the relief was enormous. But I knew throughout that he would leave again. And when I awakened, he had.

Draw a circle in your head. This is you. Now, fill the circle in with black marker. This is grieving you. Make sure to colour all the way to the edges; don't miss a spot. Grief affects every part of your circle. Now. Get used to it. You will never not have that black blotch. *You will never not grieve.* Where people used to believe that the passage of time would shrink the tumour of grief, new thinking says it never does, that our lives just grow around it. In the comments beneath an eight-minute BBC Stories YouTube video describing this revised understanding, mourners express passionate relief. "Ppl say to me 'you need to get over that and move on,'" September Dan shares. "Shit burns me up."

The burn has simmered for eons of human history. It was 1917 when Sigmund Freud got to it, before grief even had its own field of study. But the damage of this pioneer's tidy conclusions on its management endures. It was the standard in those days to pitch a narrative that grief could be overcome and, more than that, that it could be overcome with a prescription of simply forgetting or getting over the people whose absence was causing the grief.

Grief, Freud declared in his essay "Mourning and Melancholia," has an *end point* toward which people can work. You might be feeling blue today, but take heart: there'll be brighter hues tomorrow. One must only deposit their source of grief by the wayside to emerge cured. It's thanks to Freud that we talk about closure and letting go. We work through, we detach, we move on. Or at least we should, he said. And this first sanctioned foray into a complicated field amounted to an invitation to failure for anyone who couldn't shake their ghosts.

Just as guilty is Erich Lindemann and the cure-all promise he extended from his 1940s research on the long-term impact of grief and trauma. This Harvard psychiatrist was called in to work with survivors of the Cocoanut Grove nightclub fire in Boston, which killed 492 people in 1942 and was the deadliest nightclub fire in history. These patients, who had seen their companions killed (and almost died themselves), their improving conditions notwithstanding, were acting unexpectedly. They weren't grateful for their doctors and struck out in violence often, one smashing glass, another knocking her surgeon to the floor. It was a reaction to loss in its most elemental form, Lindemann said, and it echoed the work he'd done with soldiers who'd had their limbs blown off and with patients who'd had their gall bladders and uteruses removed. Losing a human relationship, he said, especially one central to your social structures, is like losing a part of yourself. Partial death.

More than that, said the shrink, these thrashing hospital patients were expressing grief—an extraordinary suggestion to a medical community that had yet to label the experience *psychiatric*. But the "grief work" Lindemann proposed for them undermined the consequence of his discovery. He suggested four to six weeks of sessions with a psychiatrist to shake not only the strong attachment to the person but the grief associated with their loss. It was an aggressive agenda, but he was adamant. Lickety-split, he said. A full recovery awaits. Another set-up for disappointment.

But the most damning prescription for grief recovery was Dr. Elisabeth Kübler-Ross's. In her 1969 book *On Death and Dying*, the Swiss-American scientist nominated five stages for the emotions people experience when they're dying: denial, anger, bargaining, depression and the hard-won prize of acceptance. When this orderly sequence was subsequently applied to grief, it suggested a progressive pathway to *fine*. It's a model that's dragged a lot of sufferers into the gallows, convinced their inability to outrun it means they're doing grief wrong. Outsiders' tsking appraisal of the time they're spending on the chase to recovery reinforces the bereaved's self-censure.

Kübler-Ross recanted this prescription near the end of her life, regretting the pressure it loaded on getting over it— but the template was well set.

The concept of closure comes from Gestalt psychology, among whose therapeutic techniques is "the empty chair," which invites participants to imagine the source of their "unfinished business" in a chair across from them. It's kind of a moot point anyway, says Ashley Davis Bush, in *Hope and Healing for Transcending Loss.* "We want to believe there's an end to pain. In reality, it's not that the pain ends, but it changes over time." It's why she doesn't talk about "closure," but "healing," "growth" and "living with the love," with the person left behind honouring the relationship and gathering wisdom from it.

It's what American psychologist William J. Worden suggested in 1982 when he urged mourners to find an enduring connection with their loss. It was an extraordinary idea: suddenly, sad souls were allowed to hold on to a missing love. With it, they could imagine a recovered life that was both meaningful *and* inclusive of the person who went away. Relief.

In 1996, Dennis Klass cemented the idea with *Continuing Bonds: New Understandings of Grief.* The linear models, Klass wrote, were short-sighted, particularly for their preoccupation with getting over the loss. In his theory, healthy grief is resolved not by letting go of anyone but by creating a new relationship with them in their absent form. Like Taoists, who believe deceased family members live on, grievers were now permitted to make room in their emotions for someone who was no longer there. To preserve them in the cage of their chest, to stroke their guitar picks and remember them preciously.

Grief, said C.S. Lewis, is like waiting. "It gives life a permanently provisional feeling." That was my milieu as the winter that started *with* Sam thawed into a spring *without*. Sadness swamped my psyche, stole my focus from everything. But tangled in the sadness was the waiting, which I couldn't help. My spirit was infected with not only the world's upset but my tyrannous conviction that all would be righted soon. If I was just patient. If I could just live another day.

My expectation that Sam would come back was enormous. How could he not? We had met in a star storm. We had marvelled at our good fortune for years; imagine a union that leaves both partners feeling lucky, we would say to each other. Now imagine that union and all its fortune being scattered to the ether. One day, months after Sam went away, my father said, "This can't be sitting well with him either," and it made my heart leap. *Of course it couldn't be. Of course he must be feeling like shit. Of course he'd be back.*

But such conviction made me anxious. I was plagued by a pulse keeping me in a state of hyper-alertness that anticipated his reappearance in every text, every email, every ringing phone. I fantasized about my response in the instant I saw he'd tried to contact me. Imagined his email dropping in or his name lighting up my cell. I wouldn't look at it right away, I decided. I would breathe for a bit. *I would savour.* But then one evening when I was sitting on the cold wooden floor outside my daughter's dance class, I got a text from someone my phone identified as "maybe: Sam" that exploded my brain, and I couldn't open fast enough. (It *was* a Sam. But not the one who'd shotgun-kissed me and shared his poutine.)

I'll hear from him today, I would think. *Every day.* Marking the date and its potential significance for a person sorry for having hurt another person, a person on the hunt for a slick withdrawal from a reckless act. My birthday. The three-month mark. Spring. My heart sped at ten thirty every night, when he'd called for six years. But nothing dropped in or lit up at all.

There was a precedent here, and in the early stretch it drove me nuts. A long time ago, when we were maybe three years into our relationship, Sam and I got in a blistering fight and he clammed up and told me we were done, and I thought I would die—every bit as much as the next time. But then he returned. "Maybe we can at least talk," he texted me out of the blue after he'd gone to ground for weeks, just a few days before a Christmas I had been dreading.

I was in my basement with my friend Alexandra when the text came through, and I jumped up and down and cried. It was one of my life's happiest moments, and it made me think of Adrian. Adrian was Sam's "Seasons in the Sun" friend, and his loss from Sam's life was a constant infection. They got into teenage trouble together, these two, and learned guitar with the same mad fuel. Sam used to rhapsodize about their friendship and Adrian made regular appearances in his tales of his Montreal adolescence, like the one where his father found them smoking weed in his garden shed and the two towering teens had to skulk past him on their way out. But

Adrian let Sam epically down not long before I came along and so was a subject shrouded in complicated emotions. Sam was too proud to surrender his vow to cut this turncoat off but too thoughtful not to lament his friend's absence. He declared regularly that he *would* get in touch again, that *one day* would be the right one to reach across the divide.

I imagined, with this pre-Christmas text, he'd reached such a tipping point with me, and had picked up his phone and written his quick message and pressed Send before he reconsidered.

We talked on Christmas Day when the kids were having lunch with their father and I took the new dog, adopted for comfort, to the schoolyard. Presli gnawed at her leash while I perched on a sunny picnic table and Sam and I took turns exchanging careful grievances. The conversation was long, but I knew from the start that we were going to be repaired; our time apart had alarmed us. We told each other we were sorry, said *I missed you*, made plans to meet. At some point the dog worked through her restraint and escaped, but I didn't want to break the spell by hollering for her, even when she took off through a gate. I spied her after from up in the air, where that redemptive call had floated me.

We planned to meet in Montreal in a couple of days, and I reserved a hotel room out of decorum. But I cancelled the second night's stay after a feverish reunion on the first and we got into his little white Toyota and drove across town to his apartment. It was mild, above zero, though the city was blanketed in snow. I watched beautiful Montreal outside our windows and couldn't believe my luck. Inside was our own aquarium, the delicate threads that had connected us re-forming, criss-crossing our bodies with silk.

We left his car in the underground lot at the end of his block and scaled the steep driveway together in slow motion. At its summit everything was the same: the red brick and wrought iron, the park across the street. But when we mounted the snowbanks and walked up the concrete steps to his build-ing, it felt like the first time. Then we entered his little foyer and the whiff of indoor winter and weed came at me in gusts of all those sunny Saturdays when we'd tumble into his apart-ment between afternoon and evening to occupy his bed. It ferried me across the pizza flyers scattered like leaves beneath the mailboxes and along the painted hallway to Apartment Number Four. I had been so hungry for this.

Inside his apartment was a feast. The out-of-date calendar on the back of his door, the cross-country skis in the kitchen, the row of guitars beside the couch: I devoured them all. After I put down my bag, he asked how I was and wrapped his arms around me for as long as I wanted, like he used to. I felt all the parts of my body realigning. Then we played Santana and smoked a joint and climbed back into our story.

In the weeks to follow, Sam told me some things about how he'd been in the break. Like how he'd cried listening to k.d. lang sing "Hallelujah" and how he'd kept his favourite photo of me, the one where I'm smiling in the canoe, on his fridge, even though he'd told me we were done. I'd thought about those things for all those years since he clammed up the second time and about the precedent they set and the likeli-hood of another hallelujah.

In this, my more recent heartbreak, I continued to write Sam emails and letters about my expectation. To make him bear some responsibility for it. To compel him to respond. He had left too abruptly and the irritated text he'd flung me on Valentine's Day to advise me "We are not together anymore" was not substantial enough to end a six-year relationship. I deserved more. *I deserved a conversation. At least.* Eventually, I got explicit. Put me out of my misery, I said. All will be forgiven. Tell me I'll never see you again if that's what you intend. Just don't let me blow in this loneliness, believing. Say *something*—or I'll interpret your silence as reservation.

At least, that's what I wrote. What I meant was: *Don't say anything.* Please God don't say anything—*and* I'll interpret your silence as reservation. Hope, Dickinson's "little bird that kept so many warm," was my only source of heat.

When he didn't say anything, the inevitability of his return became more likely. This was the algebra of my waiting. The salvation of the elimination method, which confirmed mathematically the link between his silence and his failure to endorse the permanence of his silence. If he was too chicken (or unsure) to confirm that we were finished, I would reserve a pocket of my heart for the possibility he was just being reactive and angry, and could regret his impulsive conduct at any minute. Even now.

Stop writing to him, friends urged me. *Preserve your pride.* But my pride was not on the table. I wrote Sam when it was the only thing I could do. When my body was so filled with grief there was barely room for blood or breath to pass. The idea of reaching out to him loosened my skeleton. And the lift I got from crafting a letter whose pristine message I designed to, at last, convince Sam to return conveyed me to coffee shops and libraries in something like exaltation. There, I would bend over a dozen drafts, devoting entire afternoons to agonizing, poignant missives, until I had said what I needed to say. Until I had drained the poison from my veins. "All sorrows can be borne if you ... tell a story about them," said the writer Isak Dinesen. These notes to Sam were my stories.

"My darling one," I wrote him in one, some months after he left. "I am a wreck. I only love you." Then, four days later, I wrote: "Sob. Miss you so much, love. Miss you so so so much." And, five days after that: "I'm having a hard morning. I am hurting so much. Please talk to me. I am in so much pain."

He never wrote back. Never responded to my emails or texts. Never acknowledged my letters. Never picked up my calls. But I didn't stop—I had no choice. I was sick with grief. And I believed his drought would end on this day, or—*surely*—that. Maybe this note would be the one that caught him in a moment of wondering. Or regret. Or this note. Or this one.

"This is the hour of lead," Emily Dickinson said, as if observing my early foray into this disaster. "Remembered, if outlived, as freezing persons recollect the snow." But the snow in my story had frozen us in the winter of my tragedy. And when it began to melt, it left a new layer of sediment in my heartbreak. We had been away from each other for more than a season. My instincts kicked in as the days grew long. The sun on my arms made my mood leap, filled me with an unspecific euphoria. And then I'd remember that Sam had left and the drop back into the dirt would be from a new height.

I saw us under that same sun, winding through Montreal's summers with our fingers hooked. Walking on leaf-dappled sidewalks en route to this pleasure or that. Always on a high, filled up with each other. A weekend ahead, unfolding plans, me in the passenger seat, loving his lead. The Lebanese take-out, the canoe rentals in the Lachine Canal and the Blizzards at the Dairy Queen on Saint-Joseph to follow. All those trips up our mountain, the grand houses he had stories about mapped in my brain. I was transported back there by this blooming season, my first April for half a dozen years without his seawater eyes on me.

And I was at last so overcome with want and sorrow that I couldn't properly exist. My doctor, whom I'd telephoned to say I needed to talk about mental health, told me I'd lost weight when I sat at his desk and I heard my dull lips say something about silver linings. I didn't tell him about going six weeks without food. Or about wanting to die, but not. I did tell him that Sam had left and that I was in trouble. I cried, as I knew I would, crumpling in his sunny office with its desktop ivies and graduation photos. I'm in such bad shape, I told him.

The doctor made his voice singsongy as he tapped out prescriptions—for Ativan, for sleeping pills, for antidepressants—which I filled at the pharmacy on my way home. I took the anti-anxiety right away, and let it slip into my bloodstream like Sam's voice used to when I'd flip to him in panic. The storm raged on, but now I watched it from a shelter. After, I'd take the bottle with me when I left the house in the morning, and swallow a pill after dropping the kids at school. And sometimes in the afternoons too, so I could stay alive till dinner. The drug filled my insides with cotton. Airbags for a life that had exploded through the windshield and skidded across the highway.

The boundary between grief and illness has long been a woolly one. When Margaret Radcliffe, Queen Elizabeth I's maid of honour, died in 1599, soon after her beloved brother Alexander was killed in the Irish wars, doctors performed an autopsy on her. They found her body, according to an essay published in the *Lancet* in 2013, "all well and sound, saving certain strings striped all over her heart." Her passing was recorded as "death from sorrow."

In ancient Greece, no one would have batted an eye. There, *melaina kole*, or black bile, was the murkiest of fluid humours responsible for the healthy functioning of the body, including digestion, respiration and nutrition. The trick to avoiding sickness was balancing these fluids—especially challenging when up against so-called prolonged passions, the worst of which was sadness.

"Expel sadness far from thee; for sadness hath killed many," Thomas Wright advised his mortal peers in his 1601 book *The Passions of the Minde in General.* "There is nothing more enemy to life than sorrow," his contemporary Thomas Elyot agreed. So lethal did the world consider grief that the city of London included it as a cause of death in its weekly "bills of mortality," published from the plague years up to the mid-nineteenth century. In 1632, alongside 1,797 cases of consumption and thirty-eight cases of "King's Evil," grief is pinned for eleven deaths. Eight years later, moral philosopher Edward Reynolds compared grief in the heart to a moth in a garment, "which . . . stoppeth the voice, looseth the joints, withereth the flesh, shrivelleth the skin, dimmeth the eyes, cloudeth the countenance, deflowereth the beauty, troubleth the bowels [and] disordereth the whole frame."

Nicolas Coeffeteau, a French theologian in the early seventeenth century, was fascinated by the idea of death from sorrow. In his *Table of Human Passions*, this father of French eloquence described the autopsied insides of deceased grievers as "smothered with melancholy." Instead of a heart, he wrote, "they find nothing but a dry skin like to the leaves in autumn."

In 2018, a study out of Rice University published in *Psychoneuroendocrinology* was more prosaic. Grief can kill you, it declared. After interviewing and examining the blood of ninety-nine people whose spouses had recently died, researchers concluded that elevated grief symptoms—pining, difficulty moving on, a sense that life is meaningless, an inability to accept the loss—produce up to 17 percent more bodily inflammation than in less rattled souls. They were first to confirm that grief, irrespective of attendant depression, can promote inflammation, a contributor to almost every disease in older adulthood.

Still, there is little consensus among the disciplines of psychology, psychiatry, sociology and anthropology on the specifics of grief's relationship with pathology. When does "sorrow" become "depression"? "Carving nature at its joints," as Plato urged, is thorny work. Take the controversy the DSM-5 agitated with an amendment that opened "sadness" up to medical intervention.

Based on research showing that major depressive syndromes after the loss of a loved one were common, were often transient and didn't require treatment, the DSM-III excluded "bereavement" from the depression diagnosis in 1980. But in 2013, the fifth (and current) edition of this medical stalwart retracted the bereavement exclusion, arguing this denied some grieving patients proper treatment. This, says Jerome Wakefield, who wrote *The Loss of Sadness: How Psychiatry Transformed Normal Sorrow into Depressive Disorder* with Allan Horwitz, was "a gross error of psychiatric classification."

Such an ordinary human phenomenon as grief, the authors argue, has no business in this mental health guidebook. Including it encourages doctors to abandon common sense in favour of medication and throws the psyches of normal grievers into peril. In this new universe, heartbroken humans are mentally ill, their demolished souls plugged with medicine, their ancient impulses to mourn and cope trampled by diagnosis.

A surprising thing happened to my pain in the first year after Sam left: I got comfortable with it. This wretched companion was not Sam. But it was a relic of him, the wrapper he'd shed in his hasty exit that still bore his shape. If Sam's presence was the best thing, second best was the reassuring, constant companionship of his absence. "What I am is alive in me because of you," wrote the intense and lyrical Bohemian-Austrian poet Rainer Maria Rilke. "I do not reinvent you / at sadly cooled-off places you have left behind. / Even your absence is filled / with your warmth and is more real / than your not-existing." Now, in my car, coasting between places to wait out the daytimes till the nighttimes obliterated me, I had company.

And this company—an ache that vibrated with him—was effortless. Familiar sorrow that was in such easy reach. A habit that knew my story. Sitting at a light after depositing the children back at their schools after lunch, I would watch pedestrians march past me, and wrap this gloom around my shoulders. With it, I wasn't so terrifyingly alone. I didn't have my darling one, but I had the sorrow that connected me to him—and that sorrow was so palpable it was almost flesh and blood.

You make the most surprising friends when you're all alone.

Science shrugs at the idea of addiction to grief, not really sure where to land. It could be a question of comfort. With grief your new familiar, you know the territory, how to sustain yourself inside its perimeters—even if it's a graveyard of trouble. Or maybe you linger there because it feels good. Reporting in the journal *NeuroImage*, scientists at UCLA suggest that the pleasure once stirred by certain thoughts and memories persists after their reality has shifted, conferring the neural excursions with addictive properties. Going there keeps tickling our nucleus accumbens, a cluster of front-bottom brain neurons that host effervescent dopamine and are key players in determining which actions deliver rewards. The fact that someone we love is gone doesn't stop us from going for the same old prize.

Enter Dr. Freud, and his crushing death drive. In his 1920 opus *Beyond the Pleasure Principle*, Freud wrote of a force—later called Thanatos—that opposes Eros, which keeps us animate and multiplying. Freud identified this concept when he stumbled upon impulses that contravened his pronouncement that life seeks only pleasure. The death drive is a reflexive impulse to dwell in discomfort because we humans are perverse creatures. It pushes a person toward extinction, destruction, repetition, aggression, compulsion and an "inanimate state." It's why we insist on revisiting things that bring us sorrow. A sombre yin to the sunny yang.

As spring yielded to summer and summer yielded to fall in my first year on my own, I set up house in that snug, sad yin. Sank into its embrace. Fell in love. "If heartbreak is inevitable and inescapable," mused poet David Whyte, who may as well have been looking in on my plight, "it might be asking us to . . . make friends with it, to see it as our constant and instructive companion, and strangely perhaps, in the depth of its impact as well as in its hindsight, to see it as its own reward."

5

Ego

Before the universe could account for it, I was closing in on my second year without him, so many days of disregard in my wake. Knowing that each contained Sam's conscious election not to talk to me was a reliable reminder of my value. Which was to say none. I felt denied participation in our demise, I wailed to anyone who would listen, but damaged again by his refusal to acknowledge me. My one-time darling deciding to deprive me of not only affection but an existence was as good as daggers. Death by erasure. As he'd tried before. Only then he'd resurrected me.

I rarely told him about *this* pain, instead continuing my convention of tortured but blameless missives on my sorrow. It was so heavy to mention, so awful to talk about. But I some-times couldn't help it. Bottomless afternoons at the library when my speeding brain couldn't conceive of any reason for joy, when my need for his comfort overpowered everything, including my traction on the high road. "How terrible not to be fought for," I wrote him, one swerving occasion. "To be abandoned so effortlessly."

"I am just tears and memory now," I wrote in another.

"Ego is built on fear," American spiritual teacher Ram Dass declared in 2015. Dass, who studied LSD with his Harvard University psychology department buddy Timothy Leary, said we're all terrified of "non-survival" and that's why we construct a cage around our ego. Unguarded, the ego is vulnerable to everything, always in peril. When you give a speech or apply for work or fall in love, you put your ego in the winch. No wonder it's such a casualty of heartbreak, the fallout of one person determining to no longer cherish another, the way we fold that into our psyche. To be rejected by your lover, who carries some of your value in their cells, is to be rejected by yourself.

Diana Athill knew that. In *Because of a Letter*, the 1962 memoir the *Guardian* called "the kind of detergent autobiography that scours the soul," she told the story of her own life tragedy. When she was fifteen, she fell in love with Tony Irvine, an Oxford grad who came to tutor her brother. They went riding and punting and sailing together, and drank whiskey in pubs with cultured friends. He gave her Oscar Wilde's and T.S. Eliot's collected works, and happiness "crept up like a rising tide." Tony proposed to Diana before accepting his RAF post in Egypt, and then transferred there with a plan for her to join him in a year. Their imagined future hung over their separation for a time. And then Tony, quite suddenly, cut Diana off.

His decision to quit communication with her, to no longer write, to ignore her letters, devastated her enough that Diana still described it in searing terms three decades later. She waited, she said, for her erstwhile love in "a swamp of incredulous misery" for two years. Her agony in that stretch, she said, was like "a finger crushed under the door, or a tooth under a drill." In 1941 Tony resurfaced—but only to ask to be released from their engagement so he might marry someone else. This further thump to her sense of self pitched Diana into "a long, flat unhappiness."

Tony was killed in action soon after and never married anyone. And Diana Athill, whose rejection by him altered her DNA, spent the next two decades lost and dreadful. Her soul, she said, "shrank to the size of a pea."

At lunchtime, after feeding the kids, I would drive to a sandwich shop north of my house and set myself up in its fluorescent midst for the afternoon. I'd sit at a laminate table in front of my laptop and push lettuce around a plastic container and cry into napkins. I would just skim the surface of my writing and editing work; my waterline was so high with mourning him, there was only room in me for the shallowest of outside thought. My productivity had compressed to a tight knot of predictable employment. I couldn't get invested in anything.

Every few minutes my eye would snag on the time and my brain would flip to where Sam might be at that moment. On a bench press in the shiny gym pants I used to tease him about. Bent over his guitar teaching a student harmonic stress.

Climbing the mountain in his little white Toyota, his sheet music on the passenger seat in the buckled satchel I gave him. I'd summon his face to my brain: his smooth skin, his deep smile lines, his seawater eyes. I'd play out one of our "lasts." Our last hotel room or dinner around his parents' table or time we fucked on his couch. And I'd wonder: *Is he thinking of me, too?*

Rupert Sheldrake, who invented a field of study around such questions, might be inclined to say yes. Telephone telepathy is the telepathic communication that takes place when you think of someone and they call. As he describes on his website, he asked sixty-three people in 571 trials to guess which of four potential people might be phoning and had a success rate of 40 percent—well above the presumed 25. After kissing his wife on New Year's Eve in his New York nightclub in the final scene of *Café Society*, Jesse Eisenberg thinks of Kristen Stewart, who broke his heart years before. Pan to Stewart at her Hollywood house party with her husband, who's asked why her "eyes look so dreamy"—and see that she's thinking of him, too. I love this movie for this final scene. *Maybe*, I think. Maybe.

Freud did "ego" first. He called it *Ich*—or *I*—and declared it the mediator of other human urges, charged with keeping id from blowing it all in the casino without ceding so much to superego's prudence that no one ever even leaves the hotel room to step into the bar. It is the brain's problem-solving system, concerned with moderating instinct and conscience, and with keeping its host alive. The ego's on point when the id's tamped to socially acceptable levels and the personality's operating in the real world.

But our concept of ego has changed since Freud unveiled the term. Where he used it in reference to the conscious part of our psychoanalytic brain, we talk about egos as boastful negatives that crowd a character. We cluck at their size and self-importance. But huge egos simply belong to people with huge senses of self. And maybe the oversized models are lucky for the protection they offer against assaults from the outside world—among their most essential functions. "The human ego prefers just about anything to falling or changing or dying," American ecumenical teacher Richard Rohr wrote in *Falling Upward.* "The ego is that part of you that loves the status quo. . . . It attaches to past and present and fears the future."

When I'd feared the future for almost two years, I wrote my friend Kyla. It was a Saturday night and I was home alone, eating yellow rice and watching *House of Cards* in my bed. "Thursday is the goddamn second anniversary of his deciding I wasn't the one for him, and taking his fucking leave, and the launch of the Revised Version of Me, this iteration sadder and more despondent than any of the earlier ones," I said, invoking the various wretched editions of my personality since the heartbreak had set in. "I miss him desperately and fiercely and always. I am so injured by how he rejected me that I don't know how to move forward."

I'd tried. I'd taken the kids to *Phantom of the Opera* on the weekend and started painting my little girl's room pink.

I'd volunteered on a yearbook for the hundredth anniversary of the children's elementary school. I'd harked back to my old life on the boards by signing up to audition for Muriel Bingham at my community theatre's production of *Fox on the Fairway* and practised a monologue from *Our Town*.

"Just for a moment let's be happy," I recited in the car, tears streaming. "It goes so fast. We don't have time to look at one another."

I woke up on audition day wishing he knew what I was up to. I was starving for his delight, which had fed me for six years. I got to the theatre fifteen minutes before my two o'clock slot. The group was an urban version of community theatre: not as quaint but just as catty. I sat in the waiting room on a set-piece couch beside another would-be Muriel Bingham. She knew where to sign in and was chummy with the guy at the desk. I faced the wall and studied the head-shots. The lights were watery in this basement room and the place felt dingy. Its stewards had a taste for British farce and insisted upon authentic accents so I'd mostly steered clear. This pivot to American romp was a crack in the doorway to a possible revived amateur acting stint.

Still, I was nervous as hell. I wasn't inclined to make small talk with the competition and avoided their eye contact. I followed the cheerful woman who'd called my name through the black velvet curtains and onto the stage, which was just a painted floor in a rehearsal room. The two people smiling at the desk in front of me said to take my time, and I did. But I got self-conscious in the silence and leapt into my speech prematurely. I felt as if they noticed so focused on that for half of it, my lines tumbling like gravel. Then I thanked them for their smile-plastered indulgence, parted the black velvet again and came back into the waiting room. I didn't make eye contact this time either.

When I failed to win the part of Muriel Bingham, my ego's pilot light, already so faintly lit, blew out. The blackness of rejection was closing in. "Please don't leave me alone out here in the dark," I wrote Sam after. "I have had all of my confidence knocked out of me, all my sense of self, any idea that I might have value." *It goes so fast. We don't have time to look at one another.*

In the 1990s, Mark Leary, a professor of psychology and neuroscience at Duke University in North Carolina, uncovered a link between how accepted or rejected by others a person feels and their self-esteem, and published an article about it in *Current Directions in Psychological Science*. It was a revelation that flew in the face of almost all the prevailing theories about that critical marker of life experience. Up till then, we'd conceptualized self-esteem as a person's private self-evaluation only. And we'd believed we should have lots of it, regardless of how others treated us. *Buck up*, people said. *Feel good about yourself.*

As if we could.

Leary sought to prove it by bringing subjects into his lab five at a time to study how we mess with each other's self-concept. After inviting everyone to introduce themselves, he had them rate preferred partners for an upcoming task. When people learned they'd been rejected by these near strangers, their self-esteem dove.

James Baldwin, a Princeton psychology professor whose contributions to early discussions of developmental psychology were seminal, dug in. He called our sense of self the product of "suggestions from others"—an extraordinary idea in an empowered age. "The ego and the alter are born together," he famously said, just before the twentieth century launched. So treat a person like a hero and she'll drape herself in silk; treat her like a loser and she'll strip off all her pride. "He himself at every stage is really in part someone else, even in his own thought of himself," he wrote in his 1897 *Social and Ethical Interpretations in Mental Development.*

It's a terrifying notion, that other people get to determine how we define ourselves, that our well-being and sense of self are at the mercy of someone else's carelessness and intention. It means that another (whether stranger or lover) can injure our precious ego. It means that they can murder it.

Dr. Karl Albrecht called ego death "the fear of the shattering or disintegration of one's constructed sense of lovability, capability and worthiness" and included it in his list of human's five essential fears. Another, built on the same scaffolding, is the fear of abandonment, rejection and loss of connectedness. It's the dread, said this American executive coach and author, "of becoming a non-person."

"What can I do, baby?" I asked Sam in a dread-filled email I sent across the bawling air currents between Toronto and Montreal when he'd been gone two years. "Please help me. I am in so much pain. Please don't make me beg. Please, at least respond. Please release me from this torment."

And he did release me, a little. Though not from my torment.

One day, I went on Facebook and Sam wasn't my friend anymore. His profile page stared back at me generically, set off by a green bar suggesting I *add* this contact—this man who'd made my feet burn in his bed, who could read my mood in a word—as a *friend*. And with that, my pea-sized soul contracted further.

That he'd kept that social line open for all this time had fuelled me. It had given me hope. It had permitted me orbiting—the ability for socially obsessed humans to hover weightless above each other's lives—before it was a cultural trend. Now I was truly cut loose. Space dust. *It goes so fast. We don't have time to look at one another.*

Complicating this, of course, was the fact that we still shared cyber connections, including my children. I exploited that after the excision by convincing my youngest to give me her Facebook password under an unlikely premise, so I could see him through her. Sam stayed pretty silent on social media; I mostly used this access to send him secret messages in postings to her page, which I knew he'd see. Like effusive birthday wishes to her that I loaded with memories that were his too. And photos—of me, my hair perfect, and my kids, and Mr. Cat, all of whom Sam had loved—so he could still see us out there, doing our thing. It was part gift to me, this idea that his eyes were on us. And it was part gift to him, because I knew he must miss this little band, his other family for half a dozen years.

Romantic rejection, said a study on "heartbreak, anger, guilt, scriptlessness and humiliation" published in the *Journal of Personality and Social Psychology* in 1993, damages a person's sense of attractiveness, desirability and deservingness. It "carries a symbolic message of inferiority" and the injury to a person's ego can be significant.

The extent of the injury? Depends on your DNA. Scientists already knew that the OPRM1 factor makes us more sensitive to physical pain, and that people with a G allele variant on this gene need more morphine than others to extinguish the pain. If emotional pain travels the same pathways, they pondered, maybe G allele carriers also experience more intense versions of *emotional pain*. Heartbreak on drugs. In 2009, they—psychology professors at UCLA, including Naomi Eisenberger—published a groundbreaking study that proved they do. So-called G carriers have less capacity to compensate for negative emotion—whether it's in response to physical *or* social pain. Infant rhesus monkeys (whose relevant opioid receptor resembles ours) with G allele genes are louder with their vocalized distress when they're away from their mothers, and cling to them longer when they come back. Freighted with two years of such afflictive loss, I was evidently hauling heavy G.

DNA aside, the intensity of the damage rejection inflicts hangs on the intensity of the romance. Jumping off evidence that new relationships expand their participants' self-concepts, scientists discovered that the chemistry extends to the opposite periphery, when a relationship ends. The more a relationship *expanded* a person's idea of themselves, they wrote in a

2006 issue of the journal *Personal Relationships*, the more that idea shrinks when it's over. This, along with earlier science confirming what the poets already knew—that we knit our romantic partners' selves with our own—is bad news for sops like me who'd had their self-concepts, now thoroughly deflated, expanded so magnificently in the days when their unions filled them up.

My friends, alarmed by the persistence of my grief, suggested I replace him. Get over one guy by getting under another and all that. I couldn't imagine how that could make anything better. Like losing a hen and buying a lawn mower. Another man was not Sam. The hole he'd left in my life had his dimensions.

But I was reeling. I felt so lonely and smashed up all the time. The ache I dragged behind me was enormous. I would've done anything for relief.

I wrote an online dating profile that was filled with woe, each sentence wincing with apology. I said I couldn't believe I was on such a site, that it was an experiment, being there. I said I always thought someone would feel lucky to be loved by me, and other things that tipped experienced profile readers off that they were dealing with someone who'd been left behind. I sounded angry and sad.

Still, because I was fresh, I got notes from men who were interested in meeting up. And because I was spinning in amorphous despair, I met them. Maybe they could still the spin.

For a long stretch, many months, I saw a different man almost every night. Four or five or six nights a week I left my children (between fourteen and twenty by this point) in our house and met men at the bar near the bottom of my street. I generally sat in the same window seat, a wingback turned slightly toward a more modest, wingless companion. A spider needs a commanding post from which to cast her web. At least that's how it looked—especially to the doorman, who smiled like Idris Elba to say he'd noticed my quarry. Truly, my superior armchair was more about emotional comfort: I could duck into its winged embrace as required and pretend this wasn't my life.

I'd drink wine at these rickety meetings with strangers, glass after glass in quick succession. In between glasses I'd go to the bathroom and cry. Once, I stumbled out from the bar into the neighbourhood and threw up on someone's front lawn. My date, who was shocked, left me sprawled on the grass while he rushed off to get water. I told him I was fine and that I'd make my own way home. I didn't care a bit.

The men, as far as my vantage point suggested, were ridiculous. Shapeless and shifty-looking. Too young or too old. "Between jobs" and living in their mothers' basements. One guy was four hundred pounds, on a liquid diet. He told me he couldn't ride a bike because he'd break it. Another, labelled "Swiss" in his profile, had such an impenetrable Polish accent I couldn't understand him. I could never recognize my dates when they came squinting into the pub because I'd not really looked at their photos. I'd forget their names as soon as they said them. Sometimes I'd keep a note of their information on my phone that I'd flip to.

We'd ask our questions. Who is your family? What was your childhood? Why are you here? I developed a patter that was easy to drop into. It wasn't joyful, this patter. It was sardonic and self-defeating. I told everybody about Sam. Confessed that I loved someone who lived in Montreal and had left me in tatters. I couldn't help it. It seemed terrifically disloyal to be meeting another man without him there. So I brought Sam out and introduced him to my company.

Once, I brought my friend Alexandra too. The guy was surprised to find his date waiting for him with some other woman, but I was just too lonely to be doing this cheerless assignment on my own. Sometimes I'd have my kids phone me at a predetermined time so I could feign distress over an imagined calamity at the house and race back there.

I rarely left the comfort of my neighbourhood. I met one guy at a downtown wine bar who had declared himself a childless, non-smoking PhD of a certain age and height. But he was a high school dropout whose three kids presumably knew their father to be ten years older than I did. He'd also shrunk half a foot since filling out his profile and taken up smoking. His cellphone wallpaper was a topless beach selfie before he'd added the pot belly, presumably the product of the expensive wine he favoured, whose sticker price he announced as he ordered bottles to our table. At the end of our date, he was surprised I was heading home and couldn't be convinced to join him at the hotel room he'd reserved for us.

I saw a couple of the guys more than once. One of them lived in the country, and he invited me out to have dinner with him on a Saturday night. He lived on a grand property, set back from the road and behind a gate he had to open with a remote control. I drove there in a stupor. It was something to do, a way to fill an empty evening. Could be he'd save me.

When I arrived, he opened his garage and showed me his Porsche. Then he took me into his place and gave me wine. I gulped it back and so did he. In short order, he excused himself, bolted down to his basement bathroom and began retching profusely. I sat at his kitchen table and listened while night fell across his yard. The retching continued. I drank more wine and texted my friends that my date was in the basement, vomiting. The Chinese food he'd gotten for us sat on the counter, the top of the paper bag still folded under itself.

After an hour, I decided to leave. I didn't know this guy and couldn't imagine creeping downstairs and embarrassing the both of us to discover him in a puddle of puke. But when I drove to the bottom of the driveway, the gate was locked, and so I had to skulk into the basement after all to ask for the remote control. I found him in bed in the dark, mortified by what had happened. He begged for a second chance. When I came back for dinner a month later, the quiet drive out just as lonely as before, exactly the same thing happened. We drank, he bolted, he vomited, I weighed my options a floor above him, and I fled. I had to finagle the gate remote a second time too.

My longest encounter was with a guy named Matt who told me he loved me on our first date. He also told me he'd been pulled back from leaping off a subway platform a couple of weeks earlier, and that he'd had to call his dad over once to keep him from murdering his ex-wife. I stayed with Matt for six weeks.

Matt gave me a winter coat and a cute black hat and a card that said he couldn't wait to spend his life with me. In him, I had Friday nights out and someone to text. But he liked to do things I didn't, like ice-skate and care about stuff. I never once let him into my house—that was Sam's space. At his spotless condo I couldn't put my feet on his coffee table and he made me smoke my weed on his balcony while he wrinkled his nose inside. He did not approve. I did not care. I was reeling, paddling so wildly, just trying to stay afloat.

One afternoon, he got pissed off when I paused our telephone conversation to address my daughter and he told me it was over, that I'd disrespected him. He blocked all our social connections and clammed up. That was that and I barely noticed. When he'd been gone a month, I couldn't even remember what he looked like.

I stopped trying to replace Sam after that because there wasn't any point.

But make no mistake, I—a flattened ego on legs—was no prize either. Two and a half silent years after sustaining the assault, I was still smarting and yearning. He'd never said a word and I let that injure me constantly. Disregard, says Kipling D. Williams, an American psych prof who's studied the subject extensively, is the ego's cruellest assailant. He calls ostracism "among the most devastating experiences a person can endure." Animals who are ostracized don't survive. Once set adrift by their crew, they lack both the resources to find food and the pack for protection. For humans, exceptionally social creatures whose dependence on others is arguably bigger than anyone else's, close relationships are equally critical. If our ancestors couldn't sustain associations with intimates, they perished.

No wonder psychology emphasizes the importance of creating and maintaining relationships. "Without friends, no one would choose to live, though he had all other goods," Aristotle said. "There is something in staying close to men and women, and looking on them, and in the contact and odour of them, that pleases the soul," said Walt Whitman, twenty-two centuries later.

In the book he wrote with Erika J. Koch, *Emotional Responses to Interpersonal Rejection*, Mark Leary considers the consequences of a soul denied that pleasure. If you've been left behind, he says, you might suffer sadness, jealousy, isolation, envy, guilt and embarrassment. In the moment, people who've been rejected experience anxiety and depression; in the longer term, they internalize low levels of self-esteem and a general lack of well-being. Rejection slows their heart rate. Some try to kill themselves; some succeed. My children and parents, to whom I was deeply connected, kept me from even considering that option.

To the list add aggression, linked to rejection in a 2001 Surgeon General of the US report. Think of school shootings and dismissed employees going postal. Still, the research is clear: much of the aggression that rejection arouses is pointed inward. Same with disdain. "I was rejected," we say, the passive participants in our own tragedies. It's a hell of a posture to take: just when our ego is at its lowest, we heave up a sack of self-loathing. Rejection does half the damage, says American psychologist and author Guy Winch; we do the rest.

Research also uncovered a connection between social exclusion and reduced intellectual functioning. Multiple studies reveal that our cerebral performance dries up if we think we're going to be rebuffed. Participants told they would end up alone performed significantly worse on general intelligence tests—were less able to retrieve information from memory and bombed the logic—than those who believed their future would be filled with belonging and meaningful relationships.

Perhaps most significantly, researchers learned that we castoffs feel the pain of it in our muscles and bones as much as our psyches. Scientists confirmed in 2012 that physical and social pain experiences rely on shared neural substrates, in the first study of social exclusion in humans.

They believe that's so because, a thousand generations of rejection ago, our ancestors' social attachment systems co-opted the pain system's siren to prevent the species-ending consequences of social separation. This mingling of our social and physical needs, said American neuroscientist Paul MacLean, helps explain why "a sense of separation is a condition that makes being a mammal so painful."

Christmases had turned painful when my kids' dad and I split. It was lonely overseeing the season by myself, and I suffered the usual guilt separated parents feel about stealing their family's easy experience with it. But when I met Sam, from that very first holiday and for six more after, my joy returned.

We didn't see each other at Christmas, holding out for Boxing Day reunions that kicked off animated week-long holidays to the south. But we were part of each other's celebrations just the same. We both had traditions of attending

Christmas Eve services—once-a-year appearances at respective neighbourhood churches, me before dinner in Toronto, him at midnight in Montreal. Christmas magic could collapse geography and time, so when we lit our candles off our neighbours' and sang "Silent Night" in the flickering ambience they cast across our programs, we could have been together, our thighs touching on the same pew.

There's nothing like Christmas Eve. No night's so crisp or huge or enchanted as the one that delivers the world across into Christmas. Our conversations on these nights were always intimate and effervescent, both of us still fairy-dusted from our church visits and the walks home in the snow after, chatting breathlessly to people we hadn't spoken to in a year. I'd put Sam on speakerphone so I could wrap presents while we talked. I loved hearing about his Christmas Eves in the cozy church he'd visited since he was a kid. It was within walking distance of both his apartment and his childhood home, where his parents still lived. Years earlier, Sam had stepped up for the resident caretaker, whom the church was mistreating, and he served for a time on its board. Sometimes he'd play at a special occasion there, releasing all his elaborate music into the hallowed rafters. When the little church closed from lack of business, Sam was so sad. I tracked down a brass offering plate from the congregation and got it engraved for him.

After the Christmas Eve service, Sam used to walk a grateful widow home, lending her his arm across the snowbanks, basking in the community of the special night in his beloved city. He would tell me about that, his annual encounter with this woman he'd known since he was young, and I would cut wrapping paper and write tags and feel grateful. "I wish you were here," I'd say, and he would tell me something like "I am, baby. I want you to feel it." And I would.

Then I'd tuck the phone under my ear and deliver all the gifts to the tree and drink Santa's milk and fill the stockings. And all the while Sam would talk to me and make my solitary maternal labours—bloated this night with so much expectation—less solitary. When it was at last all set up for morning, I'd head upstairs. "Look outside now," I would tell him from my dark bedroom window before we said good night, and Sam and I would peer across the crackling Christmas Eve at each other as though there was no sky between us at all.

I thought about all this on the second Christmas Eve after he left. About the candles and the carols, the widow and the snowbank. His arm. I thought of it while I went through my Christmas rituals in silence, arranging the presents under the tree, tucking oranges and lottery tickets into stockings, writing Santa's blocky notes of thanks for the cookies. Then I turned out the lights and went up the stairs alone, no one in my ear saying I'd done a good job putting on another Christmas for my children, no one who noticed, no one who knew.

When I looked out the window into the deep magic sky the second Christmas Eve after Sam left, my gaze went on and on, didn't meet up with anything at all.

"My dear little love," I wrote Sam one afternoon when he'd been quiet for more than two years. "I think it would help me, if your heart and soul are utterly and undeniably convinced that they are done with me, if you would write and tell me so.

This silence has been crazy for me." Elie Wiesel's comment about the opposite of love being indifference was never far from me in this stillness.

The silent treatment is the most insidious quill in ostracism's quiver. When someone expecting a door gets a wall, the blow to the ego is tremendous. It generates the special quality of suffering that comes with being erased. Here is soundless rebuke—an ancient tool of psychological punishment—and its power to steal its victims' identity and voice and value. To send them spinning in squalls of isolation and grief. To make them question not only the relationship they had but the person they are. Here is disregard, and the layer it adds to rejection, the combination confirming that you matter not at all.

Even a fiery argument grants both participants the dignity of voice—there's a sense of control inside the flinging invective. That's not the case with the silent treatment, which shuts one party up and down. "Silence," said George Bernard Shaw, "is the most perfect expression of scorn." Mark Leary's theory says self-esteem actually bottoms out not when people believe others despise them, but when they believe others feel neutrally about them. So we feel just as badly about ourselves when people ignore us as when they hate us.

Various academics have taken a run at the subject over the years. One of them, Paul Schrodt, a communications prof from Texas Christian University, reviewed the relationships of fourteen thousand people. Afterward, he declared the silent treatment "the most common pattern of conflict" they contain.

"It does tremendous damage," he said.

In *Ostracism: The Power of Silence*, social scientist Kipling D. Williams tells the story of Lee, a woman in her seventies from the American Midwest whose husband had silenced her for the last forty years of his life. She couldn't even remember what had inspired the punishment, but she wept when she recounted the years she'd spent in its grip. "I wish he would've beaten me instead of giving me the silent treatment, because at least it would have been a response," she told Williams. "This has ruined my life. . . . It's the meanest thing that you can do to someone."

With Meidung, an exercise of shunning practised in the Amish faith, individuals are actively singled out for comprehensive neglect. Practitioners conspire to ignore other humans—refusing to speak with them or eat with them or even acknowledge them. The victims, accused of violating the Ordnung, the church's unwritten expectations for adherents' daily living, suffer a "slow death," said American lawyer Margaret Gruter. The faithful defend Meidung with a biblical prophecy: "And if any man obey not our words by this epistle, note that man, and have no company with him, that he may be ashamed," says 2 Thessalonians 3:14. Mennonites, Hutterites and Jehovah's Witnesses also practise forms of shunning.

In 1947, a court in the heart of Ohio's Amish country heard a case of Meidung. The plaintiff, a thirty-three-year-old Amish farmer named Andrew J. Yoder, sued a bishop and two preachers from his old-order Amish church for $40,000 in damages and a court injunction against a "boycott" he alleged they'd arranged for him. Yoder claimed the church had "mited" him for five years for purchasing a car so he could transport his polio-stricken daughter to medical appointments, a move that contravened church doctrine. The community disregard made him feel like a "whipped dog," Yoder told the jury at his civil trial. But his opponents were convinced that this man had broken the pact he'd made with God with this acquisition, and that their actions complied with the commandments.

Yoder said he was satisfied with the verdict, which awarded him $5,000, but the payout allegedly did nothing to mitigate the Meidung of this man whose ego had been flattened under the boots of loved ones fleeing him. "In the end, we will remember not the words of our enemies," Martin Luther King Jr. said, "but the silence of our friends."

And so I wasn't alone. Nor were the helpful people who pointed out that if I didn't write to Sam, I wouldn't be shunned by Sam. But if I didn't write to Sam, I wouldn't be okay. *Be quiet,* he'd declared with his retreat—but I still had things to say. And I would say them until I didn't care to anymore. I had no other valve. My head was jammed and I had to unload. It was a perverse delight, this unorthodox exercise of calling to someone who never called back, and I would draw it out, savouring the purpose it gifted my indifferent life for a day or longer while I worked on my note, always anxious, always hopeful. He never said a word. My ego never knew what hit it.

6

Happiness

"Joy and woe," wrote William Blake, "are woven fine." I could have said as much in that third year without Sam, when their needles pricked me all the time. I'd soar with the memory of us sharing red wine at a bring-your-own joint in Montreal or making each other howl on the beach in Grand Bend, then dive to know the moments were over. I rode the spectrum like a pro, keeping the woe in check while I made appearances at the house and in the car and at the libraries. I spoke and I reacted. I worked and went to restaurants and talked about other things. But I was wholly occupied with thoughts of him.

I went to the cottage in the fall, just me and my dog, to run and write. The path to Sam was short here in this site of childhood idyll. We'd burned through so many summers on its ancient beach at the crook of Huron's embrace. I thought of him as I ran, my feet pounding the lake road, guarded by pines and shafts of sun. I saw a mother and her toddler, just up from the beach in a green hat, and thought: that child was not even imagined last we were together. That woman with the red shovel hadn't even conceived of this love yet, its vibrations hadn't started. And now on this autumn retreat I ran through them, watched them stir the leaves beside the road. I thought of the impossibility of their love and the miracle of its conjuring, my steps dropping hard. And I thought of our miracle too, mine and Sam's, and how it was as much for its evaporation as its appearance.

My turnaround point was the end of the beach road, where the provincial park begins. Sam had hidden in the bushes there in our last summer, ducking away on an evening walk and jumping out at me for fun. I'd shrieked, and when he'd emerged from the brambles, he was laughing and covered in scratches. I thought about that on this solo turnaround all those years later, my dog already heading back the other way. My life had become dull in his absence. No more fizzing anticipation or scratchy surprise. Just my childhood beach road and my footfalls and my memory. What about all *our* vibrations, which had thrummed for years before that mother knew any with her child? What about all our happiness? Where'd it go? Where does nature store all of humanity's joy, once it's released to the ether?

Happiness is heartbreak's critical counterpoint, illuminating the darkness with contrast. We have to know one to appreciate the other. So say psychologists, parsing our mental forays between the two. Does returning to past states of contentedness fill us with gratitude for remembered pleasure or pain for what we no longer have? In the former, the *endowment effect* deposits experiences in a memory bank whose contents enrich our ongoing bliss. In the latter, the *contrast effect* ensures a constant point of nostalgic reference for more fortunate times.

What we'll remember and in what light is a crapshoot—everything on these cerebral excursions might as likely inspire surges of joy as descents into sadness. Still, science gives us a pretty reliable clue. Happier people, says Sonja Lyubomirsky, a distinguished professor at the University of California Riverside, who has devoted most of her research career to the study of happiness, endow past events with positivity, extracting pleasure from what they *were*, and contrast negative ones, highlighting the improvement of their present; while unhappy people endow events with negativity, letting their sour tastes persist, and contrast good times bitterly, furious at the universe for turning off the lights.

The subject of happiness turns us all into philosophers. Everyone has something to say on this elusive, essential condition, this charmed state of being in whose company days are weightless, and in whose absence a bag of stones. And why not—the benefits happiness bestows are huge. Life satisfaction, mental stability, enhanced creativity, even fatter paycheques. Compared with their downcast peers, says Lyubomirsky and other happiness researchers, happy people are more sociable, charitable and co-operative. They're more likely to get married and stay there. They're more grateful and philanthropic, more optimistic about the future, more comfortable with the present. They have expanded world views—confirmed with experiments in which people given sweet treats had wider perspectives and were better at integrating complex information in decisions. Doctors who'd had their "positive affect" spiked with a bag of candies bested their not-treated peers in creative problem solving—important, say the study's authors, because it could help with diagnosis, where spying connections is the point.

Happy people are deeply committed to goals. They're more productive, are better negotiators and enjoy higher-quality work. They're more creative and innovative. They're more energetic and have better immune systems. Happiness reduces pain, controls blood pressure and may offer protection against disease. Happy people live longer.

We know about the longevity because of the nun study, among the most famous contemplations of happiness and age. In 2001, scientists from the University of Kentucky scrutinized autobiographic essays Catholic nuns had hand-written upon taking their vows six decades earlier, when they were mostly in their twenties. The sisters who'd expressed the most positive feelings lived seven to ten years longer than their more sullen counterparts.

Had I been invited to write an autobiographic essay in that third solo year, it would've been a study in despair. All this time past, all those summers my skin went brown outside his gaze, all those bedtimes without him in my ear, and still my heart was broken.

The "still" part bothered me. At least as far as optics went. I always felt a stab of shame for failing to abide society's expectations for my recovery.

The recovery part bothered me too. Who was to say I would ever have one? And what it would mean if I didn't. That it was too big to swallow, or I was just incapable of it?

I'd test myself on these points regularly, mentally screening expired versions of us to see if I could sustain them. I'd summon us around a campfire outside the summer cottage we rented, Sam playing "Hey There, Delilah" for my kids in their jammies. Night-swimming at that Cuba hotel pool until we got kicked out for being there after hours. In that Crescent Street bar overlooking the race cars that soaring sunshiny Montreal day. They never lost their ink, no matter how often I ran them through the projector.

That confused me. I thought it would be nice to feel happier. To not wake up to that weight on my chest, to not fill the car's drink holders with napkins I'd wept into. But I also thought it would be a disgrace. If I'd reached a place where his impact on me had flattened, our value flattened too.

I once knew a man who moved through women like a ghost, never lingering on how they'd changed him. My relationships were the Trembling Giant, a sprawling clonal grove in the middle of Utah whose trees all share a root system. In its subterranean tangle, almost the oldest living organism, the roots of one tree entwine themselves in the roots of another, their ancient, sinewy arms looped and clinging. The braided embrace linking Sam and me was buried the deepest.

But things were different for us on top of the dirt, where our trees had been separate for more than two years, their branches twisting away from each other abruptly. Sorrow growing out of buried joy.

Before it was an emotional state, happiness was the province of the divine and the moral, the product of effort, discipline and devotion. "Happiness is a life lived according to virtue," Aristotle declared, and said few would achieve it, the ethical elite. The Stoics agreed: virtue was sufficient for happiness. Even, said Epictetus, one of Stoicism's principal practitioners, if you were in danger, exile or disgrace—if you had virtue, you had a life worth living.

But Homer called happiness a function of providence alone—happy people were lucky, full stop. Many of the world's languages back him up: every Indo-European tongue traces happiness's roots to luck. "Fortune's wheel turn[s] treacherously," said the Monk in *Canterbury Tales*. "And out of happiness bring[s] men to sorrow." By medieval times, happiness was heaven, only achievable, said Thomas Aquinas, through the bliss of union with God. And then the Enlightenment reinvented happiness as an entitlement, and Jacobin leader Louis Antoine Léon de Saint-Just called it "a new idea in Europe." At the end of the seventeenth century English philosopher John Locke was plain: the "business of man is to be happy," he said. Across the ocean, Thomas Jefferson declared its pursuit a self-evident truth.

With this hedonistic recasting, happiness was democratized. The masses, freed to claim their earthly pleasures, did so without apology—and made concrete some of our most noble humanitarian sentiments (including the belief that suffering is wrong and that all people deserve happiness) along the way. But this transformation also launched a mad scramble for emotional highs that produced a culture of disappointment. "Happiness today is not just a possibility or an option but a requirement and a duty," writes Pascal Bruckner in *Perpetual Euphoria: On the Duty to Be Happy*. Keep striving, said nineteenth-century German nihilist Arthur Schopenhauer, but know your efforts will nosedive in a crucible of craving.

The scramble persisted and attaining happiness became a global goal, launching philosophers, theologians, psychologists, even economists on expeditions into its wilderness. They discovered that happiness is complicated and awash in confusion. And that most of us don't even *know* if we're happy, given the absence of empirical measures to confirm it. "As much as the scientist might wish for it, there isn't a view from nowhere," writes prominent Harvard psychologist Daniel Gilbert in his book *Stumbling on Happiness*. Happiness hit its zenith in the 1990s, when positive psychology emerged and Bhutan introduced the concept of Gross National Happiness to the United Nations as a paradigm for alternative development. In 2013, the United Nations declared March 20 International Day of Happiness, and Sam messaged me from Europe. "I am so looking forward to seeing you," he said. "I have missed you so much and am ready to come home to my girl. Has felt very long without you."

There was a time when happiness was everywhere.

In the beginning, when the skies were cheap, Sam and I would travel to each other by plane, alternating the flights and airport pickups every second week. Each destination had its charms, but for me nothing beat my visits to Sam. Where a weekend in Toronto stuck me with routine and obligation, a weekend in Montreal was everything else.

The Wednesday evening was for packing, my giraffe-print duffle open on my bed, my children sprawled around it. I'd try on outfits then twirl in the hallway light so my daughters (who were pretty young at the beginning of the relationship but almost all teenagers by the end) could make their picks. Tops that wound around me twice and tied at my hip. Boots and jeans. Silver. I'd picture myself wearing each of them inside Montreal's milieu, imagine Sam's pleasure, expand with anticipation. "The first or the second?" I'd ask my girls, giddy because I knew both were good.

Everything was.

Once my bag was packed, I'd float down to the kitchen to make the next day's lunches and finish the weekend's note for their father, who took over with the children every other weekend. The kids would drift in my wake, accidental beneficiaries of my joy. We'd talk about school and summer and then congregate around my laptop to take photos that stretched our faces and made everybody laugh.

Later, after I'd squared the instructions on the kitchen table and kissed my dear housemates good night, Sam would phone. He'd be home from work by then and flying too. So we'd light up the stratosphere with five hundred kilometres of fizzing imminence. Then we'd close our conversations with incredulous pronouncements that we'd see each other *tomor-row*. We never lost the excitement of having reached this part of our cycle; it always lit us up.

I would feel, on those Wednesday nights, lovely and adored. Filled up to the top. Here on this day would be my children and all of their delights and there on the next would be my love and all of his. I would always struggle to fall asleep; I couldn't believe my luck.

But the Thursdays were even better. Anticipation can blow your mind, said a 2013 study that found wanting things makes us happier than having them—and the Thursdays were all about the want. I would swim in it all through the workday's industry, the trundle to the airport, the hauling across various points of entry, the business of boarding a plane. And then there I'd be, suspended in the final hour before him, before us. The last scented gusts that inflate the waiting of something amazing. *Voorpret*, the vigorous Dutch called it: the sense of enjoyment before a party or event—*pre-fun*.

My routine at the other end was automatic, and it was just as well—my head was full of stars: retrieve my carry-on from the overhead bin, sail up the aisle in a river of French, skirt past the Tim Hortons and down the escalator, duck into the bathroom just this side of the airport exit. There, after I'd shrugged off my coat and dug my hairbrush from my bag, I'd look at myself in the mirror and see a firecracker, its wick lit since Wednesday.

I'd been set off before in other relationships and other men had loved me. But none had made me explode like Sam. And none had so well understood how you had to blow up the sky while you could. We did it with food and sex and weed and whatever parts of the world we could get to before our ashes rained down. We did it with language, cast in knotted ropes across our cities. Sam let me fill his inbox with poetry, which was such a gift. Mine had been a life in search of people whose mouths liked the taste of my words, and so here was a rare specimen. And such a beautiful one.

We did it with music, which was always behind our story. In Arabic, *tarab* is "musically induced ecstasy or enchantment." When we went to Cuba, Sam invoked it with his travelling guitar, all the sunburnt tourists cocking their heads at our balcony when he played there at happy hour. *The thing is,* I would think, tipping my wine and regarding his audience, *I get to take this music home with me. Our hours are always happy.*

And so we fed on each other, writing and playing and fucking, a thousand points of light. And we did it all inside the exquisite torture of a long-distance relationship, the inherent privation, privilege and prolonging of which cannot be overstated. Extraordinary circumstances breed extraordinary experiences and our intermittent encounters were feverish. I was overheated as I brushed my hair in the airport bathroom on those brilliant Thursday evenings, my sparks glancing off the tiles. I was beautiful and couldn't wait to show him, to step out of those sliding doors and into the Montreal evening and his Toyota. To light up the sky with our happiness.

The ancient Greeks assigned happiness two houses: eudaimonic and hedonic. In eudaimonia, happiness is the consequence of meaningful pursuits and is accorded moral value. Dwell in states of self-control, justice, wisdom and courage, said Socrates, and you dwell in eudaimonia. And while eudaimonia's gifts extend to our physical well-being—boosting immune systems, lowering reactivity to stress—it's an objective condition. Humans participate in it irrespective of their emotional states.

Hedonic happiness is a whole different place on the map. Here, happiness is the sticky sum of all the sensory pleasures. Proponents of hedonism, which takes its name from the ancient Greek's *pleasure*, believe the experience of living should spring from indulgence alone. Maximize happiness, minimize hurt, à la Wolf of Wall Street Jordan Belfort. Hedonists dig in to carnal delights without restraint, filling their bellies, actual and metaphoric, with every extravagance they can reach.

The concept started with Epicurus, who considered pleasure the very idea of existence. In his philosophy, the sun on your face, the syrup from a peach, the trill of a sparrow were cause for a swooning heart. But this bearded logician recommended a sober take on pleasure and urged his contemporaries to live modest lives of limited desires. In a letter summarizing his position to his chum Menoeceus, Epicurus was specific: "By pleasure we mean the absence of pain in the body and of trouble in the soul. It is not by an unbroken succession of drinking bouts and of revelry, not by sexual lust, nor the enjoyment of fish and other delicacies of a luxurious table."

So, different from hedonism after all, which promotes gorging on that fish and staging an orgy in its bones.

I used to know a thing or two about hedonism.

Ours would start in the car, into which I'd so giddily hop outside the Montreal airport's doors on the weekends we'd nest in that city. And there'd be Sam. After eleven days of yearning, in the flesh. His whole self would hit me as Lara did Zhivago, "like the first wave of the seas as you run down over the sandy beach in the dark." He was beautiful; he had such a gentle soul. He'd kiss me and tell me it was me who was beautiful. And then we'd put my things in the back seat with his guitar—along for the ride after his last class—and roar off into our weekend under all these pyrotechnics.

Sam would keep his hand on mine all the way to Amir. We'd stop there to pick up shish taouk and crack jokes in the restaurant's glare while they packed up our little pots of tzatziki. Then it was home at last and it felt like the lights switched on. We'd park in the basement lot where he rented a space on King Edward. If it was icy, Sam would go up the steep drive first and reach down his hand for mine.

He'd carry my duffle and the treats he'd bought me on the way to the airport—gummies and chocolates that I never ate at home, Diet Coke—and we'd cross the street and climb the snowbanks and say things to make each other laugh. My heart would be beating so hard. I'd feel Montreal on my skin again, take her breath into my lungs. And then there we'd be at his red-brick apartment and Sam would be up the two steps and unlocking the big front door, my bag and his guitar across his shoulder, his long body twisted like a clef.

The hall smell, which would hit me first, was of weed from the dealer on the second floor. Of a heating system exhaling through seventy years of dust. Of so much winter and humanity crossing through. I used to love to breathe it in. It reminded me of Sam. His apartment was Number Four, way at the end of the hall, the door on the right I could never reach fast enough. When he did he would put down the bags and take out his key and swing it open. The party would begin after that.

It was an apartment for a man, an apartment for a Montreal musician who'd tidied it for his girlfriend. The main room was where he had his desk with his computer and all his papers. Stacks of bank statements and junk mail and notes about music lessons he'd scrawled in his longhand: "Cordelia: Friday, 4 p.m." It dog-legged into a long living space with a bookcase whose lower shelves were packed with sheet music. So many stacks of loose pages, but Sam could pluck "In My Time of Dying" or "If Troubles Were Money" from its midst in a beat. Farther in was a couch and a crowded shelving unit for his TV and all his music—both sheet and CD.

At one end of the room was Sam's little balcony, whose doors he opened in the summer to extend his living space. At the other was his bedroom, the site of so many of my Montreal pleasures. In the middle were Sam's guitars, a half-dozen or more. He knew them intimately, and could unpack from its battered case whichever was the most appropriate for his musical intention.

Our arrival ritual was always the same. We'd drop our things and take off our coats and lay a kind of psychic claim to the weekend ahead. We'd stand there for a minute, savouring, knowing this was the start of something. And then we'd drift into the living room together and he'd lock my eyes. "How are you doing?" he'd ask, and put his arms around me when he did. It was a hell of a question he intended. He wanted me to lay down that Thursday evening the burdens of all our time apart, the accumulated cargo of a week and a half of loneliness and single-mother martyrdom. And so I'd do that, deep inside his embrace, until I'd emptied everything onto his floor.

After that, we'd smoke a joint and devour each other on his couch like we'd come out of lockdown. We'd watch *Jeopardy!* and share our shish taouk with Tigger, the cat who never loved me. We'd drink beer and laugh like drains in front of video games, skiing on TV and doing running commentaries. We'd watch Letterman tucked so close we only took up one cushion. And then we'd tumble into the bedroom and love each other so much again I would sometimes cry when it was over.

It was Thursday night in Montreal and we had three more days of this stuff. I used to know a thing or two about hedonism.

Like other happiness variants, hedonism unspools in the company of others. Our happiness very much relies on other people—relationships are key to happiness, and happy people are good at them. In a big study on the happiness of teenagers, happiness research pioneer Ed Diener found that "the most salient characteristics shared by the ten percent of students with the highest levels of happiness and the fewest signs of depression were their strong ties to friends and family."

All of this is enormously backed up by the Harvard Happiness Study, a monster research project that uncovered that social connections—more than genes, social class or IQ—are among the best predictors of long and happy stays on the planet. The project began tracking the health, happiness and broader lives of 268 Harvard sophomores—including their personal and professional triumphs and failures—in 1938. It stuck with them for nearly eighty years, amassing mountains of medical records, in-person interviews and questionnaires. The study's revelations shocked everyone, including its administrators. "It wasn't their middle-age cholesterol levels that predicted how they were going to grow old," marvelled study director Robert Waldinger, a psychiatry professor at Harvard Medical School in a popular TED Talk (viewed more than 40 million times). "It was how satisfied they were in their relationships. The people who were the most satisfied . . . at age fifty were the healthiest at age eighty."

Even our biology tips off the happiness-social link. The love hormone oxytocin is celebrated for inspiring empathy and trust in our fellows. In one study, participants played a game where they gave resources to a stranger, but first took a whiff of either oxytocin or saline spray. Half the oxytocin whiffers handed over all the loot they could; the saline whiffers only gave up 20 percent.

Every winter for lots of years, Sam and I had found happiness in Mont-Tremblant, an ornamental ski resort town in the Laurentians that's everyone's secret playground. A mix of tourtière Québécois and Gore-Tex jet-setters come here to wander among the pedestrian village's bistros, antique shops and toytown boutiques. In the winter, twinkly lights make the buildings' exteriors glow yellow and rust; from the chairlift you can see their red and green roofs. When you spy the conspicuous clock tower with all those painted buildings around its shoulders, it looks like the centrepiece of a ceramic town you might have on your sideboard.

Sam and I went there in the winter to ski, though for me it was mostly about the holiday and the views. Sam would book us a room on the mountain or past the roundabouts down on the highway near the *casse-croûte* we went to with his sister. I loved the rides up in the lift after we'd installed ourselves in our temporary quarters, pressed against each other in those swaying chairs, me feigning alarm, him offering reassurance. My toes in those space boots, once we started down the hill, were claws all the way to the bottom. Sam, who grew up in these mountains, used to love to go for it and I always knew he wished for a more athletic partner.

One winter visit he was there to play at a resort and we languished in its hot tub before he went onstage, watching the mountains through the rising steam. After the concert a perspiring girl stopped me in the hall to ask if I was Sam's groupie and I flipped my hair in haughty response. But I secretly loved it. What stoked my happiness more than his music?

Still, it could only stoke until nature took over. Happiness is written in your bones. A series of studies measuring the happiness of pairs of identical and non-identical twins, raised either together or apart, identified a characteristic potential for happiness that's genetic, no matter the misfortunes and windfalls of the life. This "set level" of happiness accounts for 50 percent of our likelihood for it, keeping half out of our reach. "Trying to be happier is like trying to be taller," said the researchers, including Sonja Lyubomirsky, behind one of the twin studies.

Meanwhile, just 10 percent of our happiness is a function of our perks. Hardly worth the energy we put into landing the job, moving into the house, marrying the prince. Multiple studies confirm that beautiful people are no happier than schlubs. And while money makes people in poor countries happier, it does so in developed countries only up to $75,000 a year. A *New Yorker* cartoon published after the twin study shows a pair of big-beaked men in leisurewear sipping cocktails. One says to the other, "I could cry when I think of the years I wasted accumulating money, only to learn that my cheerful disposition is genetic."

Still, that leaves 40 percent in our control—open to intentional activity and strategy. This is a dynamic arena, historically thrumming with messages of confident encouragement. "Happiness depends upon ourselves," Aristotle said. "Just choose happiness," reiterated Norman Vincent Peale, a sunny-minded American minister, in his book *The Power of Positive Thinking*, 2,300 years after. "Say to yourself, 'Things are going nicely. Life is good. I choose happiness,' and you can be quite certain of having your choice."

And if you can't get there on your own, outspoken British philosopher David Pearce has a plan. In his philosophy, transhumanism, it's all happiness all the time. There's no grief or heartbreak or suffering at all—mental, physical, spiritual. There's only "superhappiness," the third tenet (with superintelligence and superlongevity) of a three-pronged intellectual movement whose followers believe the future might just be sublime.

"The human species can, if it wishes, transcend itself,"

wrote the British evolutionary biologist and philosopher Julian Huxley (Aldous's big brother) in a 1957 essay that coined transhumanism. You bet, says Pearce, who co-founded the World Transhumanist Association four decades later. He thinks it behooves humans to apply every resource our collective psychic development has put in our reach—genetic engineering, nanotechnology, neurosurgery, "psychoactive wonder-drug" therapy—to end suffering in all sentient life, and replace it with "information-sensitive gradients of bliss." He believes the biologic rationale for malaise has run its course and that humans should animate their lives in this technologically enriched present with multifaceted MAO inhibitors, intravenous cocaine and heroin cocktails, kappa opioid receptor antagonists, dopamine bursts, and other "potent, long-acting mood-brighteners"—all ingested into synapses enlightened physicians have modified to optimize their reception. Furnishing all living things with lifelong happiness is nothing short of our duty, Pearce says. He thinks it behooves humankind to take advantage of all the help available and calls his project *paradise engineering*.

Critics call it ambitious and implausible—like all efforts to manipulate happiness, a bootless pursuit. "Ask yourself whether you are happy, and you cease to be so," nineteenth-century philosopher John Stuart Mill once said. Indeed, agreed Stanford psychology prof Iris Mauss: the more we strive for happiness, the more likely we'll set a standard that's too high to meet. Which is why the whole business is such a tyranny. "Life is so constructed," Charlotte Brontë clucked, "that the event does not, cannot, will not, match the expectation."

It's just as well. The positive psychologists say unadulterated happiness might blind us to warning signs and make us reckless. Happiness is "only possible as an episodic phenomenon," said Freud in his 1929 *Civilization and Its Discontents*, and our ceaseless bids for it are unnatural. "The intention that man should be 'happy' is not included in the plan of 'Creation,'" he reminded.

But Sam and I had been happy for six years and I was close enough to them in that third year after he left to feel confident about this. Like any couple, we had fights, but not a lot. We were too conscious of our dwindling weekends to squander many hours pouting. Because so much of our relationship was conducted by phone, we had a few phone skirmishes, some with hang-ups and silence till the next day, when they sometimes flared again. And he was impatient with me our last autumn. Snapping at me for bringing road salt in on my boots or getting up too early on Sunday morning. But our foundation was pure joy. In phone or flesh, we never lost sight of our solemn objective: to make the other laugh. We filled hotel rooms and bedrooms and cities with laughter like they were conch shells. And if you held them to your ear in the years after we'd gone, you could still hear our joy. At the summer respites we spent in Tremblant the locals would complain about our gales.

We'd invoke our sunny Tremblant memories all year, dangling them in front of each other from snow heaps. And then warm weather would return and so would we, climbing the mountain from Montreal in the Toyota, curving upward along narrow *chemins* lined by cyclists and chateaux. It's a puzzle to locate the town along the indistinguishable highways in this part of Quebec, chiselled into rock and guarded with vigilant evergreen, so we'd sometimes lose our way. But Sam is good with directions and he'd always deliver us to the site of our mountainside escapades. We'd play the Stones and Black Crowes on the radio and I'd keep my hand on his leg the entire ride, loving his proximity and the electrified air.

In the middle of Tremblant is a body of water with a likely name. Lac Tremblant is a magical lake, sparkling and deep, the watery boot at the end of the ski slopes' leg. This special spot, where the deciduous fringes of the St. Lawrence Valley brush against Canada's first boreal forests, had epic proportions for Sam and me. We took such deep dives into each other there.

We'd head to the beach first thing on our summer visits, and spread our towels on the yellow sand, fine as turmeric. We wouldn't sit on them long, though, looking out at the flashing lake, which we were there to be in. Sam hated entering all water of dubious temperature—he called the transition from dry to wet "the shock," and was always keen to accelerate it. I would make my way in more slowly. But when we had left our towels and were fully immersed, the rest was a breeze. Did I want to go for a swim? he'd ask when we were up to our ribs, as if there was a question. That's what we were there for, the sacrament we'd established as the pinnacle of our summer exploits in this holy place. *I did,* I would tell him.

With that, we'd take off into the very centre of the lake, slicing the water with our arms and legs in shows of athleticism that invigorated us both. The excursion took a few minutes, and we wouldn't speak or break the effort. How satisfying it was to use our muscles under a big sky with our very best friend alongside.

When we'd reach our destination, halfway between the waterfront and the green island beyond, we'd tread water and marvel at the vista between gulps of breath. And then we'd talk. We'd have long, sun-baked conversations in the middle of a lake, our feet paddling like ducks beneath us. We'd talk about our worries and futures and secrets. About our parents and our fears for when they were no longer here. About the fawns we'd thrilled to see on our way to the beach, and how their trembling existence made us think about our own. Out there in that cold mountain water, the only ones around, we'd share ourselves with each other like nowhere else. It was as if that bright lake gave us permission for intimacy you couldn't pull off on land. And when we'd return to the towels and turmeric sand, it'd be as if the waves had stirred all our stories together.

How grateful I was for those Tremblant summers with the man who spread my towel first, all those years after the last. Grateful for the pool of memory I could swim for all the days of my life. Grateful his dear mountain was part of my story.

Gratitude is central to Greek and Chinese dogma, but it didn't emerge as a Western obsession until the eighteenth century. Age of Enlightenment philosophers, wrestling to understand why people make sacrifices for one another, pronounced it a cardinal moral emotion. Adam Smith called it the glue that ties people together. University of California Davis psych prof Robert Emmons said it was "a felt sense of wonder, thankfulness and appreciation for life."

Today, gratitude remains a focus for a pack of researchers eager to understand its influence on our moods. Emmons, who's one of them, writes in his 2008 book *Thanks!: How Practicing Gratitude Can Make You Happier* that gratitude exists along a continuum, spanning simple expressions of thanks to deep and abiding appreciation. At its apex, gratitude has the power to heal, energize and change lives.

His studies of more than 1,000 eight-to-eighty-year-olds have found that grateful people are less lonely, more helpful, forgiving and outgoing. Gratitude makes us more optimistic, co-operative and compassionate; less envious, possessive and depressed. Grateful people sleep better, and have stronger immune systems and lower blood pressure. They have higher good cholesterol, lower bad cholesterol. They're less beset by aches and pains. Grateful people have a higher sense of self-worth, transformed by others' acknowledgement of value in them. "It's hard to feel like the world is terrible when we notice all the things that other people are doing for us," Emmons says. Despair and gratitude are incompatible roommates.

Gratitude's consequences are enduring. When we feel grateful, we return the kindness, and a circuit of generosity is born. Gratitude counteracts adaptation and habituation so we can access positive memories and relish their reminiscence. Best, gratitude has a positivity bias, writes psychology prof Phil Watkins in his 2014 book *Gratitude and the Good Life*. So where ungrateful people home in on what they don't have, gratitude grants a lens of abundance.

Sam and I were abundantly grateful. We used to say that the best thing about us was that we felt mutually lucky. I had a constellation above my hot tub in the winter whose stars made an L shape. "Lucky," I'd tell him in our nighttime conversations beneath it. "Lucky," he'd say back.

I believed it fiercely, that our appreciation for the ways the other enriched our life kept us invested. "Your rare beauty gives me so much to be thankful for," Sam wrote me, a couple of years after we met. I, with my children and house and diction, was a novelty to him. We were home and family. And he, a broad-shouldered rock-and-roll poet from Montreal, was a novelty to me. "What's so special about him?" his sister once asked mourning me in exasperation after Sam had gone. "He's magic," I'd said. Tanya had thought about it and then changed her tone. "He *is* magic," she'd agreed.

After he left, my sense of gratitude was challenged. "It's better to have loved and lost than never to have loved," people purred at me when I'd been three years on my own. Like my mother, in occasional frustration now that the sorrow had hung on this long. And my friends, who'd run out of other platitudes. I'd always have to go away to think about it, I could never be sure. It pissed me off that our story had run out; it was hard to feel thankful for what we'd had when there was still so much to go. I felt cheated. Not like Dostoevsky in *White Nights*, who was satisfied with a meagre serving: "Good Lord, only a moment of bliss? Isn't such a moment sufficient for the whole of a man's life?"

What would it have been like to have never known Sam, to have tripped back into the November night outside the

Chick 'n' Deli before his friend found the nerve to send those green drinks? I wouldn't have understood how it felt to slow-dance in your lover's living room on a Friday night, rocking back and forth to Sia's swelling assurances, "I know we're lost, but soon we'll be found," electrified by Montreal and two weeks of absence and bracing wintertime darkness, our bodies together at last. I wouldn't have had that pleasure reference in my repertoire, couldn't have subpoenaed its rapture in an emotional inventory. How narrow my collection would have been, constricted on either end of the scale.

How would I be different if I hadn't spent six years in his company? It would mean never suffering his loss, never dropping from the clouds. Having a story not made tragic by exclusion and erasure. It would mean a lighter soul, surely, without the weight of his rejection. But surely, too, a darker one.

"I'm sorry you're sick and are having a rough day with the kids," Sam emailed me one afternoon when he still loved me. "I wish I could be there to take care of you." *Imagine that. Being adored that much.* I was so fucking lucky and knew it. But that was before something changed with the *mutual* part of our arrangement. "I don't think you've felt so lucky about me lately," I wrote Sam, much later, after he'd taken off. After he'd left with my happiness.

7

Missing

When Diana Athill's mother delivered the letter in which Diana's deserting fiancé, Tony, applied for release from their two-years-silent engagement, Diana's body "went cold and limp in the bed at the image it suggested of what [she] had become in Tony's memory." She dropped the "horrible piece of paper and thought, Well, anyway, it's over now."

But the final desolation, the author writes in *Instead of a Letter*, was to realize that it was not over at all. "The picture which came into my mind was of a long bridge suspended between two towers. One of the towers was knocked away, so surely the bridge must fall—but it did not. Senselessly, absurdly, it went on extending into space."

So went my bridge too, in the days and years after Sam's tower came down. An endless road of missing, my eyes trained on its vanishing point, my ears tuned for every sound. In the mists, presumably, was Sam, beaming at students lucky enough to be learning his guitar, ordering pizza, all-dressed, on Friday nights. Sleeping and laughing and playing. Living his life.

But I had not heard a word and my bridge went on.

The years had blunted the agony, though it shamed me to admit it, and the raging inferno of our story's sad ending was tamped down and grafted to my soul. But rising from the embers was something palpable: *the missing*.

A subset of grief, a neighbour of obsession, an engine for memory, the missing is what's left in the fireplace when the injury has burned away. It is the asbestos core of heartbreak. The missing does not burn. "We never forget," I wrote his sister years after her brother's train pulled out of my station. "No one can outlive human connection."

When we miss, we desire another reality so badly it breaks our bones. Here is wishing and praying and mourning at once, all hands on deck for a strenuous swell of emotion that crashes over the hull in waves infected with lunacy. Magical thinking, Joan Didion called it, in her meticulous account of the first year after her husband John Gregory Dunne's death. "I was thinking as small children think, as if my thoughts or wishes had the power to reverse the narrative, change the outcome."

It's this delusion that sends the missing knocking about your skull, suffusing your dreams, waking and sleeping. We miss and we miss and we miss, our focus fervent on a lone target. But there's nowhere to go with it, no satisfaction at all. Only the tortured company of memories, which pin us down, force every neuron into yearning. "O for the touch of a vanish'd hand," Tennyson bawled in 1833. "And the sound of a voice that is still!" This is the tributary of grief, the one rushing with memory, that will drown you if you go too deep. Could be they find my body washed up in Mile End, swollen with our strolls through its vintage breezes. Or taking in water on Bourbon Street, which in truth we usually floated above.

Ideally, the memories drown first, in the watercolour brume they become. Milky photographs whose images have lost their power to haunt. And the players? They are heroes or stoics or crazy. Part of humans' vibrating history of missing. Here find Heathcliff, drenching the moors in longing, Miss Havisham going to bed in a wedding dress. Me, in a silent solo slog along an infinite bridge with no one waiting at the other end.

"I think you must have reached a place where you can think of me and not feel sad," I emailed Sam, when I'd languished three years on that steely bridge. Like Athill, I was plagued by imaginings of what it was like for him, the vision of what I had become in his memory. Surely ash, light as anything, lifted in any breeze.

"That makes me sad but I understand it. It's survival. You have reached a place of survival. Not me. I miss you so much. I cannot forget the force we were. I wish you hadn't disappeared into the ether. I wish I could pull you back."

The rituals I'd introduced to replace the ones tethered to him were pretty established by then. I'd changed my coffee shop and library to surrender the whiff of Sam that had lived with me there, when my days were strung with his texts and calls and anticipation. I'd adopted a policy of going out any night I could, to get stoned or drunk with whichever acquaintance I could convince to join my mission of forgetting, whichever unwitting vessel I might tip my soul into. On nights at home, I'd gotten used to an earlier bedtime, so I'd be asleep when my ten-thirty phone didn't ring.

But still I wasn't safe. There was no spot in time or space that was beyond his reach. Beyond *my* reach, really—for him. Not his for me. His arms, I imagined, were always at his sides.

I turned fifty about this time. Three birthdays since the one I'd spent puddled in McDonald's writing an epic letter I secretly believed would bring him back. But here was another with this altered chemistry, another year passed outside his orbit. The thought made my muscles go slack. So many empty Saturdays and sinking mornings and silent nights, every one a trial. "O aching time!" John Keats howled in *Hyperion*. "O moments big as years!"

I divided my moments according to which side of the breakup their scenes occupied. I could identify whether a family trip to the cottage had happened *before* or *after* by how Lake Huron felt around my heart. I knew if a song had come out when Sam wasn't with me by the rivers of sadness it set loose in my veins.

My horoscope for the year of the rooster predicted "plenty to look forward to, as limitations of the past lift and openings appear." I couldn't wait. I spent the week before my birthday in Cuba, a milestone gift from my kids' dad. Aside from the travel-writing gigs of my youth, it was the first time I'd travelled on my own. My trips had long been Sam's pleasure to plan and mine to enjoy. I was terrified of the flight and secretly felt sorry for the version of myself that would take a solo expedition to a place couples go to reconnect. "I am going on an adventure," I texted him from the airport. "Wish you were beside me."

Sam believed everyone should always have a trip in the works—the secret to happiness. And so we'd taken lots together. Las Vegas and Amsterdam, Spain and Washington, New Jersey and New Orleans, so many times. And Cuba too, my first visit there, when we'd flowed through each other like water.

Cuba, this time, was hard. Solo everything, including vomiting up the Black Russians the guy at the lobby bar had suggested when I'd asked what would get me drunk fastest. My selfies from that trip are sad and brave. I took a series in sunshine and lipstick for a new Facebook photo I knew he'd see. Days I'd spend poolside—conspicuously alone. I'd peer over my book at holidaying men standing belly deep in the pool, holding their travellers' mugs above the water and moving only for rum refills at the swim-up bar. Nights I'd force myself into the enthusiastic tourists—smile-plastered and self-consciously swaying in front of the band or staring out at it from a drink-clutching bar seat.

Back home, my children threw me a birthday party that was a surprise till one of them let it slip. So many people were there, wave after wave of my life: high school, theatre school, journalism school. Friends from work and the schoolyard and the neighbourhood, jamming up my kitchen with their craft beer and prattle. My daughters staged a trivia game to test who knew me best and everyone, drunk by then, roared with laughter. My parents came, my father stationed like a general in the living room armchair, my mother buzzing among the guests, her voice rising with every recalled acquaintance. My friends all wrote their favourite memories of me on little scrolls that they slipped into test tubes and closed with a cork. Trivial Pursuit and the cottage and something unsigned about a kiss.

It was a tremendous event and I felt enormously loved. But I missed Sam so much that night it's a wonder I didn't combust. I felt ravenous for him, like my hunger had peaked on this landmark day and now I was starving. Like all the time up till then was all that was available to me, all I'd been allotted in these post-breakup years. And now something *had* to happen—an apocalypse at least—because I'd hit a wall. Three years of missing was all I could handle, it had turned out.

Nothing happened. And so I mounted the stairs and arranged my heavy body in the impression that Sam, my fiftieth birthday party's most absent guest, had left in my bed when I was three years younger. I looked out my back window at the same view he'd seen on his very last visit. The moon's face, on the opposite side of the Earth from the sun, was fully illuminated. It was February's full moon, called the Hunger Moon by early Native American tribes for the animal appetites that rage at this time of year.

When I got up in the morning, I couldn't find the silver key or the silver chain on which it had hung around my neck since Sam gave it to me four years earlier, a year before he left. This was the second silver key—I'd lost the first, a birthday gift, to my colossal despair. He'd sought out this polished replacement in Amsterdam when he was in Holland for his grandmother's funeral. I'd worn it, swinging just below my heart, ever since. I never took it off, running or sleeping, before or after. When my children drew pictures of me, they always drew my silver key.

But now it was gone and so was he. And I was fifty.

I turned the world upside down for my missing treasure. I shook out my clothes and my bed, swept every floor, retraced every step. Nothing. All the time my rib cage consoled me, protected my heart. If it was gone, it was meant to be gone, I resigned, in its embrace. The magic I'd granted that lost-love artifact had been fake and nonsense. And so what? Onward.

But it tore me up, the idea of losing this link to him. Of it reducing us to meaninglessness. Because what was the value of meaninglessness? If we were to be extinguished, what had we been for? All those rituals and pleasures and stones. Our pockets filled with each other's childhoods. I knew his Dutch aunts and teaching schedule and secrets. To what end? If oblivion was the destination (*It's time to getoverhimforgethim-moveon*, the voices persevered), why had the universe even erected the bridge?

It was a last resort when I dragged the garbage bag into the living room to fish through its party-soaked entrails. I'd been out walking in the sun by then, my bare neck gleaming, and had reached a Buddhist acceptance of the loss. *We would have meaning, even if I had no talisman to confirm it.* But then my fingers found the silver key at the bottom of the garbage bag and I lifted it from the intestines of wine-soaked paper towel and sodden pretzels and was flooded with relief. I put the chain around my neck—switch-flipping its magic back on—and, oblivion skirted, reboarded the bridge.

Missing is considered a contranym—a word freighted with opposing meaning. In one missing, you allow something to pass you by—you miss the plane or the point—and the missing is done as soon as it happens. The other kind of missing, which will wring out your soul, is the one that endures. Possibly forever. At least it does for complicated grievers, the people Freud identified as incapable of surfacing from prolonged, unabated sorrow. According to Dr. Katherine Shear, an American researcher who quantified the condition in 2011, these inconsolables have a number of qualifiers that make their grief complicated, including "persistent intense yearning" for someone who is no longer around. I had no shortage of these.

More than that, they're good at remembering these absent someones, which is remarkable given the generalized issues with memory loss scientists have identified in complicated grievers. Intrigued by this paradox, two Harvard University psychological scientists, Donald Robinaugh and Richard McNally, considered how these past piners might think about the future. Their poignant findings unearthed people with complicated grief struggling to conceive of a tomorrow without their loved ones in it—but able to imagine fake futures with them. This research points to a cognitive mechanism underlying yearning that's characteristic of complicated grief.

That grief and yearning share an umbrella doesn't diminish the stigma of either. I, whose failure to evolve from a now more than three-year-old tragedy to most people's satisfaction, could have said something on that. The world wants tidy sadness only. Dwell too long in a black humour and risk getting stuck in its tar. What's *too long*? Who knows. The line separating normal and not is tricky here; people have only so much patience for our recovery, and we complicated grievers, who can miss others endlessly, wear out welcomes fast.

There's a street in the suburb of Margao, the largest city in Goa, with a Christian cemetery at one end and a Muslim cemetery at the other. Across the road, Hindus bring their dead to a *shmashana* to be burnt on a pyre. Grief and loss, from tip to tail. This is Rua de Saudades. Street of yearning.

Saudade is a Portuguese word that—author Aubrey Bell's assignment of "a vague and constant desire for something . . . other than the present" notwithstanding—is broadly considered untranslatable. It could be its chronological complexities, as Portuguese philosopher António Quadros talked about in *The Idea of Portugal in Portuguese Literature of the Last Hundred Years*. He believed every language has expressions that are "mothers"—words that simultaneously obscure and uncover "a long and mysterious experience that is supra-individual and trans-temporal." He called *saudade* such a word.

It exists in the present, he said, "in the form of eternity, attached to the past by memory, to the future by desire." *The Origin of the Portuguese Language* touched on this too, in 1606, calling *saudade* "memory of a thing with the desire for this same thing."

The word, which won sixth spot in the German Institute for Foreign Cultural Relations' 2007 competition for the most beautiful word in the world, dates back to the High Middle Ages. It showed up then within the first texts of Portuguese literature, the Galician-Portuguese poems of the *Vatican Songbook*. In these troubadour laments of those left behind by adventurers and soldiers, the idea of extreme personal longing was assigned lyric language.

The poetically enlightened kingdom of Denis of Portugal also exploited *saudade* in the thirteenth century, and its emphatic sentiment helped boost the country's literary credibility.

Later, *saudade* became a prevalent motif in popular Portuguese music and poetry of the sixteenth century. "Tears of yearning, Come, do not hold back, For, if you fail to appear, you will be my death," goes an anonymous example of the latter.

In countries whose citizens have been exiled to other places, *saudade* is mostly about homesickness. Like Galicia, a rainy knot of Spanish estuaries novelist Gabriel García Márquez called "mythical." In Turkish, it's *hasret*. In German, it's *Sehnsucht*. The French just call it *nostalgie*. The closest English gets is *missing-ness*, but that's not strong enough. *Saudade* is missing, *but more*.

Fernando Santoro is one of the scholars who've picked at the word's particulars through the ages. In *Dictionary of Untranslatables: A Philosophical Lexicon*, this Brazilian philosopher and poet grants *saudade* massive distinction, calling it a "delectable melancholic philosophy" in whose shadow "the whole history of philosophy can be woven and deconstructed."

Most recently, the concept has become associated with *fado*, a Portuguese musical style known for its profound sorrow. Julio Iglesias sings about *saudade* and Cesária Évora, a pop singer from Cape Verde, built her career around it. In 2001, the novel Portuguese writer Fernando Pessoa wrote in the tone of *saudade* was published posthumously. In *The Book of Disquiet*, Pessoa talks about the "bluish, forlorn indefiniteness of everything."

That sounded right to me. Especially the forlorn indefiniteness. Especially the blue. Like the sky in Málaga when his whole family flew to Spain the spring I was forty-four and we celebrated his parents' anniversary on the terrace of that restaurant and I wore those sandals and had that point of view. When I was excited by these ideas. When I spent my days that way. I missed it all.

Because as much as *saudade* occupied me with missing for him, it occupied me with missing for me. And for the universe that had contained the two.

In the tissue-paper layers of time and place, missing captures every detail. Not just the missed one but the particular summer day that bore him along. The particular summer day when the world was talking about these things. When your hair flew back like a scarf and you were thinking about that. When the clouds were just so and the radio played that song and your parents were this young and your worries were this few. "It is Margaret you mourn for," concludes Gerard Manley Hopkins in his lengthy poetic inquiry into the source of grief for a girl named Margaret.

The Margaret I mourned for was the one who ducked the rain with Sam to drink his client's whiskey and watch the Stones documentary in his apartment that afternoon when I was a decade younger and adored. Of course I missed Sam and his sturdy presence and the way his fingers always imagined frets. But I also missed the Stones and the whiskey and the rain. And me, when I was a rock star's girlfriend and kitted out in all the swagger that went with it. I missed me and my envious weekends in a city where I could be anyone I wanted, including a hippie chick who didn't look like she drove a minivan and tucked in four children. Outside my house and family and town, the Montreal me was a free agent. No one to pick up or calm down or worry over. I missed that anonymity and absolution from responsibility—a vivid dynamic of a new relationship for a parent sharing children with an ex.

And of course I missed the youth, which is irretrievably tangled with missing. We are all ghosts of ourselves from first missing. Fluttering, effervescent relics from a more vibrant time, when every sense was on fire. "Yesterday when I was young, the taste of life was sweet as rain upon my tongue," said Charles Aznavour. "Kodachrome," said Paul Simon.

That's what you get with missing. All the actors in juicier states, front-lit, their tongues wet with rain. "Green and carefree," wrote Dylan Thomas in "Fern Hill," his 1945 autobiographical poem about the journey from innocence to experience. In the "lamb white days" of his childhood, time let him "play and be Golden."

Golden like I was in my youthful conjurings of us forty months after he left—a vigorous, gilded version of me that wore that sureness of smile and had that firmness of flesh. That lightness of being.

I missed that me like anything.

Phantom limb syndrome was first identified by a French physician called Ambroise Paré in 1552, although the term wasn't coined until American surgeon Silas Weir Mitchell did it, in the late 1860s. Paré was a barber who doubled as a maverick neurosurgeon in a quartet of French kingdoms, raising the profile of the combo profession with this reign. A deeply philosophical man, Paré was known for medical innovations and eccentric treatments that offered an alternative to barbarism. It's thanks to him doctors no longer cauterize wounds with boiling oil.

When Paré was tending to the victims of sixteenth-century feudal Europe's battlefields, he noticed soldiers complaining about pain in limbs they no longer had. "Verily it is a thing wondrous strange and prodigious," the military surgeon wrote in his 1564 *Dix livres de la Chirurgie.* "Patients, who have many moneths after the cutting away of the Legge, grievously complained that they yet felt exceeding great paine of that Leg so cut of."

René Descartes mentioned phantom limbs next, in the sixth of his *Meditations on First Philosophy*, published in Paris in 1641. Descartes believed this pain wasn't phantom at all, but a response to peripheral stimulation of the same nerve that had run through the amputated tissue, experienced through the soul. But it's American Civil War physician Mitchell who's most closely associated with describing this disorder. Mitchell served the North as a contract surgeon specializing in nervous system complaints and was celebrated for inventing the "rest cure" for "nervous" patients. He also dabbled in fiction, and first mentioned phantom limbs in *The Strange Case of George Dedlow*. In this page-turner, published in the *Atlantic Monthly* in 1866, the protagonist awakens from an amputation and asks an attendant for help with a cramp in his leg: "'Just rub my left calf,' said I, 'if you please.' 'Calf?' said he, 'you ain't none, pardner. It's took off.'"

The phantom limb phenomenon remains an ongoing subject of inquiry. Today, an astonishing 60 to 80 percent of amputees are said to experience it. For some, the sensations diminish. But for the rest of us, the pain of those parts of us that were there but went missing won't ever go away.

When it had been almost four years, I had dental surgery to reinforce my gums' hold on my teeth. My unhealthy gums had been receding from my healthy teeth for a long time, and I had started putting the procedure off when Sam was still around. We'd talked about it. *I'll make sure I'm in Toronto that day,* he'd said. Then he left and things got dire in my mouth and my dreams filled with falling teeth. I made the appointment and entered a scary new room inside my empty house.

The idea of a doctor propping my jaw open so he might scrape bloody reinforcements from my most susceptible flesh and stitch them into my gum line horrified me. It made me feel as if I was plummeting past the floors of a high-rise, gathering speed. Alone. Having to endure the operation without Sam had been one of the first thoughts to light up my brain when he left. *Who would break my fall?*

Being alive includes a regular parade of terrifying events that send your soul over a cliff. But at the bottom is the person who loves you and he is a mattress. When you are afraid but also loved, this person absorbs some of your terror in his tissues, lets its anxiety bend his knees some, to lessen the burden in you.

If you hit the bottom and have no mattress, you could explode. Your blood vessels could rupture, your oxygen could still, your brain could shut down. Your skull could shatter. Your aorta could disconnect from your ruined heart.

I arrived at the periodontist's office a half-hour early that overcast January morning so the drugs I'd ordered would have a chance to warm my blood. I'd made various practical arrangements to accommodate the event, but I hadn't been able to find relief for my fear. All I could do was remember what it felt like when Sam was out there, and how it used to make things better. Focus my buzzing brain so hard on him he was as good as there. My soul had considered the alternative and rejected it; I could not do this alone.

So I sat in that waiting room on an upholstered chair and let the lady from behind the desk give me two pills and some water in paper cups. And then I melted into the upholstery until I was a midnight candle and Sam was there beside me. In me. Across the Saturday morning diner table, bacon and eggs, no beans, extra fruit, the waitress noticing his beauty, his eyes locked on mine, that guy beside us boasting to his girlfriend how fast he could run to the pharmacy if he went into anaphylactic shock, us laughing forever. Him saying *I love you* all through the day, the texts, the emails, always with his initial and three *x*'s, the lunchtime call, the nighttime call, a velvet ribbon of *I love you*s and *xxx*'s leading me up from the waxy waiting room and down the bright hall and into the dental chair. But now it's a Toronto Friday and Sam and I are picking up my littlest girl from school and he's holding her hand as we cross the streets and the dentist is hoisting open my jaw and wielding a massive cartoon needle and we are almost home, the three of us, the brightness in his eyes a giveaway to his bliss, the neighbourhood springtime, miracles everywhere you look.

But Sam had disappeared again when the surgery was over and I was home spitting up blood on my mattress. My mattress, not his. His mattress was gone, long gone. All that was left was the missing.

8

Place

On the first night of May in 2017, when the moon was a waxing crescent between Castor and Procyon, I, with one of my daughters, arrived by plane in the most unlikely of places.

Our flight from Chicago home to Toronto had been cancelled due to runway construction at Pearson, the harried Air Canada rep at O'Hare's check-in desk told us after we'd waited in line for two hours to hear the news. It was the same news we'd heard the night before, on our first attempt to catch a flight home. We'd had to get a hotel then, irritable and thwarted. Now we were back.

"There's nothing we can do," the agent said. There were no more flights to Toronto that night. They would help us book another hotel room. At our expense.

No way, I told him. I had children and work in Toronto and wouldn't pay for another night away. He would have to do better. So the guy said he'd try, and bent over his computer to review our options again, occasionally muttering "maybe" and then "nope." I could feel the throngs in line behind me, juiced for their turn. And then the clerk lifted his head. "I can get you to Toronto on a flight through Montreal," he said. And I couldn't believe my ears.

Montreal?

Of all places.

For so long, Montreal had been a miracle to me. I'd gone there every month for six years and was never not humbled to be in its midst, never not grateful for its oblivious grandeur. Toronto was my companion, but I'd never had a lover like Montreal. I was always so warm under its mantle of snow.

But for me the city had turned, in the last long stretch, into a toxic thing. Something to subvert, to sidestep in public discourse. As far as I was concerned, its mantle had washed into the Gulf of St. Lawrence, taking in its crystalline molecules all the occasions it had sustained. From outer space, the astronauts had seen Montreal go dark when Sam left me on a January Tuesday all those years before.

And now, a thousand Tuesdays hence, a series of travel glitches had me contemplating a return. *This* fragile package of flesh. To *that* city. Of all places.

The flight, the guy at the desk told us, was supposed to have left Chicago already but had been waylaid. He could get us on it *and* a connecting flight to Toronto on its tail—if we ran. This was the only way to get us home that night, the guy said, looking up from his screen. To have to go through Montreal. I started crying at the counter.

My twenty-two-year-old daughter, who'd come with me to a social gathering in Chicago, put her hand on my back. I felt silly and exposed but still unravelled. "It'll be okay," she said, and waited to hear my decision. So did the clerk, his fingers hovering above his keyboard. Behind me, the throngs waited too. And above it all hung this vast proposal, gigantic in its unlikeliness. A return to the city I'd sworn myself off.

All right, I finally told the guy with the fingers, and he handed boarding passes with YUL stamped on them to my daughter, the more capable traveller.

I boarded the plane and plugged in my seat belt as soon as I could, pretending all my muscles didn't remember how this ritual made them jump, loaded their springs for a reunion with someone whose love thrilled me, whom I'd thrilled to love. Who was gone now, tearing around that city in a car I'd never been inside, teaching students whose names I didn't know, anticipating an evening in which I wouldn't play a part. I shut down my nerves in that airplane seat to this truth. I would outlive this ordeal by turning to stone.

I wrote a text to Sam while we flew. I hadn't texted him since his birthday three months before, but this disaster could not go unobserved. I told him about the glitches and said I was shocked to find myself arriving in Montreal. Then I struggled, my gut in turbulence, to convey just how massive this accidental appearance in this charged site was for me, writing and rewriting sentences that couldn't possibly contain my pain. "All my thoughts are with you in our city, baby," I texted at last. "What a difference it is to land here without you waiting on the other side." I pressed Send as soon as our wheels hit the tarmac and I could switch out of airplane mode. Then I wept into my tiny cocktail napkin and twisted my head toward the window to watch the moisture collect between the panes. Outside, I saw all the things I used to see, felt all the things I used to feel.

Our delayed departure meant we arrived in Montreal ten minutes *after* our flight to Toronto was to have taken off. The flight attendant made an announcement about our priority exit and said they were holding the plane for us. *Run,* she said, and we bolted into that familiar airport. Through that shuddering metal hallway, past the ads in both official languages, under the signs where *arrivées* and *départs* outranked the English options—and my heart was always stone. Our bags knocking against our bodies, we thundered across known terrain, enduring the grey-vinyl sprawl of the passenger lounge, the predictability of the escalator. I even saw the bathroom where I would brush my hair while his car idled outside.

But it was a drawn-out ordeal, and by the time we reached the gate, almost an hour after setting out for it, I had a river of sweat down my spine and a view of the empty passenger lounge. They'd had to let our flight go, said the airline people, who were locking up shop. They'd waited as long as they could.

At the airline counter they directed us to, where we stood in another line for another hour, I didn't say a word to anyone, stone. When I reached the front and the attendant saw the tears I'd made no effort to conceal, he was rude. "After this lady," he hissed to his co-workers, making a slashing motion across his throat, "I'm done." I asked him why he couldn't just be nice and he said they'd cancelled seventy flights to Toronto that day and he'd had all these angry customers. "It was one of the worst days of my life," he said.

Mine too, I told him.

He just shrugged and said there were no more planes to Toronto that evening but he could get us on one in the morning. Then he handed me a brochure of hotel rooms for "displaced passengers" who had to stay the night in Montreal. I reached around behind his desk and stuffed the brochure into his garbage.

The city closing in then, we made a run for it. I could sense Montreal in the air. Her disinterested dignity, her shaggy soul. How I had loved to have her in my lungs. But my stony defence would shatter if I inhaled her now. I'd be quarry dust, lost to the breezes of the Pierre Elliott Trudeau International Airport.

At the basement car-rental desk where I'd hustled with my daughter, I paid $350 for an escape. It was almost midnight when we located our car in the underground lot and threw our bags in the back. But I couldn't figure out the keyless ignition and my daughter had to run for an attendant to help her mother, whose boiling energy was entirely consumed by a getaway.

We started for home at last, our inconsequential vehicle emerging into Montreal's enormous nighttime, an unexpected apparition piloted by a resolute driver, her attention hard on the distance, a hundred miles into the dark, anywhere but this place, where the edges of another reality still flashed from the roadsides and bridges. I drove with my foot heavy under that city's sky, whose fibres trapped all our vapours, only exhaling, not daring a whiff, still stone.

But then there was the road that would take us to his place, the sharp left onto the highway and leafy neighbourhood and long park beyond; then onto his brick apartment and its crucible of music and sex and other lush things. There was my past, six years long, tracks that must still show on some map. *What if I took that road?* I thought, as I feverishly took the other. *What if I drove my rental car to him, all these months and years after we said our last things to each other, and what if I rang his bell? What would he say? Would he invite me in? Would he shut me out? Would the earth crack down the middle?*

I missed Sam so much that night I was so close to him that I almost lost my mind. One of the worst days.

We got home just after four in the morning, when Jupiter and her brightest star, Spica, were high in the sky. I had stayed stone till Toronto, till the road signs were English, the radio stations mine. We parked on our street and let our slamming doors scatter the particles of Montreal we'd carried back on the paint.

Montreal was one of our places. A space we inhabited for a spell, a rambling urban landscape we painted with our time together, dragging our brushes across its contours with the days and nights we lingered. Its example offers a pristine illustration of place's significance in the formation of memory and identity and meaning. We understand how setting is the base coat, an experience's first layer. The city or elevator or living room whose carpet brightens with blocks of afternoon sun informs a moment, is a critical piece of its architecture. The classrooms inside which we write our stories are automatically part of the plot.

This is the geography of experience, the map of moments that mark the passage of our lives, the iterations of ourselves we leave behind. "And Deering's Woods are fresh and fair, / And with joy that is almost pain," wrote Henry Wadsworth Longfellow, "My heart goes back to wander there, / And among the dreams of the days that were, / I find my lost youth again." *Where were you when . . . ?* people ask, keen to fill their head with pictures. We need to know the physical pillars to understand the action that unfolded around them. Where you were standing or sitting or floating above when something happened is inextricable from its happening.

It's why the white palaces of East Egg belong to Daisy Buchanan forever. And why the Yorkshire moors are as much about a windswept wildness as they are its Gothic casualty, Catherine Earnshaw. "My love for Linton is like the foliage in the woods," she said. "Time will change it, I'm well aware, as winter changes the trees. My love for Heathcliff resembles the eternal rocks beneath: a source of little visible delight, but necessary."

Necessary like gravity, which guarantees this fact of association humans make with certain milieux. "Make us as Newton was," W.H. Auden wrote in his prologue to *Look, Stranger!*, "who in his garden watching / The apple falling towards England, became aware / Between himself and her of an eternal tie." Whether the tie's blessing or curse is another matter. The rush of emotion an infused place inspires could delight or kill you—and not a blade of grass would care. "You'll always end up in this city. Don't hope for things elsewhere," wrote Egyptian poet C.P. Cavafy in 1894, a brutal review of the inevitability of an environment's hold. "Now that you've wasted your life here, in this small corner, / you've destroyed it everywhere in the world."

We destroyed Montreal, Sam and I, by filling its cracks with us (swanning among its thoroughfares, climbing its hills, flattening its parks). But the arrangement was reciprocal because Montreal filled our cracks too. Like Amsterdam did. And New Orleans and Grand Bend and the little white Toyota that ferried us through all the years of our life together. We were just as destroyed by spending time with these places as they were spending time with us. This, in heartbreak, is the power a place wields.

"To be rooted," the philosopher Simone Weil wrote, "is perhaps the most important and least recognized need of the human soul." Serious business given all the ropes we can't help tying to where we are. This is place attachment, and it's a big deal.

Place attachment has two pieces: place dependence and place identity. The former considers the functional aspects of our connection to a place—how well it meets our needs or facilitates our activities, and the amount of time we spend there. The latter, the concept's cognitive aspect, is more concerned with our bones. Place identity is the influence we allow *where* we are to determine *who* we are.

When American environmental and social psychologist Harold M. Proshansky introduced the notion in 1978, he called place identity—our ideas, beliefs, feelings, values and behavioural tendencies relevant to a particular environment—a substructure of self-identity. The logic linking self-identity with how we distinguish ourselves from others can be extended to how we distinguish ourselves from our environments, he said. In other words: where we hang has the same influence on who we become as our mothers do, can safeguard us just as she might.

Near the end of the third year on my own, the Tragically Hip performed their final tour. Lead singer Gord Downie had been diagnosed with terminal brain cancer, and the ferocious Canadian band was winding down. No one was explicit, but everyone knew it was the end. The Hip had scored my lifetime, saturating my angst with theirs, and the looming demise of the bellowing Downie was a blow. In late August, the CBC streamed their last concert live, without any breaks, a tremendous event that unified the country in pathos.

I was at the cottage that night, an early visit to Grand Bend after Sam left. It wasn't my first time. I'd built up to it with a day trip, to test my mettle for a longer one, and it had been an ordeal. I'd found the place as we'd left it, sun-baked and fortified from a week of its medicine. But I'd found us too, on the sand and in the water and strolling the main street, taut and tan and together. Our ambling apparitions had infuriated me. How improbable to have pulsed with such joy in this space and now to know it in flatline. How insane that humans must endure such wrenching change.

"I am at the cottage with the kids," I wrote my friend Melody the first summer after he'd gone. "It is so hard." Sam had left his fingerprints everywhere. The burger dive on the highway, the minigolf course that had old-timey photos of the town at each hole, in every grain of sand at the beach, where we would dry in the sun between swims, where I told him about my conversations with God, where we sketched out all these plans. Maybe he would move to Toronto one day, become a studio musician. Maybe I would move to Montreal, when the kids got older. Maybe we would open a restaurant with tables that spun. Maybe we would write a song. Everything seemed possible with Sam in Grand Bend all those indelible summers we'd loved each other there and the sun had shone down. It was so hard to come back after he'd gone.

Still, I'd stayed steady for the kids who'd accompanied me on that quick turnaround to their favourite place. I'd bought them french fries and sunglasses, and laughed and laughed. I'd waited until they were way out in the lake before allowing the sand-slapping sorrow to swallow me. I wept on my towel the whole time they swam, overcome with grief for days spent and wasted and never to return.

But *I* returned, because it was my place before it was ours. I returned to reclaim it.

And when I did, in that summer of the Hip's last tour, when I ventured to the bottom of the main street alone to watch the concert on the big screen they'd set up on the public beach, I missed him again. If Sam had been with me, we'd have gone together and it would've been amazing to have him there. I thought about that the whole time.

It was pouring, and only the area in front of the stage was sheltered. But the people were gathered everywhere, even on the dark sand, even with the rain soaking their hair and beach cover-ups. We sang "O Canada" together, pitching our voices into the weather like Gord Downie deserved. We kept a beach ball aloft and squinted at the melancholy when he belted out "Courage (for Hugh MacLennan)." And then we became a mourning collective, committed to "wait and see what tomorrow brings."

I spent some time there, swaying in the tempest with everyone else. It was one of those moments and we all knew it. It had to do with togetherness, the community of our grief. Here was an entire country immersed in my mood. And we in this throbbing beachfront scene, drenched in tears and rain, were soulmates. I felt less alone that night than I had in so many years.

"I honestly believed that at the lowest moment in my adult life I'd been rescued by a building," Nora Ephron wrote in the essay "Moving On," the writer's love letter to the Upper West Side apartment she discovered after her marriage to Carl Bernstein blew up. Celebrated human geographer Yi-Fu Tuan would have named that *topophilia*, an abstract psychological concept he purported to have invented in 1974 that includes all of "the human being's affective ties with the material environment." In fact, W.H. Auden ventured this neologism years earlier, assigning nomenclature with Greek roots to the sense of being connected to your space. *Topophilia* takes *tapos*, or place, and *philia*, love, to make *place love*, and Auden used it in his introduction to a book of poems he'd edited for John Betjeman. Auden said he hoped this British poet's mastery of *topophilia* would inspire other poets.

Could be such wordplay just added to the confusion. Dissension brews about the concept of place attachment, and how we might define and measure an idea that is part emotion and part pattern of thought. There's no substantive body of research, well-established developmental theory or precise understanding of the neurological changes it activates. It is social science's mud patch.

A 2017 study published in *Environment and Behavior* was the first to isolate the subject. When participants were asked to visualize a place to which they felt attached, their self-esteem and sense of belonging spiked. Scientists testing the waters of geography's emotional undertow discovered themselves awash in a room of empaths, their hearts swelling to think of home. "Oh, to be in England / now that April's there," Robert Browning once trilled.

People feel that sense of attachment, said an American scientist named Herbert W. Schroeder in 1991, according to a place's *meaning*. These "thoughts, feelings, memories and interpretations" a landscape evokes are essential to stirring ties, and are all the more pronounced with the passage of time. (It's an idea Schroeder took pains to distinguish from *preference*, a more aesthetic appraisal he called "the degree of liking for one landscape compared to another.") Settings acquire meaning, Tuan once said, through "the steady secretion of sentiment." Each experience in a place plumps the glands of emotional connection.

New Orleans was our third city. After Montreal and Toronto, we spent more time there than anywhere. We visited three times, engorged by nights bingeing *Treme* on HBO. We visited a plantation and a bayou and could talk to bartenders about Katrina. We had our own taxi driver who gave us her private number and took us to Bullet's, a yellow clapboard tavern in the Seventh Ward, to see Kermit Ruffins play. Music was everywhere in those New Orleans visits, drifting through the slits in all the painted shutters.

We took our second trip to that city in late spring 2009, and stayed this time at the Pelham, on Common Street, a four-storey landmark close to the French Quarter. The bedspread, which we stripped upon arrival, was worn, but the room was clean and the price was great—another of Sam's finds. But the Pelham had no pool, and we were sweltering. The second visit was a broiling one, and the days felt hotter after choppy nights of midnight jackhammers down on Magazine Street. Surely there was salvation to be found in this sizzling town, we reasoned through the steam, even for budget travellers. So we schlepped ourselves to the front desk at the majestic Sheraton, past the fountain and its semicircle of Cobb salad eaters, and asked if we might have a swim in their pool. We might not, they told us—the pool was just for guests. Same thing at the majestic Marriott's fifth-floor double dip. But the Hail Mary pass we made to the concierge on our way out connected: he told us the secret of the city's hidden pool.

The Hotel Provincial on Chartres Street, just down from New Orleans's Old Ursuline Convent, has the French flag and a curlicue balcony above its entrance. During the Civil War, it was a medical facility for wounded Confederate soldiers, and their restive spirits are still said to wander its hallways and bloody its sheets. But we were infused with the promise of a swim by a sanguine concierge when we visited, and so hastened through the lobby of that hotel like we owned the place, our eyes on its checkered floors all the way to the back. Then at the other end we busted through a door into the sunshine of a sudden courtyard with a red-brick patio framing a postage-stamp pool that invited us, only us.

The tiny pool was surrounded by trees that dipped their fronds into the turquoise undulations veined white where the sunlight penetrated the canopy. There was a hush to the space, interrupted only by the tinkling fountain that arced from a stone lion's lips along one perimeter. Along another, wrought iron chairs scattered beside a table. We dropped our things there and hustled into a leafy corner to change into our bathing suits, hunched over and moving fast in case the doorman had loose lips. The water, which we dropped into like stones, was the answer to all our boiling questions. We stayed in there for a long time, never accustomed to its miracle, our conversations dense with gratitude.

After a time, Sam climbed out, his nylon swimsuit gathering in wet pleats around his legs, and dragged a chair to the edge. He dropped into it and flipped in his magazine to a story about Dennis Hopper. "Read it to me," I said from the water, and he did. While I read to him often, this was the only time I remember him reading to me. And each word, which dried in that sun with his muscles, became memory, warranted in my hippocampus and imbued with a potency that would crackle for years.

In 1970, Dennis Hopper directed and starred in *The Last Movie*, a *deus ex machina* about a Hollywood crew making a western in a remote Peruvian village. When production wraps in the film's plot, Hopper's stuntman character hangs back, looking for redemption in the Incan isolation. It was a cocky, coked-up second act to the counterculture epic *Easy Rider*, which had thrilled Dennis Hopper. He bragged that *The Last Movie* had no script, that it was all the product of his improvisation.

Hopper shot the film in Chinchero, Peru, and recruited several hundred locals as extras he paid about a dollar a day. For the sacrifice scene, the extras crouch over seven sheep with their legs tied together and slit their throats. Hopper, in stovepipe boots and high on blow, watched the blood spill before yelling, "Cut." It was 1970, the same year Sam was born. Forty years later, in one of the special places that offered locale to our own love story, he told me this one.

We spent the whole afternoon there at that private pool, alternately chilling our flesh in its waters and warming beside it in our private square of Louisiana sun. No one ever joined us, no hotel guests ever broke our idyll with their legitimacy. Only Dennis Hopper, whose story in Sam's mouth was the loveliest thing.

"Place makes memories cohere in complex ways," American urban historian Dolores Hayden wrote. Anybody who's been swept in a tsunami of location-loosed sentiment could've said as much. But the grey-matter particulars of the place–memory cohesion have been more of a mystery. Which part of the brain lights up in that café or swimming pool or brown cottage whose bedsheet has snapped corners? And how do the lights get hung in the first place? American researchers from the University of California San Diego figured it out in 2015 with a study, published in the *Proceedings of the National Academy of Sciences*, that isolated the neural mechanics behind episodic memory formation in the human brain for the first time.

Episodic memory, called a "marvel of nature" by Endel Tulving, the Estonian-born Canadian cognitive neuroscientist who identified it, is the neurocognitive system that enables humans to consciously recollect past experiences. It gets encoded in response to a combination of stimuli—the more spurs, the higher the likelihood we'll remember the event they showcase—and the place piece is a fundamental one.

The retrosplenial cortex, a key member of a brain region pool that underpins a range of cognitive functions and keeps an ongoing low-level acknowledgement of our physical surroundings in its cerebral shallows, is the likely site that locks place with memory. In 2014, researchers at the universities of Dartmouth and North Carolina injected the retrosplenial cortex in a rat's brain with a man-made virus that shut it down. Without its functionality, the rodent couldn't associate a location with its consequence. The rat's inability to link his physical surroundings with food meant two things: scientists could see where sense assimilation took place and the rat missed his dinner.

Episodic memory gets stored in the hippocampus, an emotional pair of seahorses in the middle of our head. In 2015, scientists at Ohio State University proved it with a study that revealed lightning storms going off in the left anterior skies of people's brains when they were asked to talk about a memory's time and place. There, episodic memory shares real estate with so-called "place cells," neurons that help animals navigate the world. They fire when a rat occupies a particular place and act as a representation of specific locations, known as the cognitive map. Developed in 1948 by American psychologist Edward Tolman, the cognitive map is a phyllo pastry of soft tissue whose layers, subsequent research uncovered, are distinguished by sentiment. Locations with important meanings, where maybe romance brewed or tragedy struck, are drenched in emotional honey and baked into the hippocampus's densest tiers.

Montreal was more drenched for Sam and me than any other place. The city and I had fed off each other's energy for six years, mine a live wire that jolted her chill circuitry, hers an effortless *joie* that slowed my pulse. A lifelong dweller of Canada's biggest metropolis and its most ardent fan, I couldn't help the inborn smug I dragged into my relationship with the second biggest. Toronto and Montreal were always in contention, circling each other's manners and money, each returning home convinced of its dominance. But there was a secret and here's what it was: Montreal was always the winner.

How could she not be, with all her wrought iron loveliness, her silver maples and massage parlours, her metal staircases reaching for the street like triplex spaceships inviting earthlings aboard? Montreal was a city that made no apology. Not for her titty bars or churches or wood-oven grittiness. Not for her potholes or shady deals or fixation with hockey, whose fortunes you could sniff in the air. She was ever the cool kid, smoking Pall Malls in the schoolyard; I was ever the beholden interloper, in awe of her language and style, grateful for her shrug to my arrival, thrilled to be noticed at all. This was the knowledge I kept under my toque for all those six years. That I spent my days with Montreal in a state of grace.

I wondered, all that time after our last schoolyard tryst, if Sam ever told her why we couldn't be together anymore. I wondered if he knew.

9

Obsession

One Sunday of that first winter when I was hurting so badly, probably in March, maybe just February, I went to a travel agency on Bloor Street and was a sad robot, plucking glossy travel brochures from the walls, their azure covers catching the fluorescents. I backed out of the store with a smile for the glancing attendants, like booking a resort vacation was my next natural step, and took the magazines to a submarine sandwich place in an industrial-neighbourhood strip mall. There, I let them slide across a table I'd set up on after ordering something to buy my time. I took a glue stick and pair of scissors out of my bag and watched the sub guy's eyes flick over. I unpacked a stack of photos I'd printed at home when the kids were upstairs so I wouldn't have to answer questions, pictures of me and Sam I'd yanked from Facebook for their clarity and forward faces. And I spread all of this obsession on the table in front of me and set about turning it into something that would make everything better.

I spent the whole afternoon there under the sub guy's watch, carving up photos and gluing our smiling faces onto the faces of the giddy vacationers in the brochures. Now it was Sam and me who were sprayed by the ocean and reclined on beach loungers, *our* joy memorialized in page after page of fantasy holiday that I slipped into clear plastic sheets in a plastic book with a blue cover. I made so many pages that afternoon— the industry, the sweet, deep dive into him such a pleasure. A homemade tourism catalogue with a personalized message: *Don't forget, my darling one, that we were going to do that trip.*

Don't forget that we were going to do *everything.*

I wrote our names on the cover, but I'm not sure what else. Something persuasive, something begging for mercy. When I was done and thought I'd made an exceptional thing, immune to disregard, I tucked my blue plastic book into a big envelope and put his name on the front. I sealed it later and brought it to the post office, where the clerk and I both pretended it didn't smell like French perfume. And with this scrupulous, aching creation, obsession twenty pages deep, I'd seen through a salvation plea I'd scraped from the inside of my body. *Travel with me again.*

Be *with me again.*

This was an act of desperation so enormous, it would have shocked me to hear of anyone else undertaking it. It was a glimpse into the oven of my mind, a cast iron container for whirling memory, stirred up by a poker I couldn't keep out of the fire. My focus on him was red-hot, searing with psychic insistence that I remember the days when I was someone's great love, when I had conversations with another person that were weathered and layered with joyful, easy reference.

Obsession saw to it that I dwelled there, four years after he'd left, my membranes filled with our accumulated stones. Here we were fucking in the shower of that Ottawa hotel room and, after, wearing the hotel robes like kings. Driving everywhere, past Montreal's muffler shops and strip clubs, up her beautiful crag, me always watching his hands on the wheel. Walking the Alhambra under the brightest sun and seeing amazement in each other's eyes. This and that and everything. I thought about him all the time.

I thought about him and I thought about whether it was possible I might never stop thinking about him. Mourning, morning to night and all the leaden minutes between. He was, for me, Mary Shelley's "great object, which swallowed up every habit of my nature." The first of my thoughts as my brain sparked to consciousness and the disastrous last when I closed my eyes in front of babbling television so someone else could write the script to my dreams. "Extinguish my eyes, I'll go on seeing you / Seal my ears, I'll go on hearing you," Rainer Maria Rilke wrote in the early twentieth century. I knew such conviction.

There is something in conceding an obsession that damns it. When you don't merely think but think obsessively, your pathology changes. Eventually, you traverse the blood–brain barrier, the tightly stitched mesh of endothelial cells that spares your good sense. "I never noticed anything but you / But you but you," wrote Dorothea Lasky, in a poem from the other side.

Around 1600, obsession was tantamount to possession, the hostile action of an evil spirit. Your fixations in those days were considered the work of a fiend, outside your control.

Jean-Étienne Dominique Esquirol, a nineteenth-century psychiatric clinician who was into crazy, called people like me "madmen who do not appear so" and, in 1819, coined the concept of monomania, where a fixed idea takes over someone's otherwise sound mind—a focused delirium.

By 2002, thinking had changed and obsession was downgraded to "an intrusive thought," said American psychotherapist Eric Maisel. "Recurrent, unwanted and inappropriate." Recurrent and unwanted are the things. Obsession's vapours infect the brain insidiously, even while your rational thought is running around throwing open all the windows. "I must get my soul from you," Sylvia Plath wrote in her journal in 1956. "I am killing my flesh without it."

I filled my eyes and my arms with my children and my work, but my thoughts were still so much of him. *Everyone's had heartbreak*, people said, stunned by mine, keen to highlight my failure to wrap things up as others had. Lots of personalities can't sustain obsession, though it took me a long time to realize it. When I did grasp how challenging this was for others to bear, understand and witness, I counted my friends. "I so appreciate your response," I wrote one of my dearest, Kyla, after she'd fielded another desolate email with forbearance. "I appreciate, particularly, that you don't peg me as sick or extraordinary and can simply recognize that feelings this deep aren't fleeting. And that the recovery process is long, long, long." The long, long, long was insurance. I was laying the groundwork for more of her indulgence, which I knew I was going to need.

In *A Grief Observed*, the feral lament he wrote after his wife died, C.S. Lewis called this kind of indulgence vanity, and scoffed at our efforts "to prove to ourselves that we are lovers on the grand scale, tragic heroes; not just ordinary privates in the huge army of the bereaved, slogging along and making the best of a bad job." My friend John grew so impatient with my grand lament for Sam and the implication that my heartbreak outranked any of his that he just took off.

As for the rest, they stopped asking and I stopped telling. My fixation on this long-ago misfortune became the fodder of their boozy klatches when I wasn't there, or so I imagined. And why not? This kind of psychosis went well with wine. *What is wrong with her?* I pictured them tsking. *She's crazy.*

I was. Four full years and all their seasons had passed and still I sat among the changing trees, picking at the fluff snagged in their branches. His ongoing silence had cultivated in me a powerful belief in magic. I imagined he was sending messages into the universe and always cocked an ear. And I continued to hear in all that quiet a million reasons to believe in Sam's rueful reappearance. *Really?* said my friends. *You still believe that?*

His reliable lack of response had turned him into my confidant. Into his pit, which had no floor, I pitched my starkest confessions. "Since you left," I wrote, "I talk to spirits that I imagine are around me when I find a dime on the sidewalk. If the parking machine feeds me money back I think: today is the day you're going to reach out to me again."

There was no question I'd let myself slip into caricature. Obsession had given me a brand. I was the eccentric woman who'd had her heart broken—an easy shorthand for the neighbours.

Among the things with which I was obsessed, the following:

Numbers. Specifically, thirty-three. In licence plates, gas station signs, odometers, treadmill readouts, restaurant cheques, wait-list assignments at the blood donor clinic, hydro bills, laptop power percentages and all the digital clocks in the world. Their random appearances were messages to me. He'd be back. Of course he would—thirty-three wasn't only my favourite number, it was his, so was a sure bet.

Time. Particularly times with thirty-threes in them. There was one of those an hour, and so that kept me busy. I'd see the 7:33 or 10:33 or 3:33 (the motherlode) and pause to register its auspiciousness. But the best time was 11:11, a twice-daily minute of great good fortune, especially if caught unawares—as if I ever could, the way I hung around the stove clock before heading to bed. I wished for Sam on every 11:11 I saw since he left. Years and years of magic-time wishes.

Signs. Like a car with a Montreal licence plate pulling in front of me. Or my lone win at a fair when I stopped at a felt table where they spin a stack of arrows around named wedges—and the wedge I'd spied and slapped with my coin was called "Sam in the Future."

Obsession.

In the early years, I'd sent him things in the mail. A Dutch team jersey for a World Cup we wouldn't watch together. *The Flintstones* DVD collection, because its cozy associations had been a shared touchstone. The book about the tiger and the boy and Sistine Bailey that I'd read to him at the start.

I stopped the presents but never the Christmas stocking, filled with socks and gift cards and shaving cream. I'd track its delivery till I saw he'd picked my package up from the post office and then lose an afternoon to daydreaming about it on the passenger seat beside him, him smelling my perfume through the envelope's folds, me filling his senses.

I never stopped talking to him either, even though he'd not talked back for four years, even though he'd not given me reason to believe he would. "Miss you so much tonight, baby. And our easy way," I emailed, like it had only been a week or a year. "Maybe we can just talk, and finally set this thing straight. Contact me when you can."

I didn't need much, just his acknowledgement. Just a word or two to give me back my whole self, the one that included who I was with him, so recently shuttered. Just "I'm sorry" or "It's okay" or "I'll never forget." That would've been enough. But I didn't get anything at all.

Sam and I had a joke where we'd regard a situation that was only halfway victorious and declare it a success. One out of two actually wasn't *that* bad, we'd say to each other reasonably, and then fall into gales. That sometimes occurred to me as I was sending him emails and envelopes and watching his intentional absence accumulate on the same clocks in whose enchanted numbers I invested wishes. And never hearing a word. *At least* one *of us was engaged,* I would think, which Sam would've loved. One out of two ain't bad. And then I would think: *obsessed.*

Crying, which I still did, was a relief. Every day, at least once, I would let myself tumble down the other side of my thoughts, which climbed to him habitually. Mostly it was music that sent me over. Or a scrap of public dialogue he could've spoken. "Until soon," he used to say. "Piping hot." "Love you, baby." My brain went to him by default, filling in the absence of any pressing alternative with my regret and missing and memory. The crying paid homage to the idea of us, threw a penny into our fountain and then sent me along. At least the jags were less frequent and over more quickly. But I was always propped up by the fact of him. He may not have been available to me, but he was alive and I was working on making that enough.

On the fourth anniversary of his bugout, I sent him a ribboning email telling him so. "Sometimes," I wrote, "when I can barely breathe for the grief of it all, I console myself with the last thing, the only thing left to me in a world where you pretend I no longer exist. And that is *that we were.* That we were. That we loved and laughed and sang and played. That we ate and drank and drove and travelled. That we experienced. That we shared. That we were. And that somewhere out there, you still are. Your long body with its lobe-less ears and seawater eyes. Your leather sandals and brown Thai T-shirt and Spanish leather jacket. Your #4 apartment with its out-of-date door calendar and broken aquarium and high-pressure shower. Your beautiful guitars and ridiculous table-top Christmas tree and the word 'love' on your bedroom mirror. You are out there somewhere, Sam. And, at last, in the absence of everything, everything, everything else, I land on that. You exist. You are. You loved me. *And we were.*"

Charlotte Brontë was twenty-six in February 1842, when she lit for Brussels with her sister Emily to attend the Pensionnat Héger. They were at this "maison d'éducation pour les jeunes demoiselles" to brush up on their European languages, particularly French, of which they knew little. In exchange for room and board, Charlotte would teach English there and Emily music. When they'd polished their tongues, their plan was to return to Yorkshire and open their own school.

The Brontës—including Patrick, who accompanied his daughters to the city and stayed one night—found the *pensionnat* among eighteenth-century homes on the ancient rue d'Isabelle. Their school was in the shadow of King Leopold I's palace and across from the bottom of a flight of stairs guarded by a marble General Augustin-Daniel Comte Belliard in full military dress. But the *pensionnat*'s fortune was behind the house where the Brontës stayed, the garden Charlotte described so tenderly in her 1853 novel *Villette*, where vines gathered "their tendrils in a knot of beauty," and hung "their clusters in loving profusion about the favoured spot, where jasmine and ivy met and married them."

It was perhaps in that romantic setting that the sisters received instruction from one of the handful of teachers at this small school, Constantin Héger, a man historians credit with their literary discovery. Héger, who had fought in the Belgian Revolution and lost his first wife and a child to cholera by the time he met the sisters, was considered noble, a friend to the poor. "He has an easy speech, and possesses to a high degree the eloquence of good sense and heart," an old woman who knew Héger wrote Elizabeth Gaskell for her biography of Charlotte Brontë. Héger taught the Brontës French and literature, but his academic reach was wide. Together, writes Gaskell, Héger and the girls read Casimir Delavigne's rousing ode to Joan of Arc, Saint Ignatius's letter to the Roman Christians and some of Bossuet's fine oratory. He told them Victor Hugo's story of Mirabeau, the dubious hero of the early French Revolution. And he assigned them to write, themselves, on something that excited their hearts and minds.

Charlotte's heart and mind were excited by Héger.

In an effusive letter she wrote three months after arriving, Charlotte described her teacher as a "professor of rhetoric, a man of power as to mind, but very choleric and irritable in temperament." She talked about him upbraiding her for a poor translation, and revealed that he'd given the girls private lessons, which she felt had "excited much spite and jealousy in the school." Monsieur Héger lent his young protege books and engaged her in regular conversation. He gave her gifts— her own copies of *Das Neue Testament* and *Les Fleurs de la Poésie Française*—and let Charlotte assume the tutor role and teach him English after Emily left. On the first day of Lent in 1843, he took Charlotte and another pupil to see the masks at the Brussels Carnival. "It was animating to see the immense crowds and general gaiety," Charlotte wrote. "But the masks were nothing."

Charlotte Brontë fell in love with Constantin Héger, who was now married to the school's proprietress, Mademoiselle Claire Zoë. This aching secret was only fully revealed in 1913, when the Héger family donated her letters to the British

Library and they were published for the first time. But, as Elizabeth Gaskell explains in her 1857 *Life of Charlotte Brontë*, Madame Héger saw it then and told her husband to do something about it. The teacher acceded, cutting off the books, cancelling the language lessons and stepping back from this blossoming English flower. Charlotte Brontë was crushed.

"However long I live, I shall not forget what the parting with M. Héger cost me," the young author told her friend Ellen Nussey, when she joined her sister back home. There, in Haworth, a remote Yorkshire town at the end of a steep and cobbled road, she wrote to the professor often, in language that made beautiful the torture of her addiction. She told him she wrote to him in French, which he had taught her, "because it reminds me of you—I love French for your sake with all my heart and soul."

Her letters were emotional, full of intimacy and apology for the trouble of her persistent presence. They grew in intensity as she awaited his replies, which dwindled. In 1845, Constantin instructed Charlotte not to write him except with news about her studies and family—and that not more than twice a year. She complied, but in one breathless letter, let loose after six months of restraint, she told him how wrenching the estrangement was for her. She'd done everything to get him out of her head, she said, but hadn't been successful. She was humiliated "to be unable to control one's thoughts, to be the slave of a regret, of a memory, the slave of a fixed and dominant idea which has become a tyrant over one's mind."

The tyranny produced, for Charlotte, "a prolonged and gloomy silence" that she dwelled inside, awaiting word from the man at the centre of her thoughts, a man who had six children with his second wife and allegedly never wrote his besotted pupil again. He was "mute as is the grave," Charlotte grieved in a poem she wrote of this anguish years later. In the margin of the last page of her final letter, which Héger may have kept open on his desk, he at some point scribbled a cobbler's address, a scrap-paper scrawl alongside the closing lines his swooning disciple had penned to him with such yearning. "Fever claims me," she had written. "I lose appetite and sleep. I pine away."

Stories about pining made me feel sorry for their victims. Including me, who was also a victim, who also pined. Who still slogged her sorrows through every city block, still bent conversations to an absent actor, still listened for someone mute as the grave. My story was sad, no question. Abandonment, bewilderment, yearning. Left at a train station, every plea for interaction unanswered. Rejection big as a tide. And then this dangling despair. If I had met me in a park and heard about it, I would have wanted to take me in my arms. "However long you live, you shall not forget what the parting cost you," I might have told myself. But behind my consolation I would also have thought: *Enough already.*

That was the trouble, in my brewing brain: I felt two things about my obsession with this man who'd gone away—pity and disdain.

The pity was for this girl with such a broken heart, whose life had been so cracked by somebody's dismissal of her, who was so stuck. The disdain was for this loser who couldn't recover. *You're* still *obsessed with Sam?* people would ask, four years out, their voices hitching on the *still* and adding a syllable. They had no idea.

Obsession's only redemption is the art that's so often created in its glare. In poems and paintings that the world wouldn't know had the artist been able to drag himself away, we understand how madness can produce something sublime. "The willingness to risk excess on behalf of one's obsessions is . . . what makes some artists adventurers on behalf of us all," John Updike said of J.D. Salinger. But there are consequences to art by immersion. Like insanity and suicide and roaring, lifelong despair.

Expressionist artist Oskar Kokoschka was such an adventurer. This avant-garde fascist's feverish brush strokes told a story about life in the time of Freud, when dreams were revered and the bourgeois disdained. He was twenty-six when he met socialite Alma Mahler in Vienna in 1912. Mahler, freshly widowed by composer Gustav Mahler, was allegedly charmed by a drawing of her Kokoschka had dynamically dashed off while she played piano at a mutual friend's party. Afterward, they fell in love.

The couple blazed through a passionate relationship for three years—living together, travelling to Italy and the Swiss Alps, playing their parts in the studio. Kokoschka painted his lover often, including in his most famous piece, *Bride of the Wind.* Here, the couple reclines in a storm of bedclothes, Mahler serene, Kokoschka intense. Mahler got pregnant and aborted the baby, a tragedy Kokoschka also observed with his art. Eventually, Mahler freed herself from Kokoschka's hold and returned to an earlier lover, Bauhaus architect Walter Gropius, whom she married. Devastated, Kokoschka decided to duplicate her.

The sketches, paintings and descriptions the Austrian painter sent to the Munich doll maker Hermine Moos, whom Kokoschka had commissioned to make a life-sized Alma doll, were precise. "Pay special attention to the dimensions of the head and neck, to the ribcage, the rump and the limbs," he wrote in a note that's still preserved, on August 20, 1918. "And take to heart the contours of body. . . . The point of all this for me is an experience which I must be able to embrace!" Four months later, Kokoschka sent Moos another note: "Can the mouth be opened? Are there teeth and a tongue inside? I hope."

When the order arrived at last, Kokoschka unpacked his effigy "in a state of feverish anticipation, like Orpheus calling Eurydice back from the Underworld," he wrote in his 1962 autobiography, *A Sea Ringed with Visions*. He wasn't entirely satisfied with the final product, but got his servant to drop word around town about her just the same, the new woman in his life, and how he'd hired a horse and carriage for her and rented a box at the opera. He also set about painting the doll with the same fervour he'd painted her inspiration, often arranging her horsehair-plump limbs, a mottled patchwork of ochre, brown and pink, in sexually suggestive poses.

And then, just like that, Kokoschka surfaced. "I decided to do away with it," he said. "It had managed to cure me completely of my passion." He marked his recovery by hiring a chamber orchestra from the Vienna Court Opera to play in the middle of a baroque fountain, and throwing a drunken garden party around them that culminated with Kokoschka beheading the Alma doll and dousing her in red wine. The next day, a police patrol burst into the artist's house when they thought they'd discovered the body of a naked, headless woman covered with blood in the yard. And so ended the obsessive love story of Oskar Kokoschka and Alma Mahler. As for my own obsessive love story, it was still ringed by chamber music in the yard.

There was a bookstore at the bottom of my street with tables on the second floor, to encourage people to sit and sample before making a purchase. I used to go there a lot in the days and years after Sam left, especially in the winter dinnertimes, when the kids and their father were at the house and I needed to scat. I'd ride the escalator up and think of him because it was a Wednesday and people and books and breathing reminded me of him. I'd wonder what other folks did on cold mid-week nights when there were no parties or urgent calls for their presence. I'd forgotten what a Wednesday was like when you were loved, when you might just pad around the topography of your evening, ducking in here and there and never feeling swamped by abandonment.

I had a book I was visiting at the store in that stretch, too self-conscious to buy and bring home. It was called *How to Break Your Addiction to a Person* and the subtitle was: *When and Why Love Doesn't Work*. It was written by a clinical psychologist, Howard Halpern, who'd taught at Columbia, and

I could identify its red cover in the bottom-shelf line of books where I'd tuck it at the end of each session so I could find it the next time. When I did, I'd pluck it up and put my big winter coat over a chair and sit at a table at the end of a row of shelves, where none of the neighbourhood moms could spy me. Then I'd hunch over the pages like a thief, devouring the counsel I hoped would release me to a different kind of Wednesday night.

I had been interested in the book's promise to address sad sacks with "attachments to people who are painfully unattainable." The first chapter was called "Prisoner of Love." By the end of it, I'd become convinced of the merits of turning our relationship on its back, focusing on its shameful underbelly. If I could train my brain to the ugliest moments of our six years, I concluded, I could get on top of everything. So I'd put down my book frequently on those winter nights when everyone else was at home and loved and I'd will myself to think of Sam's worst displays. The time he broke the handle on my front door because he slammed it shut with such force. The way he'd been an asshole about buying me the Philippa Gregory book on the last Christmas, stamping around the mall two steps ahead of me. The drive home from the train station that wasted weekend when he'd whipped himself into such a random rage and I'd asked if he just wanted me to get out of the car and he'd said yes and I'd lumbered around his neighbourhood with my bag for almost an hour before phoning him and hating myself for it.

I did more of this willing on my next bookstore visit and my next, solemnly conjuring up memories of how he'd disappointed me. It was my liturgy in this neighbourhood bethel, with its paperback comfort and towering ceilings. Once, I took out a sheet and a pen and wrote a manifesto, a page of promises to myself, both sides, every statement "I will." "I will not crumble," I wrote. "I will be who I'd like my daughters to be." "I will remember who I am and my long life and my value." "I will read and listen to music and make fresh plans." "I will stop dwelling where there is no hope." "I will be enough." I folded the page up and carried it in my bag until it tore at its folds into six shabby squares, and even then I carried it.

But I had a lot of trouble keeping my eyes locked on the underbelly. Generally, by the time the bookstore was closing and I was pushing through its doors in my big winter coat, I was sifting through our stones. Remembering how soft the skin on Sam's arms was. His empathy, which his eyes gave away. The fields of poppies he used to take me to in his bed.

"I think of you throughout my days and hold you close," Sam wrote me once. But when he left, it felt like he'd gone on with his Montreal life, playing his music and ordering his weekend eggs (with bacon, no beans, extra fruit), and I had turned into a speck in the distance, adoring him still. "The one you love and the one who loves you are never, ever the same person," wrote Chuck Palahniuk, miserably, in *Invisible Monsters.* Addiction, classically defined, is pursuing something compulsively, no matter how it makes you yowl. To the usual addictions, add extraordinary things. Tattoos and cat fur and sorrow. "Be careful with sadness," Gustave Flaubert warned. "It's a vice." The Vietnamese Buddhist monk and peace activist

Thich Nhat Hanh knew this business. "People have a hard time letting go of suffering," he said. "Out of fear of the unknown, they prefer suffering that is familiar."

I began to understand that, thinking of Sam, whom I craved so urgently, whose absence was unacceptable, whose remembered presence, in lieu of anything else, was my only succour. So did Lucy Brown, a neurology prof from the Albert Einstein College of Medicine in New York City, who was so convinced people could get addicted to each other—and that it would set them up for searing withdrawal—that she put fifteen victims of unwelcome breakups inside MRI machines and measured their brain activity to prove it. When the subjects were shown photos of their lost loves, their brains' reward centres, where the same dopamine that gratifies drug addicts is doled out, started to buzz. This suggested that people can experience cravings for their ex-partners that are similar to the ones junkies feel for a hit they're missing. The distress they produce is psychological *and* physiological.

Professor Albert Wakin, who teaches psychology at Sacred Heart University in Fairfield, Connecticut, thinks the human addiction is actually a combination of addiction *and* OCD. Only this addiction is worse than the average addiction because the alcoholic can have their needs met with booze but the spinning derelict who's wild with heartbreak never gets a reward. And this OCD is worse than the average OCD because this sufferer, says Wakin, could obsess for 95 percent of their waking hours. The two or three years it usually takes to get over lost love can stretch into decades when one person is addicted to another person.

So says a surprising strand of research identifying this cohort's trials. In their 1998 book *The Dark Side of Close Relationships*, American communications profs William Cupach and Brian Spitzberg introduced the idea of *obsessive relational intrusion*, a "repeated and unwanted pursuit and invasion of one's sense of physical and symbolic privacy by another person . . . who desires and/or presumes an intimate relationship." In this phenomenon, the perpetrators could be "stalkers, obsessional followers, love addicts or erotomaniacs," but are mostly former romantic partners whose busted self-esteem explains the unwanted emails, gifts and pleas for forgiveness we hurl into the universe. Obsessive relational intrusion, which doesn't feature a pattern of threatening behaviour and so isn't quite stalking but kind of is, has three characteristics: it's persistent; it might be psychological, symbolic or physical; and it's predicated on a relationship that's "nonmutual."

But the most surprising thing we know about humans' obsessions with each other? It leaves a mark on *both* guys. As much as I was dragging a two-ton sorrow, it could be that Sam was hauling heavy emotions of his own. In "Stopping the Stalker: Victim Responses to Stalking," an article in the *Griffin Journal of Law & Human Dignity*, Dr. Terry Goldsworthy and Matthew Raj reported that being a victim of obsessive relational intrusion can make someone less outgoing—more frightened, paranoid and aggressive. They feel tangled in guilt and frustration, stressed, anxious and violated. Depressed. Annoyed. They engage in self-blame and report feeling a loss of trust in people. And, said researchers Sara

R. Watman and Roy F. Baumeister in *Breaking Hearts: The Two Sides of Unrequited Love*, they consider their pursuers self-deceptive and unreasonable. The title of their 1992 book is meaningful, because that's what's at the crux of this, their research revealed: *both* hearts break in a love that's unrequited.

I could contemplate Sam's point of view, when my bones felt hard enough, and I had allowed myself to consider what these four years had been like for him, in the delta of my whitewater. I'd always counted on Sam suffering a bit. (It made me less lonely to know there was someone else in the universe grieving the precise uncoupling I was.) But I didn't like him as a "victim," made depressed or anxious by my perfumed letters and Christmas socks. I needed to believe he received these gestures as I intended: tributes to us, which had been a spectacular thing, shared with the only other person who could know it too. So I'd mostly dismissed this notion. Instead, I'd imagined absolution for him. Still water and light, nothing dragging anything down. This was the soul of the person who'd done the abandoning, after all, not of the abandoned. And so it would surely be absolved and at ease, not twisted and starved for oxygen. The space my soul used for grieving would be empty in his, I'd think; he could use it for certitude and pride.

Anyway, it wasn't about him, this obsession. Sam's part in my fixation on him was mostly incidental. "Why should I blame her that she filled my days with misery?" William Butler Yeats wrote. "Why, what could she have done, being what she is?" It's what Ayn Rand meant when she wrote in *The Fountainhead*, "I love you so much that nothing can matter to me—not even you. Only my love—not your answer. Not even your indifference." Or W.H. Auden, when he declared in a 1957 poem: "If equal affection cannot be, / Let the more loving one be me."

As I was that freezing Saturday night when I arrived late to my friend Melody's dinner because "River" came on the radio while I was parking and I couldn't help myself from taking a ride. "Oh, I wish I had a river I could skate away on," Joni Mitchell sang, and I was swept into this tremendous current on the side of the road. "I wish I had a river so long, I would teach my feet to fly."

Joni in my ears, I let fifty months of tears rain down inside my Honda, every one a loss. His gaze, his words, his wildness. His music, his cock, his care. Five hundred kilometres away, I imagined Sam heeling through a Montreal night like a Bermuda-rigged sloop while I, the more loving one, was drowning in my car. But it could not be helped, and Joni and I both knew it. "I'm so hard to handle, I'm selfish and I'm sad," we wailed, our bodies twisting in the winter swells. "Now I've gone and lost the best baby that I've ever had. Oh, I wish I had a river I could skate away on."

When the song ended, I threw open my car door and spilled onto Roncesvalles. And when I did, I understood a third way to see my obsession that wasn't pity or disdain, but acceptance. The river had loosed in me the huge truth: Sam would always be with me. It would always feel bad. Four years out, I knew that the end point the world had dangled was a ghost. How could anyone recover from a supernatural romance? A claim to either cancelled the other out.

basement, and unloaded Sam's guitar and amp from the little white Toyota. He introduced me, the new girlfriend, while everyone set up; after, I was Pattie Boyd, my knees pulled up at the far end of a couch.

Sam was in his element under that low suburban ceiling, holding the music together like a drawstring, rescuing sloppy borders with a clean edge, playing with such skill. They did "Yellow" and "Heart of Gold" and "Sweet Home Alabama," Sam strumming the intro lick like a porn star, then belting out the anthem with such soul. I tucked up in my upholstered corner and pretended I wasn't blown away by this performance by my new boyfriend. This rock star. That I wasn't as turned on as I could be.

Sam was a great guitarist for the same reason he was a great swimmer: discipline. He'd traded his twenties for eight hours a day of practice, insisting his fingers keep learning. The guitar had kind of rescued him, as it did so many young men, teaching him self-control and giving all his restless energy a focus. I think he felt he owed it that discipline. So he'd filled his apartment with the frenetic licks and yawning bends of flamboyant guitar prodigies whose gifts inspired his own. He'd choose a riff—like "Whole Lotta Love," where the B in the A-B-A is bananas, or the semi-classical fingerpicking that launches "Babe I'm Gonna Leave You," Sam's favourite Zeppelin—and he'd play it till his muscles had memorized it. He used to say he was "practising" and it took me some time before I came to appreciate his jargon, that "practising," for him, was not for any particular event but for mastery. He mastered the jerky signature elastic lick of "Black Dog" that stretches and snaps in concert with the drums, starting on a different beat each time. He could make his guitar sound like a voice, like Hendrix's on "Machine Gun," and duplicate the robust blues bursts of his idol, B.B. King. And he could be delicate as anything, like when he'd play me Van Morrison, filling his cozy apartment with his lovely song. The crowds in those outlying towns would roar at his talent on these Saturday night gigs, rushing at him with praise between sets and buying him beer.

When he got home, Sam would phone me, late, and I'd wait for his call with my hand on my phone, under my pillow. When it rang, I'd fly awake and tumble downstairs to hear his rock star stories. We'd smoke a joint together at two or three in the morning and have phone sex and he'd tell me about their sets. I'd ask whether he thought the band had been tight, to talk his language, and he'd answer with music, all the way from Montreal.

In 1991, Eric Clapton wrote a song called "The Circus Left Town" but balked before it could be published on an album. He wrote it to grieve his four-year-old son, Conor, who had fallen from a building to his death, and it was still too soon to put it out there, went the talk, still too raw. It would be 1998 before the musician released this lyrical homage to the last night he spent with his boy, at a three-ring circus with clowns and tigers and, in its stands, a "little man with his eyes on fire." Conor was the circus of his life, Clapton said. When he died, the circus left town; he could only call out to his son with music. "What you will see and what you will hear will last you for the rest of your life," he sang. But it was poignant because he was singing it to himself too.

Music is like that. She is a doctor and a lover. A mother in whose arms we are reassured and adored. In her company, we find evidence that we're not alone. But music is also an impetuous child, setting us into little boats and sending us with a flick down all the boiling rivers of our brains. "Softly, in the dusk, a woman is singing to me," D.H. Lawrence wrote in "Piano." "Taking me back down the vista of years." The destination is always yesterday, and the music is always the way.

Like scent, music has an immediate neural pathway that can breach your thinking brain and dock in your emotions. We fill our sails with it, each song a breeze, flattening the full-length battens of our junk. Under their melodic power we tack this way and that, here where we discovered love, here where it went to shit, always at the mercy of these musical winds and the emotions they inflict—especially when it's heartbreak.

"There is no pain so great as the memory of joy in present grief," said Aeschylus, and nowhere does that intersection occur more poignantly than in a snatch of beautiful noise associated with a coveted time. These snatches, imprinted with the version we were when they played behind our pleasure, make up our lives' soundtracks. To hear them is to be dragged back there, across diamonds and rust, for the rest of our days.

No society has escaped this rough passage, no age has not felt the creep of music's reach into its tissues. Since the mid-nineteenth century, writes Alex Ross, music critic at the *New Yorker*, "audiences have routinely adopted music as a sort of secular religion or spiritual politics, investing it with messages as urgent as they are vague." Our most rough-hewn ancestors wooed with primal music before they could talk, said Darwin. And when they beat on skins and blew into flutes made from the bones of cranes, their Neanderthal audience was branded with its stamp, the smell of burning flesh lifting into the ancient air.

I wondered what Sam did about music after we fell apart. Maybe it was different for him, because he always kept his music around. It was there before me and after. Maybe the songs affected me more because I experienced them in such singular company. Sam *was* Ritchie Blackmore and Freddie King and Jimmy Page. Mick Jagger and Stevie Ray Vaughan. Jeff Beck and Buddy Guy. The dazzling Mick Taylor, tight as anything on "All Down the Line" at Weserstadion in 1972, the fifth and final leg of the Bridges to Babylon Tour. Hendrix and Duane Allman were dead, Clapton was a zombie on heroin, and at twenty-three Mick Taylor, all tone and slide, a face like a baby, was the hottest guitarist in the world. Sam was him when I visited in Montreal. And when I went away, I had to leave them all behind.

That's how I'd dealt with the music. Turned it off. Become a news junkie. Closed my ears. "To Mummy, Who Thinks All Music Is Sad," my little girl titled a CD she made me, after Sam was gone. I couldn't trust myself to listen to the radio lest "A Long December" come on. Or "Copperline," whose nostalgic throws to childhood moved him and me equally. I had cried when he'd showed me this one—increasing our repertoire, damning another song—and he'd loved it. We both aspired to the warm summer nights James Taylor sang of with such nostalgia, a tremendous feature of our connection.

But I wondered how he dealt with music after the connection broke. I wondered what he did when "Sweet Mary" came on.

"Listen to this," Sam had said when we were parked outside the Parliament Buildings in his little white Toyota, not long after we'd met. "I think you'll like it." And he'd pressed Play and we'd settled into our seats and looked out at the snow on the lawn, the same colour as the national sky, and let this deeply harmonic ballad under our skin. At the heart of the song is Mary, the *natural mystic sweet sugar plum* the freewheeling singer left to make another life, and by the end of our first listen, I had become her, Sam the lyrical lover who would never not be charmed by her magic. And the pair, and the intimate phenomenon of all of us together in the little white Toyota that Ottawa afternoon, were warranted with these honeyed strums that came in through our ears and made our organs sticky. This would be our song, one of many. And it would cheer us and connect us and devastate us in the years to come.

In the devastating years, "Sweet Mary" was listeria. The song's twist—where the freewheeling singer gets old and laments his choice to leave Mary, who has since passed away— was too dangerous for me, and so I kept my distance. Neither could I sustain the fling back to that early adventure when both of us were beautiful and leaning into a song together. We were on a weekend in Ottawa and were so new I couldn't remember Sam's last name when I checked us in at the hotel.

I knew him so much better at the end of that weekend. And all the knowing had "Sweet Mary" playing behind it.

Years later, when he was gone, I tried to remind him of us and our own lyric love by quoting the song's last line in a letter. "You never know what you've got in this cruel world until you realize it's gone," I wrote, thinking about the sweet sugar plum. I told him how exceptionally I'd learned that, hoping he would too. "How I loved our nighttime parties and morning phone calls and afternoon text exchanges and weekend escapes," I wrote. "How I loved your unswerving devotion and your arms in a T-shirt and your love. How I loved your love."

I wondered if that letter moved him. Or that song whose potency I'd stirred with it. Or if anything did at all.

Orpheus, Apollo and Calliope's boy, was a boffin with the lyre. When his beloved Eurydice was felled by a snakebite, he proved it at the gates of the Lower World, plucking the strings of his golden shell with such psychokinetic emotion that the fiery wheel of Ixion stood still and the Eumenides' cheeks turned wet with tears. Pluto and Proserpina released Eurydice to her grieving love, who almost had her back in the Region of the Light when he swung around to confirm her presence, thus breaking a promise and consigning his wife to the dark. Such pathos Virgil and Ovid couldn't take their eyes off. And music fuelled it all.

These scraps of sound organized in time and timbre fuel lots of big stories—about shipwrecked sailors enticed to the rocks by sirens' song, soldiers terrified by Scottish warriors' screaming bagpipes, lovers willing to risk it all. In 1842 an eccentric Irishman invented the glass harp, whose ethereal music, produced by running a finger around the rim of glasses filled with varying amounts of water, was said to drive people mad, even to suicide. For a time, concert halls were filled with glass harps. Marie Antoinette took lessons on it, Benjamin Franklin improved it, Mozart and Beethoven composed for it. But by the mid-1800s, the world was terrified by its alleged consequences, and the instrument was banned.

Such is the power of music, whose vibrations can shift sand, whose strains can collapse time. "In spite of myself, the insidious mastery of song / Betrays me back," D.H. Lawrence wrote of his abdication to its pull. "In the flood of remembrance, I weep like a child for the past." Music is extraordinary, said German philosopher Georg Hegel, because it contains everything. In its sphere, he said, dwell "all nuances of cheerfulness and serenity, the sallies, moods and jubilations of the soul, the degrees of anxiety, misery, mourning, lament, sorrow, grief, longing, etc., and lastly of awe, worship, love."

No wonder the subject's a favourite with the eggheads, who spool scientific and psychological studies from their towers that prove music's ability to reduce pain, in body and spirit. It could be the cozy neurochemicals with which listening to it floods the brain. That's why lifting moods is among the range of its clinical properties. So is: combatting depression, lowering stress, easing pain. It is "a sovereign remedy against despair and melancholy [that will] drive away the devil himself," said the seventeenth-century English scholar Robert Burton.

Music calms babies and soothes the symptoms of people with fibromyalgia. It can improve the outcomes of post-surgical patients and help stroke victims find their voice. And it's good for the heart in ways more than the poets flagged. In one study, the blood in a bunch of healthy adults in their mid-thirties flowed 26 percent easier when they were listening to music they defined as joyful. In another, twelve daily minutes of Mozart were prescribed for lowering blood pressure. "There is no feeling," said George Eliot, "that does not find relief in music." No wonder Apollo was god of music and medicine both.

Still, for all its appearances in ancient legends and scholarly journals, music remains a mystery. Who knows for sure why these rambling sonic sequences and patterns and rhythms dilate our pupils and hitch our breathing and speed our blood? How it is that music's trawling passage along our ocean floors, which picks up everything we were, everyone we loved, can sometimes get so heavy we have to abandon the doomed lot?

There were so many songs that heartbreak doomed for me. Music had flowed through all our time together, wrapping its staves around moments, guaranteeing the association. Sam and I had made CDs that informed our earliest meet-ups, the songs we'd each found ourselves in, extended to the other for consideration. After, there'd be music in the car at the Dorval station pickup—when I might bundle in from the cold and discover Joe Bonamassa or Steven Tyler in my seat. There'd be music on the subdued drive back when the weekend was over and it was so often raining, "Tumbling Dice" or "Oh Very

Young." And there'd be music all through the hours at Sam's apartment, where it came from the speakers and left steel and nylon depressions in his fingertips.

We'd watch performances on his computer in the afternoons, Sam dragging in a chair from the kitchen. The Black Crowes on Letterman, almost four minutes of such rocking groove, Chris Robinson loose with flapping hands, his eyes heavenward, "Don't look back my wounded bird, there's nothing for you here." The intimate Scorsese concert documentary on the Stones, *Shine a Light*, and Zeppelin's bootleg at Southampton University in 1973, when they played "Whole Lotta Love" for half an hour.

On Friday nights we'd play Tracks, a game my family had made up of alternating musical picks, one choosing the artist, the other the song. We'd listen to Aerosmith and Pearl Jam and Cream. Elton John and Fleetwood Mac. Rod Stewart and Sade. Back and forth. As wide as we could go for as long as we wanted, tight on the couch racing cars or skiing, laughing, always on top of this music, dooming it all.

We doomed Mumford and Sons, whose romantic storytelling had travelled with us on too many drives through Montreal's snowy streets, those falling-light afternoons when we'd let the radio fill the car. "I will wait, I will wait for you," they'd promised so harmoniously, and we'd both bought in. We doomed "Don't Stop Believin'," in whose lullaby were trapped the relics of me and Sam when we loved *The Sopranos* and watched its dramatic final scene together in two cities, our recordings exquisitely lined up. We doomed the Rolling Stones, which was such a huge loss.

It was Tracks that taught Sam about Gordon Lightfoot and Kris Kristofferson, my oldest friends, whose music I'd reclaim when he left, music whose roots were buried deeper than his. And where I got a master class in Led Zeppelin, whose cocksure and baroque sensibilities ran in Sam's blood. "Listen to this," he'd say when he'd had first pick, and we'd pause the video game to hear a riff whose complexity thrilled me because it thrilled him.

Sam and Led Zeppelin were always a pair. From that first basement rehearsal he was the fleet-fingered Jimmy Page, skating the rapid downstrokes of "Communication Breakdown," such a muted, chugging riff. And he was skin-tight Robert Plant, shaking his mane, strumming his buckle, low on his hips, the captain of the *Starship*, the Boeing 720 the band outfitted with a fur-decked bedroom for the 1973 and 1975 North American tours, which Plant called "oral sex in turbulence." Sam could've filled in for either of these giants.

In 2012, Led Zeppelin released *Celebration Day*, their film of a concert recorded five years before in London's O2 Arena, when the band famously reunited to commemorate the life of Atlantic Records founder Ahmet Ertegun—their first full concert in twenty-seven years. Sam showed it to me after setting up our chairs at the start of December, so keyed up. "In the days of my youth / I was told what it was to be a man," Plant sang, swaggering out of the stage darkness to start the slickly rehearsed show, and I could feel Sam, who'd seen it so many times already, buzzing beside me.

The band—its surviving trio and Jason Bonham, in his dad's old drum seat—performed sixteen songs. They played

"Ramble On" and "For Your Life" live in their entirety for the first time ever, to an audience that included Jeff Beck, Paul McCartney and Mick Jagger. The album from the 124-minute concert, whose 20,000 tickets attracted 20 million applications, won Best Rock Album at the Grammys that year.

The musicians were elder statesmen by 2012, jowls and paunches straining against more expensive textiles than in the days of Plant's other straining bulges. But the lead singer still had the mane and feral pride, and Page, in snow-white hair and morning coat, the chops. Plant kicked his mic stand right over his head and they locked "No Quarter" so tight it was like the seventies. By the second half, Page was in shirt sleeves and, sweating over pouting lips, drawing a violin bow across his Gibson Les Paul for a strobe-lit "Dazed and Confused." At its climax, Plant yelled, "On electric guitar, Jimmy Page!" like he used to when everyone was young, and a spotlight fell on this old virtuoso and the crowd went wild. Fluttering on the banners at the side of the stage, a quote from Ertegun, who died in 2006 at eighty-three: "It is a great life, this life of music."

It was poignant to observe this life of music with Sam beside me, to notice his focus on the tight shots of Page's fingers, expertly bending his notes. It felt like a solemn occasion, tucked in front of his computer that Montreal day in an apartment whose walls had Led Zeppelin in their paint, watching the band with someone with such thundering love for their power.

After Sam left, Led Zeppelin was the most doomed of all.

"The weeping of the guitar begins," writes Federico García Lorca. "Useless to silence it. Impossible to silence it. It weeps monotonously as water weeps as the wind weeps over snow-fields. Impossible to silence it. It weeps for distant things." But is it weeping for the excruciating six-four chord at the fifth or because twisted through its lilting measures is proof of God?

Lorca's guitar made his position plain: emotion and music are inseparable, equally dependent, equally inspiring of the other. We are instrument and audience both, all of us weeping. But scientists weren't convinced, and eventually snatched from the poets the mystery of whether music can be untangled from the emotions it expresses and evokes, compelled to when they saw how our blood raced between our headphones. Archaeologists and cognitive psychologists and musicologists have sifted through music's tailings ever since, looking for order and guarantees in the melodic mayhem. They've measured our skin conductivity and respiration. They've established scales and classifications. And they've discovered what the poets knew: that emotions are music's muscles, thick elastic cords where all the secrets are stored. They're what load certain songs with punch, set them up to knock you flat.

In 1959 British musicologist Deryck Cooke called music's emotional wallop its main characteristic, and said composers exploit it riotously, using the same melodic phrases, harmonies and rhythms to light us up. Drawing on examples that included Mozart's Fortieth, he submitted that music is a language with idioms and associated meanings, all of them at the musician's disposal for our emotional coercion. He identified sixteen, including that the ascending notes of a major chord convey "an outgoing, active assertion of joy."

Like lots of folks, Cooke endorsed the idea that major keys make us happy and minor keys make us sad—mostly the product of cultural conditioning, as it turns out. Emotion in music is also sprung by surprise, jerking to life when a predictability's upended. When a group of scientists watched the brains of people listening to a classical symphony, they saw "a flurry of neural activity" in the transitions between movements, as listeners endured the not knowing. "It's about expectations not being fulfilled," said John Sloboda, a British cognitive psychologist who's internationally recognized for his work on the psychology of music, "very often the basis of any emotion."

Enter the mysterious *appoggiatura*, a standout in composers' trick bags for messing with our musical anticipations. Here, listeners are thrown off the trail when a melody ducks down a side street of sudden dissonance before resolving to consonance, to everyone's relief, pounding up the harmonic front porch and busting in the door.

Intrigued by such magic and keen to organize it, Patrik N. Juslin and Daniel Västfjäll unveiled a scale that measures musically induced emotions, published in *Behavioral and Brain Sciences* in 2008. The scale's based on seven basic psychological mechanisms. In one, episodic memory, a song triggers a specific memory and we return to the emotional state we were in when it was created.

But Peter Kivy, an American musicologist who kept a clavichord in his philosophy department office at Rutgers

University, considered sad music a myth. He believed music is never sad for its own sake, only for how we load it up. Garden-variety emotions require cognitive objects, he said, and music doesn't provide them. A century and a half earlier, Austrian aesthetic theorist Eduard Hanslick had argued similarly that the "content of music, that which musical art presents in its works" is not feelings, but music itself. Music's power, he said, rests in the quality of its fabric, not in the stories we've stitched into it.

But Hanslick attracted dissent for his dispassionate view from those who knew the truth: that the fabric's beauty is immaterial once we've gotten our hands on it. That humans saturate music's density with their own emotional experiences until it's impossible to separate the cloth from its stain.

I gave Sam Blind Boys of Alabama and the Killers the second time I saw him, and we replayed them so many times that first Saturday night in Kingston, when everything was brand new. But on the first CD Sam recorded for me, "Song for Adam" was the jewel. It was the song he asked me about, the one that sent me into the lyrics for clues. There was much to construe about Sam from his love for this deeply emotional Jackson Browne tune about friends and youth and how we're apt to lose them both. About his gentle soul and willingness to sacrifice it to song. About an interior terrain as lush and romantic as my own. After, when I'd hear the violin's lament and wistful story, I'd be back in his apartment with Tigger the cat, on Sam's wavelength, feeling what he felt, loving the company on the roads music was laying down. Outside our music-lined refuge, snowy Montreal beckoned; inside, it was just us, telling each other the same story, though Jackson Browne did all the talking.

One chilly early spring evening in Toronto, Sam and I saw Jackson Browne at Massey Hall. It was a Tuesday, and Sam had stayed on after the weekend to hear this gracious troubadour, long-haired in a collared shirt, sing to us from a wooden chair in a grand concert hall whose stage was a century old. Browne opened the solo acoustic show with "The Barricades of Heaven," confiding, "I couldn't tell you what the hell those brakes were for / I was just trying to hear my song" in a rich and solemn launch to a night of 1970s southern Californian splendour. I felt Sam's focus burning all through Browne's twenty-six songs about love and mortality. I knew he was hearing this musician with ears I couldn't imagine. "The only time that seems too short / Is the time that we get to play," Browne sang, and I thought of Sam's empathy and what a rush it was to be beside it.

It felt like heat, this attention from him on the thing he did so well. It drew me into him and his virtuoso world, which was electrifying. Expertise is such an aphrodisiac, seeing someone in their natural space, watching their fingers fly because it's instinct.

After Jackson Browne, Sam and I emptied onto Victoria Street and walked through the cold Toronto night toward the subway. He was starry-eyed, amazed at how Browne had made his single acoustic, plucked from among eighteen on the stage with him, sound like a symphony. His brain hummed the whole ride back—I could see his fingers replaying riffs, churning chords, imagining a way.

Beside Sam on the train, I tried to remember the concert, so I could hear the songs as he'd interpreted them to me. I wanted to know how he experienced music, to crawl inside his complicated understanding. But its intricacies rattled in my tin ear, no match for his golden grasp. I used to do that a lot when Sam and I were together, try to hear music as he did. I never could, which would please me—it sustained my sense of luck. Tell me stories about tension and release, I'd say, and he would. It was our foreplay. He'd talk about how music builds and builds, accreting expectation, nudging us to the edge of tolerability. And about the resolution that inevitably comes, the satisfaction to follow.

I would think about those stories often in the tension of the months and years after he left. Especially what he'd said about the inevitability of a resolution.

"Music, when soft voices die," wrote Percy Bysshe Shelley, "Vibrates in the memory." So say the studies linking our stirred emotions with the songs wielding the spoon. The vibrations start in our adolescence, the peak for absorbing the music we will claim as our own. The records we listened to on our sixteenth birthday, says Daniel J. Levitin in *This Is Your Brain on Music*, had ink in their grooves that's still in our brains.

Years later, grown-ups, prone on sofas or hell bent in driver's seats, hear these tunes and, says research published in the *Journal of Biology* in 2008, are transported to the "feeling of knowing" their autobiographical elements agitate. The more emotional the event, the deeper the feeling's embedded, maybe because our amygdala and neurotransmitters tagged its memory as important. And, writes Sandra Garrido in *Music, Nostalgia and Memory*, the more vivid the pictures they project onto our screens.

This is music's sway on memory, a thud of a concept that insists you pull on galoshes and wade through the swills of nostalgia, where all our bicycles and birthday parties go. Adults find comfort in this storehouse of the past more than any other stimuli, and did even back in Odysseus's age, when our hero took respite in his slow track home after the Trojan War in the embrace of the beguiling Calypso. But he would always return to "prudent Penelope," who, though lacking the immortal charms of his mistress, was the one for whom he felt *nostos* (return) and *algos* (pain): nostalgia, among our earliest references.

Originally, nostalgia was a medical disease and psychiatric disorder, marked by bouts of weeping and anorexia, shrouded in horrified reference to middle-brain demons. But this sentimental state came into its more temperate own in the twentieth century, when its damning fragility was updated to include positive self-affect and increased self-esteem. Today, nostalgia is a whimsical concept whose sepia tones can belie the devastation of its injury—especially when there's a soundtrack to the slaughter.

There are two primary fingers on music's nostalgia trigger: a song's autobiographical salience for the listener and that person's dispositional level of *nostalgia proneness*, a delicious measure of how game someone is to board a vehicle bound for different times and places. Me, I had an open ticket. I remember my seventh birthday, sobbing to my parents that I missed being six. I missed Sam like that, when five years separated my last sight of him, hard as bedrock at a train station.

Clinically speaking, our proneness to nostalgia is predicted by our showing on two measures. One is the sadness dimension on the Affective Neuroscience Personality Scale. The ANP identifies six affective neurobiological systems that influence behaviour and experience. Sadness—conceptualized as loneliness, frequent crying, and a focus on loved ones and past relationships—is one. When he'd been gone five years, I was still sad—always, bottom layer. On top I'd flung a ton of other emotions, but I was never free of that cement in my gut.

In psychology's Big Five higher-order personality traits, neuroticism is the second predictor of proneness. Neuroticism quantifies feelings such as jealousy, worry and loneliness. While I wasn't jealous (even of the new girlfriend of whom I'd heard tell) or a worrier by nature, I was lonely enough to cover the lot. The combination made me as prone to nostalgia, especially if Carlos Santana provoked it, as anyone could be.

When I listened to music with Sam, I would take off my clothes and stand in its wind and let it have its way. That was how it was for music and me, that was what I'd learned about resisting its power. "I belong with you, you belong with me, you're my sweetheart," the Lumineers would assert, behind our conversations and all our crashing love. Or Neil Young, who sang "Because I'm still in love with you" with such emotion, feeling so hard. And I'd feel hard too, let them—Neil and Sam both—all the way in. Out there in the wind where anything could get me, I would just throw out my arms.

"It comes from heaven," Mozart said about music. And it did especially when Sam would perch on his armchair with his cat and pull his guitar onto his knees, when his voice would be an exultation, just for me. He was a big performer, singing so openly, like you could just help yourself. I used to make requests and I'd join him when I could, caught up in the moment. We'd play "I Will Follow You into the Dark" and "Brown-Eyed Girl." "Father and Son." He'd told me about how Cat Stevens's coming-of-age meditation had spoken to him when he was young and fit to burst, and I would hear his teenage sorrow in his voice when he sang about keeping epiphanic secrets.

There was so much on the line those afternoons when he would perch and take me into his gaze. My heart would race to climb atop his music and let it carry me to the sky, where I couldn't see the end, where the fall would surely kill me. "Wild horses," he'd sing, his mouth so generous, his fingers planting us a garden, his eyes meaning every word. "We'll ride them someday."

"Don't play guitar for me," I used to tell Sam. But eventually he did. Eventually I held out my wrists to him on our windy moor and he drew across a blade. It wasn't like I had any choice—I could never slip my body through all that song without getting torn by its teeth. And mingled in my blood, which stained Sam's living room hardwood and matted our hair for half a dozen years, were all these beautiful songs whose stories became ours, which multiplied the lives we lived together.

II

Memory

When you love someone, you make memories from the sun-glinting start, tuck away conversations and light and secret summits where you are the only guests. And every memory's a stone to be added to a relationship's growing stash. Every inside reference and HBO series and supermarket fight. Every joint plan and planned joint: all are stones. We carry armfuls of them from beginning to end, each a unique product of its own molten alchemy, of no value to anyone but the two in its mineral heart. Sam and I had so many stones. All those long strides along Sherbrooke, all those turns of his key in Apartment Number Four, all those hand-on-the-heart valedictions at the train station. Once, years before we ended, we got in a crazy fight and I sent him a velvet bag filled with polished rocks in the mail. I wouldn't be needing them any-more, I told him, dramatically. As if you can ever give your stones away.

I was always obsessed with remembering him. When we were apart, I would try to summon his face and despair when I couldn't. I could list his features—his silky skin and seawater eyes and insane ears—but struggled to put them together for a picture in my head. "I can't remember what you look like!" I would wail over the phone to him some nights, when we'd gotten comfortable on our couches. And he would laugh and I would laugh. But it secretly worried me, the idea that I couldn't make him bloom in my brain. And then one day I could and was so relieved. It felt as though we'd achieved a level where the universe unlocked the permanent imprints. I could never forget him after that, no matter how I tried.

Memory is our most fascinating faculty, the comfort and curse of our humanity, wildly misunderstood, delightful and disastrous. Memory is personal and universal, mercifully fleeting and mercifully persistent, subjective and objective as can be. From an evolutionary point of view, we remember to survive. We could not carry out life's most basic functions without our powers of recall, couldn't tell stories about experience coherently enough to save the next guy. "Memory and intelligence are closely connected, for unless we remember we cannot understand," wrote E.M. Forster in *Aspects of the Novel.*

We remember because our memories are buildings, constructed sure and solid as any on the pavement, and once we make them, they are always there. I'd been navigating these buildings from the moment I left Union Station that pitiless January day. The guy in Ottawa with the absurdly high voice over whom we had to stifle our snorts. The Thursday nights watching *Jeopardy!* on his couch. The time we left the car running at the Kingston hotel for eight hours while we gambolled between our room and the restaurant across the street, too giddy with each other's presence to notice the rumbling Toyota in the parking lot. Buildings, everywhere you looked.

All told, memory offers long-term accommodation for 2.5 petabytes of data, by one academic estimate—300 million hours of Netflix. No wonder scientists divide it up with such fervour, assigning categories based on its flavour and duration and lodgings. There is working memory and reference memory. Procedural memory and declarative memory. Field memory and observer memory. Semantic and episodic and autobiographical memory. The kind of memory that thrills social neurologists. The kind artists squeeze onto their trays.

When Joan Baez met Bob Dylan, she was more famous than him. She vaulted his career over her own with invitations to join her onstage and the flower children fell for their romance. But then Dylan left his idol behind and she showed him her wounds with a 1975 song: "Well, I'll be damned—here comes your ghost again," she sang. "We both know what memories can bring—they bring diamonds and rust."

The ghosts are the problem. If we couldn't remember what hurt us, we couldn't hurt. There'd be no beaches or concerts or running jokes about Uranus. No version of us when we were blazing, no chance of getting burned. Memory is integral to heartbreak. In 1937, Frida Kahlo painted herself with a metal rod run through her chest and without arms, supported by two empty dresses, hovering above her bloody heart on the beach. *Memory, the Heart* is Kahlo's depiction of the damage of her husband's affair with her sister. "Life is not what one lived, but what one remembers," Gabriel García Márquez wrote in his autobiography.

When Sam had been gone almost a year, I emailed him. "My sweet darling," I wrote. "How often I stumble upon pieces of us out there. Do you, too, love? Do you, too?" The idea that he might not consumed me. What if he never noticed our buildings? It was my greatest fear.

Same with Dido, the queen of Carthage, who loves the visiting Aeneas, the Trojan warrior whose Italy-bound ship has been blown off course to her kingdom. He loves her back in the fourth book of Virgil's *Aeneid*, and their combination is fiery. But the soldier's fate is to establish Rome, and so his return to his course is an inevitability.

When he leaves, Dido is overwhelmed with heartbreak, "an exhaustion of body and spirit, a paralysis of pride and hope, the death of ambition," wrote J. Raleigh Nelson in "Dido: A Character Study," published in the *School Review* in 1904. "We see but the wreck and ruin of her soul." Before ordering a pyre to be set ablaze so that Aeneas will know from his ship that she has killed herself, Dido sends a lament across the waves to her love. "Remember me! Remember me!" she keens, her voice leaping in register with sudden crescendo on the third time in the 1689 opera Henry Purcell wrote about her. It could be the saddest song ever written.

I sang mine through emails and texts and Christmas stockings, which slowed but never stopped. If he was to remember me, I had to be in earshot. It was my only defence against the vagaries of this impossible concept, this plague and redemption, this idea a hundred layers deep.

"Do you remember when we saw the deer at the cottage?" I wrote. "The mommy and the baby, in front of our car? Do you remember? Do you remember the light in the sky that night? Do you remember how you reached for my hand? Do you remember?"

I kept waiting to forget the name of the friend Sam jammed with on Friday nights. For almost all the time I knew him, Sam would spend the Fridays between our weekends practising with a fellow guitarist, who would drop by his apartment for a few hours and then join him at the Honey Martin for a drink. I would always ask him about his playing partner in the late night phone call that followed. But I never met his buddy, who was famously anti-social, and so only knew him by name.

But more than five years later, I felt that name was in peril. If I forgot anything, I figured, it would be the handle of this minor character whose connection to me was so tenuous. He became a benchmark; I'd test myself on it from time to time and be alarmed to sometimes struggle, to have to dive down and down and keep surfacing empty-handed. But then the answer would drift into my head and it'd feel victorious. So long as I remembered Andy, Sam and I stayed afloat.

That was memory's purpose for me, in the after years. It was a mental scull I performed every day: Blue Jays games at the Dome and the kitchen chair on his balcony and how he always looked over his shoulder at his car after parking it. I took them out all the time—exercised them so they didn't grow flabby, at one point convinced I needed to remember every moment before I could earn any more. "There is so little to remember of anyone—an anecdote, a conversation at a table," wrote Marilynne Robinson in *Housekeeping*. "But every memory is turned over and over again, every word, however chance, written in the heart in the hope that memory will fulfill itself, and become flesh, and that the wanderers will find a way home, and the perished, whose lack we always feel, will step through the door finally and stroke our hair with dreaming, habitual fondness, not having meant to keep us waiting long."

I helped that hope with triggers, which I sometimes sought out and sometimes tripped over. Like the photo that steam from boiling pots had glued to my fridge, which I stared at while stirring the sauce. We're standing at Mount Royal's look-out with the word *Montreal* spelled out behind us. I'm wearing the motorcycle jacket he bought me in Kensington—the real thing, with the reinforced leather and thick buckles—and his arm is around my shoulders. Or Facebook messages he sent while he was in Europe for his grandmother's funeral. "My love," he said in one. "How I've missed you. I so wish you were with me." I told him I couldn't wait to get my arms around him and he said, "Me, too. So much." These triggers were easy to pull.

But there's a price to be paid for this kind of attention. Every time we dip into the barrel and pull a memory out, we change it. Every activation, declared British memory psychologist Frederic Bartlett in the 1930s, simplifies it. In some ways, we ruin our memories with our plundering. It could be that the hippocampus, the wee curled marvel deep inside our temporal lobes where all memory begins, overwrites the original a little with every recall, strips it of its authenticity.

"It has been suggested that every time we, so to speak, take out, or visit a memory to look at it, we repeat the process of putting it together in the brain," writes A.S. Byatt in her introduction to *Memory: An Anthology*. "This would lead logically to the inference that there is no true or original memory to be reconstructed or discovered."

"Already, less than a month after her death, I can feel the slow, insidious beginning of a process that will make the H. I think of into a more and more imaginary woman," C.S. Lewis wrote of his late wife. "Slowly, quietly, like snow-flakes—like the small flakes that come when it is going to snow all night—little flakes of me, my impressions, my selections, are settling down on the image of her. The real shape will be quite hidden in the end." He tells the story of meeting a man he hadn't seen for ten years and being shocked to discover this version of him quite different from the one he'd carried in his head for a decade. With the years accumulating since the flakes had started settling on Sam, I had the same concern. Everyone knows memory's a revisionist. Though I'd be disabused of my inaccuracies with a single audience with the disappeared actor, my five-years-out vision of him was otherwise flecked with reinvention. A shitty hologram, ruined by yearning.

Anyway, I couldn't help it. I needed to keep stirring up the stones, right down to the bottom, where Andy's was. My memory of Andy was my proof of us.

History swells with memory's feats, starring chess players and pianists, athletes and savants. And with memory's anomalies and unknowns. Like déjà vu, where novelty inspires a lurch of familiarity. Like panoramic memory, the vivid final reel that plays when we die. Like Franco Magnani, the San Francisco artist who painted the Tuscan hill town of his childhood with astonishing accuracy in the flush of a mysterious illness, years after he'd last seen it. Like Jill Price, whose memory is so big she can recall with precision every day since her mid-childhood, including the one her forty-two-year-old husband was taken off life support.

As with so many objects of human fascination, memory reaches its dendrites back to Aristotle and his early attempts to capture its essence. The bearded polymath compared memories to physical impressions made on the waxy surface of our unlived lives. It was an analogy that made sense to lots of thoughtful humans for a long time. "Let us then suppose the mind to be, as we say, white paper, void of all characters, without any ideas," wrote John Locke, two thousand years later.

In the Renaissance, memory was magical. The disappeared rematerialized in its fog, the dead revived. But the modern age took a more prosaic look. Much-cited American psychologist Karl Lashley ran rats through mazes for a third of his life so we might understand where memories settle, only to conclude that it's not any particular place at all, that their hotspots are widely distributed across the brain.

Even more complicated than memory's whereabouts are its mechanics. How a memory becomes one. It was 1904 when German evolutionary biologist Richard Semon floated the idea that experience leaves a physical trace in our brain's neuron networks. He called these cognitive traces engrams, and said the more neurons from disparate networks that fire over a moment, the more likely the moment will imprint on the brain.

Sam and I went to a cigar-making factory in Havana once, and watched all these women roll cigars with their nimble fingers and file them according to colour. The variations in shade were infinitesimal, which impressed us. In the centre of this cavernous room, amid workers who weren't allowed time off for a doctor's visit, was a woman reading the newspaper aloud. Against a backdrop of ascending browns she read every story in emphatic Spanish, turning the broadsheet pages with ceremony, her audience rapt. It was an unexpected touch of civility in this wrung-out environment, and when Sam and I remembered it after, we lit all these little fires in our brains.

Everything is memory for an instant. This lift of the eyebrow, that plate of eggs, those bounding flights up the front porch steps. We remember dates and music and math. Faces and names and tragedies. Every last thing that caresses our brain, at least for a moment. "What should we be without memory?" François-René de Chateaubriand, father of Romanticism in French literature, once queried. "We should forget our friendships, our loves, our pleasures, our work; the genius would be unable to collect his thoughts; the most ardent lover would lose his tenderness if he could remember nothing."

What we remember is mostly a mystery. Soaring news and the opposite. Frippery and consequence, both with the same thud. "For some reason," I wrote Sam once, "I keep picturing us in that Arby's. There was nothing special about that half hour. Just a lacklustre meal in an urban fast food joint. But I think of us there, looking out the window, eating and talking, and I am humbled by the simplicity of the scene. Little pots of ketchup and laughter. Just you and me. A moment in time. You can find perfection in the most unlikely places and its memory stays with you forever."

T.S. Eliot, who may as well have been at our table, endorsed the same in his conclusion to *The Use of Poetry and the Use of Criticism*. "Why, for all of us, out of all we have heard, seen, felt, in a lifetime, do certain images recur, charged with emotion, rather than others?" he asked. "The song of one bird, the leap of one fish, at a particular place and time, the scent of one flower, an old woman on a Germany mountain path, six ruffians seen through an open window playing cards at night at a small French railway junction, where there was a water-mill: such memories may have symbolic value, but of what we cannot tell, for they come to represent the depths of feeling into which we cannot peer."

Memory increases from five, the age at which it begins. Anyone who claims to have a babyhood memory, scoff psychologists, is overlooking a home truth: children's brains aren't developed enough for such sophisticated self-recall. "As the child's mind was growing into knowledge, his mind was growing into memory," George Eliot wrote of her character Silas Marner.

Memory peaks in the late teens and early twenties. This is the *reminiscence bump*, where we cement our version of our self. When people who are a hundred screen their lives in hospice theatres, they mostly watch movies that took place between the ages of fifteen and thirty. That, says Meik Wiking,

CEO of the Happiness Research Institute in Denmark, is because this stretch of celluloid is lit up with firsts.

We also remember things that are recent, as per the rule that memories become less accessible with time. We remember things that are at the top and bottom of lists. But mostly, said American neurobiologist James L. McGaugh, we remember things that spring our emotion—and in detail because of it. In the Japanese crime drama *Rashomon*, four characters remember a samurai's murder differently—including the samurai. It's not a fantasy. Memories are famously unreliable and even given to flights of invention. "Out of a few stored bone chips," American cognitive psychologist Ulric Neisser believed, "we remember a dinosaur." Or worse. In *The Memory Illusion*, Dr. Julia Shaw wrote about how we can be convinced we committed murder or were abducted by aliens.

Or had a relationship that was always gold, never tin.

By the time I'd been remembering Sam for more than five years, I had a greatest hits reel. In it, he was never short-tempered enough to throw a remote control across the room. Or so jealous he snatched the phone from me and said something shitty to my friend. He was always the hero. The guy who bought my children Christmas chocolate. Who'd be exhilarated when we got back into the little white Toyota after a visit with his parents. Who played guitar for me in his apartment and was so good. I told him again and again. *You are so good*.

That's what I remembered, as the accumulating days layered themselves across his last appearance: how *good* he was. It's a phenomenon of being human, this gilding. Psychologists say we cultivate a practice of holding on to good memories and leaving bad ones behind because it teaches us. There was a study in the 1930s where people were invited to share stories about life events and nominate them as pleasant or unpleasant. When the researchers made a surprise request several weeks later for the subjects to recall their memories again, they'd forgotten nearly 60 percent of the bad ones but only 42 percent of the good.

But it's also a phenomenon of heartbreak. The story is more tragic if the absent player is superb and magnanimous and never out of character—it increases the loss. "I love the ground under his feet, and the air over his head, and everything he touches and every word he says," wrote Emily Brontë. "I love all his looks, and all his actions and him entirely and all together." Like me for Sam with every curated recollection. It was a justification for my mad grieving and it became increasingly necessary. My memory had to be as light as my heartbreak was heavy.

"Long after I have forgotten all my human loves I shall still remember the smell of a gooseberry leaf, or the feel of the wet grass on my bare feet," wrote Charles Darwin's granddaughter Gwen Raverat, in *Period Piece: A Cambridge Childhood*. Such is the hold of the sense memory. The bridges that senses build to memory are short—fast tracks to different worlds, where people who were, still roam; things that aren't, still are. Everything we perceive and feel is filtered into our memory by way of our five senses. In *Memory's Adventure*, in 1773, Voltaire talked about a time when "the thinking human race" believed "we had ideas only through our senses, and that memory is the only instrument by which we can put two ideas and two words together."

Marcel Proust, who shared the conviction, came from a family of physicians and might have been one himself, had he not lifted his pen. In his lengthy *À la recherche du temps perdu*, the French novelist is clinical in a consideration of the senses' impact on our memory. When the narrator dips a madeleine into his tea in *Swann's Way*, he's delivered to his aunt's old grey house before Sunday mass, the country roads of his youth. This tea-infused delicacy has sent him to another time and place so emphatically it startles him. "Where did it come from?" he asks. And: "How could I seize and apprehend it?" from Cretien van Campen's *The Proust Effect*.

The rat Remy seizes it in the 2007 movie *Ratatouille*, with a dish whose consumption flings an imperious critic back to his mother's table and the adoration she served him upon it. From the first eggplant kiss, the flinty man is a boy with a mother who loves him. "Nothing has the ability to transport a person back into their own personal past quite like food," writes Frances A. Yates in *The Art of Memory*.

We had food that transported us, Sam and I. Shish taouk and General Tao's chicken. His mother's Indonesian cooking and the beef stroganoff she made for special occasions. Stroopwafels and Blizzards and McDonald's poutine. Friday night pizza and Timbits, like the ones I spilled on the icy winter night when King Edward was a rink and I wiped out on our way back to his place, landing like a scoop of lard, surrounded by wheeling dough. Later, when he'd gone, I'd wonder if that ungainly sight of me and my skating dough-nuts made an X in his *Go* column.

Smell—set off by the 6 to 10 million olfactory cells that flower in the cortex and the trillion odours that can get caught in their petals—is at least taste's equal in the tally of senses that send us most fervently into our mental museums. Smell is primitive. Scents hit the limbic system square on, the olfac-tory nerves bypassing the conscious thalamus in a beeline for emotion. It's the only sensory apparatus that circumvents this major brain relay system, which means we're mostly unaware of the rationale for the consequences smells stir. We know only that autobiographical memories cued by odours are more emotional than everything else.

Andy Warhol knew it, and capitalized by wearing the same perfume for three months and then never again, no matter how he loved it. After, he'd have jars of vapours he could uncap to transport him to the site of their genesis—ready-made vials of memory. I knew it too. It's why I sprayed the birthday cards I sent Sam with Un Jardin sur le Nil, in whose grapefruit mist I'd identified myself. I wanted to explode in his brain when he opened the envelope. I wanted to travel up his nose into his memory, send my scented fingers into all our scenes.

Like the magnolia and geranium ones we made in Begijnhof, a patch of memory inside Spui square in the heart of Amsterdam's university district. This sacred space is among the city's oldest *hofjes*. Hofjes are courtyards, generally tucked behind historical buildings and attached to almshouses for the downtrodden—publicly funded archetypes of Holland's benevolent civic conscience. Founded in the Middle Ages, the Begijnhof was an exemplary almshouse, an enduring sanctuary for Amsterdam's poor old women.

It is also the city's "secret garden," and Sam first sampled its pleasures when he was still a boy. "You'll love it," he would say, when we knew we were going, when our trip to the Netherlands was at last drawing near. But I could not imagine this verdant oasis inside Amsterdam's innermost canal that he spoke of in the mid-pitched voice he reserved for this favourite city.

He took me there one afternoon in May 2011, under a Vermeer sky. From the street, there's no hint of the splendour that lurks behind the massive arched door at the Spui and the towering townhouses with roofs that look like funny wigs. You can't imagine the sudden stillness of the green-grass courtyard or the hidden chapel whose stained glass windows have *1347* written on them in lead. "A visit to the Begijnhof allows you to leave the city behind," says the map at one end. "For a few moments you can imagine yourself in another world, and as you move through quietly this feeling will intensify." Dogs are not allowed inside the herringboned perimeter of residential flora, and you can't feed the pigeons on the brilliant swatch of interior lawn.

In its antique tranquility, Sam lit up in the sun. This was his place as much as it was any of the seven centuries of souls who'd loved it. Amsterdam was a wonderland to him, and on this May afternoon we walked the garden-strung midst of one of its historic treasures, marking its Gothic facades and the limestone statue of Jesus they guard, Sam telling me his grandmother's stories about the pious women who'd lived there, and always breathing in its geraniums and magnolia trees. Everything about the Begijnhof is a surprise to the senses; I will always sniff this memory in the air.

"I want you always to remember me," Haruki Murakami wrote in *Norwegian Wood*. "Will you remember that I existed, and that I stood next to you here like this?"

Mnemosyne is the goddess of memory. Jupiter fell in love with her at first sight and out of their marriage were born the nine Muses, who invented all the arts. There is no goddess of forgetting—there might be, given its pull.

In Yoko Ogawa's fable-novel *The Memory Police*, the residents of an unnamed island suffer an epidemic of forgetting that steals not only the idea of things but the things themselves. Into a cloud, birds and roses and calendars disappear, and soon the memory of their existence does too. "The island will soon be nothing but absences and holes," the narrator says, "and when it's completely hollowed out, we'll all disappear without a trace."

Mathematically, we forget almost everything. Phone numbers and faces and how he used to sleep. When I harked back to Sam almost six years since I'd last seen him, touched his leg, heard his voice, he was a ghost. My memories of him were mostly gone. He was a feeling, which was a memory too. But still. "O God! can I not grasp / Them with a tighter clasp?" laments Edgar Allan Poe of the grains of sand that creep through his fingers. "O God! can I not save / One from the pitiless wave? / Is all that we see or seem / But a dream within a dream?"

Neuroscience recognizes various explanations for forgetting, including brain damage and post-traumatic amnesia. But age is memory's biggest thief, as poet Philip Larkin knew when he wrote (in "The Winter Palace") about spending his second quarter-century losing what he'd learned at university. Eventually, he wrote, ". . . there will be nothing I know. / My mind will fold into itself, like fields, like snow."

Sometimes people pray for snow, aching to have their damaging memories covered over. From ancient times, clinicians, ethicists and scientists have responded. They've tried surgery, slicing up prefrontal lobes like butchers at the counter. Lobotomy, electric shock, long-term psychotherapy. Their focus is memory reconsolidation, the process by which a recalled memory is removed from and returned to long-term memory storage—or at least the in-between stage, when the door's swinging on its hinges. Dr. Alain Brunet, a McGill University psychologist who's studied PTSD for decades, has jammed himself in the doorway. There, he and colleagues found a way to target specific memories by tracking their formation and pathways in a mouse's brain with optogenetics, which illuminate nerve activity with fluorescent light. When they gave the mouse a bad memory (a cage that administered electric shocks), they watched him assimilate the news in his cerebral cortex and hippocampus and halt his capers about a place where the memories were shocking. But then they turned off those cells and all the learning inside them, and the mouse couldn't remember his fear. He bolted into the shock cage like it was made of cheese. Bingo. Now they knew where to target their drugs.

Dr. Brunet turned his gaze to humans next, homing in on the broken ones. This scientist has a thing for the heartbroken, moved by the Greek tragedy of their lot, intrigued by its number-one ranking among the reasons people consult psychotherapists. He invited sixty heartbroken souls to write first-person accounts of their suffering. Then he gave them a beta blocker called propranolol and asked them to read their sad summaries aloud. The recitations dislodged the memories and the propranolol, which can block the strengthening of emotions if it's taken before the memories are returned to the long-term shelf, suppressed their pain. After four to six weeks, people were able to recite their narratives without getting weepy, as though the sad tales tumbling from their lips weren't even theirs.

Six years after Sam and I ended, the calendar was a duplicate of that year for the first two months of the new year, the days lining up on the same dates they'd been in our last moments. It was amazing how this coincidence greased the memory.

The temperature had dropped ten degrees over the course of our final weekend together; by the Tuesday he left from Union Station, it was minus-fourteen. Sam had pneumonia. He had been sick since arriving on the train on Friday, and we had gotten it diagnosed at the emergency room of a hospital in the west end on Saturday morning. They wouldn't process his Quebec health insurance and so he had to pay cash for the examination. They gave him a form for reimbursement and I took it and said I'd look after the paperwork for him. It made me feel like his life partner, assuming this responsibility in sight of the woman at the registration desk. Sam sagged in his vinyl chair and probably didn't notice.

The pneumonia diagnosis shocked me and whacked me with guilt. I'd been impatient with Sam that weekend, irritated by this weakness that had kept him in bed and deprived us of sex and other pleasures. I'd taken him to Emergency to make a point more than anything; I wanted a doctor to tell him he was overreacting, to get out of his office and take me to dinner.

Instead, we filled a prescription for fluoroquinolone and went back to my house. Where I was still impatient. I hung outside my bedroom deck door that evening, smoking a joint I'd rolled for both of us that he'd declined, and bitching about it being the Saturday night of our birthday weekend and being stuck. And I looked across at Sam, sweaty and silent under the duvet as I let the frigid night air invade his infected lungs, and I saw something in his eyes that shook me.

Later, after he'd left, I'd think about that look and realize it was probably resolution. He was probably coming to terms with his plan to leave me right then and there in that bacterial bed the last weekend he was in it. But I really had no idea.

When it was six years to the minute since that night, I thought about it again, pressing hard into all my brain's corners, insisting on detail. His damp, empty face. How lonely it felt to get high without him. The bite of the air rushing into my bedroom. I was stunned to remember the sharpness of my annoyance with him—in such contravention with the object of yearning he became. But the worst part was remembering that look in his eyes.

This was one of the memories I would give up if I had that drug, I reflected, when he had been gone so long. It's too hard to see endings. Like the people falling out of the World Trade Center. This is where the loved-and-lost argument flames out. I would rather never have met Sam in that freezing November star storm than have to remember how his face despised me a dozen years later.

12

Peace

When it had been six years since the end of our six-year relationship, I texted Sam: "As long in as out," I wrote. "Symmetrical but surreal. God I miss zany you."

I did, I missed him as much as ever. I didn't take the pictures of us off the fridge for such a long time, not until we got a new fridge, and by then pasta steam had so adhered them that I'd had to let the delivery guys haul our photographic evidence to their truck. I thought about him all the time—fucking in that basement bedroom, the way he got so pissy on Sunday mornings near the end, eating Friday night pizza with his cat. I thought about his Hendrix and his hands and his humour. But mostly, now, I thought about the idea of him. I marvelled at his birth and appearance in my life, at the implausibility of his having been so much here and then so much gone. It was a pounding fascination for me, an ontological mystery so massive it left a dent in my bones.

"You take my breath away and I love you more and more," Sam had written on our first Valentine's Day. We were delighted with each other then, and pointed at our first spring in each other's company. I found the card in my drawer with other relics of that life years after our future had ended.

The relics were part of how I'd gotten through, how I'd stopped crying every day and every week, how I could keep him in my head without dissolving. Part of the reason I was okay at last, six years after we ended. The comfort I derived from proof of us. The comfort I derived wherever I could.

I found it in the most amazing places. In signs that scattered like dimes across six years of silence, every number and coincidence and cosmic whiff that confirmed us. British parapsychology researcher Rupert Sheldrake says the universe hums with telepathic information. It's why plants' polygraphs spike when someone near them thinks about burning their leaves. It's why we know, 54.5 percent of the time, we're being stared at. We're all tuning forks. It thrilled me to think I could still make Sam's vibrate, five hundred kilometres and a half-dozen years out of his sight.

I got crazy about astrology, admiring the accuracy of horoscopes that predicted a rebalancing of the universe, ignoring the abstract rest. I started reviewing my dreams, poking at them for messages. I listened for every cosmic dispatch that might contain a secret, though I wasn't sure what I needed it to be. Once, a guy in a bar told me that our breath commingles on the atomic level with the breath of all living things in a year and I couldn't believe my ears. He told me it takes thirteen months for all our exhaled carbon dioxide to make contact with all the leaves on all the trees in all the world. I listened to him, my head on fire, imagining my breath kissing Sam's on an Australian frond.

I took comfort from the idea of the Akashic records, and how our story is part of this imagined compendium of all the lives that ever were, an "electromagnetic imprint," as quantum physicist Ervin Laszlo says, "of everything that's ever happened in the universe," which is eternal.

It was eternity I was after in this existential hunt. Everything following his exit felt fleeting—I needed reassurance we hadn't happened just to dissolve into air. I was not resigned, just as Edna St. Vincent Millay was not resigned in "Dirge without Music," "to the shutting away of loving hearts in the hard ground. / So it is, and so it will be, for so it has been, time out of mind: / Into the darkness they go, the wise and the lovely. Crowned with lilies and with laurel they go; but I am not resigned." Not me neither. I was not resigned to surviving heartbreak by letting it get buried—I'd survive by building it a shrine, which eternity guarantees.

Without such fastidious focus, we fade away, utterly different from who we were by the moment, even from ourselves. We replace 1 percent of our cells every day and are almost swapped out in a season. Our taste buds renew faster than our bones. It takes sixteen years for our fat cells to turn over, and the muscle cells around our heart can take even longer. We get a new liver every 150 to 500 days, new stomach cells every five. But on average, a person is the pieced-together ship of Theseus in six years. Six years since their skin last touched another person's skin on a final shared night in bed, his so hot with pneumonia.

That means the physical person I am now—the eyelashes, the blood, the fingernails—is different in every way from when Sam knew me. He's never touched this skin, never kissed these lips. That murders me, that he doesn't know my tissues, that he's been gone so long we're both reinvented.

There's no shortage of eternity in the big promises of quantum physics. In one world view, everything that happened happens still (at once, even now, even that first chicken dinner, even that last train ride); everything that was cut short carries on (even love). It's beautiful news for a person mourning a loss.

These metaphysical contemplations are sky-high, but fluttering at their comprehensible edges is a fascinating idea: that there's no proof time advances in a forward direction, or any direction at all. "Time is not an illusion," Max Tegmark wrote in *Our Mathematical Universe*, "but the flow of time is." Carlo Rovelli knew it years ago, when he dabbled with LSD and time stopped. That this Italian theoretical physicist's perception of this incontestable fact had bent so easily under chemical influence filled Rovelli with doubt for other perceptions. It also aligned him with a crew of physicists challenging our assumptions about time. "The world is nothing but change," he wrote in *The Order of Time*, his lyrical meditation on the subject that consumes him.

Enter the block universe, where space-time is the fourth dimension and we're *always* in the present, always *here*. Julian Barbour, a British theoretical physicist with an Oxford shingle, calls everything in this timeless environment a series of *nows*. Birth, death and everything in between is a *now*, and all are relative. That means Antoine de Saint-Exupéry said, "The time for action is *now*," at the same moment Julius Caesar said, "I am *now* crossing the Rubicon," at the same moment Sam said, "We are together *now*," on our way to get pralines on Decatur Street.

Parallel universes were first imagined by Princeton physicist Hugh Everett in 1957, though American philosopher William James coined the term *multiverse* sixty-two years earlier to define something less fantastic. In his many-worlds theory, Everett said measuring a quantum object splits the universe, with each possible outcome materializing in a different version. Every time you miss the train or catch it, both realities advance. When you're snatched from the jaws of death in one universe, you're swallowed in another.

The multiverse theory is still in its infancy, but the idea's got the support of some serious pillars of theoretical physics: the quantum nature of everything and the properties of cosmic inflation. If they've got legs—why not the multiverse? And as for time travelling from Caesar to Saint-Exupéry, it's possible, say the breathless physicists. It's just a matter of time.

Albert Einstein met the Swiss engineer Michele Besso, who would be his friend for fifty years, at university in Zurich at the end of the nineteenth century. They got jobs in the Swiss patent office in Bern and would walk home together in a cloud of intellectual banter. When Einstein renounced his German citizenship for political reasons and took a teaching job at Princeton, in New Jersey, the pair began trading letters. They wrote copiously—mostly about their personal lives, but also about unified field theory, the cosmological constant and "time's arrow."

When Besso died in 1955, Einstein wrote one last letter to his great friend, a eulogy to his grieving family. That Besso had departed "this strange world" before him signified nothing, wrote the scientist (who would die a month later). "For us believing physicists, the distinction between past, present and future is only a stubbornly persistent illusion."

All of this matters to heartbreak because it eviscerates it. If this *now* is the same as this one, if this life is actually many lives, Sam and I are still walking toe to heel around the concrete borders of his childhood swimming pool talking about his butterfly stroke. Somewhere. Now. And now.

There's comfort in that.

When 2020 began and we stepped into a decade that had never known our little union, which had made such noise for six years and been so mute for six years, I found our horoscope. "You are ending a twelve-year life cycle," it said. "Do not be surprised if you end that which is not working in your life. Make that okay. You are clearing the field for the better."

It felt that way to me as I packed lunches for my teenagers and pulled out my laptop at the library all those years since we began, all those years since we ended. I remembered how heavily I used to drag my feet in those black mornings, the furrows I'd make in the kitchen floor. I remembered the days of crying, the wads of sodden napkins in my car's cupholders. It felt like we'd done a full turn round the wheel. I hoped this horoscope ending for Sam was to a period of stubbornness;

I hoped the ending for me was to a period of dangling. I knew we'd both be okay either way—our horoscopes said so.

People with Sam's birthday were born on the Day of Wilfulness. They are, says *The Secret Language of Birthdays*, strong-willed, mentally quick and stubborn. Earthy and headstrong—they won't give up an inch. They're the kind of people who could make a pneumonic decision to cut short a six-year conversation with someone they loved and then not say another word. *No matter what. Not even when you're stoned or sad or hear "A Long December" on your car radio.* His grip on his decision not to be in touch had been iron. I couldn't believe his resolve, though I watched him quit smoking like a soldier.

My birthday a week later is the Day of Precognition. I am intuitive and codependent and emotionally confused. I am highly intuitive—psychic, even—but also unrealistic and unable to hold on to the right people. "Work through your problems," goes the birthday book's advice. "Not everything can come easily."

It had always made sense that Sam and I were Aquarians. Air signs, fond of idea breezes, creative gusts, talking, talking, talking. Charismatic rebels. Quirky hippies. Lovers of absurdity. Ours is the sign of the drummers marching to exclusive beats—inventing our own ways, making it all up. We are intellectual, funny, curious. Fair-minded, kind, humanitarian. Some astrologers think Aquarians represent the best of humankind.

But if they do, humankind's one solitary lot. Aquarians are famously independent, known for carving their own path and then walking it alone. Solo lives that return every night to empty apartments are kind of the point with Aquarians. We are fans of space and personal freedom—don't fence us in. It's because of our ruling planet Uranus, discovered by telescope maker William Herschel in 1781, when the world was inflamed with liberty and the individual. Uranus is the first planet beyond the orbit of Saturn, not visible to the naked eye and cold as a bastard.

I remember once a couple of guys who used to live in Sam's building dropped by on a weekend I was there. The trio of former flatmates hung in the hallway for a bit, trading loud stories about the place when it was halcyon and everyone left their doors open so that beautiful Montreal could swoop in and gaze on their youth. At some point I piped up with something small about Sam maybe one day moving to Toronto and these guys roared with laughter. No way, they said. Sam was going to die in Apartment Number Four. I laughed too, but it was fake, and Sam knew it and that we were going to have a conversation about it after his friends left.

I went through our entire relationship without realizing I was battling a natural impulse in Sam with this expectation that he'd uproot his life for me. It was what he meant in his letter—his *last letter*—when he said he was tired of waking up to the idea of disappointing me in my wishes that he move to my city. Wish I'd never said them out loud (in moments of loneliness and self-pitying comparison to other people's arrangements). But I was fired on by convention and squeezed this non-conventional Aquarian till he burst, not acknowledging till after that our mutual love of breathing room was what had sustained us. It would be years before I found out Aquarius is the sign of the long-distance relationship.

When two lovers share a sun sign, they're blessed and they're challenged. Their personalities are similar enough to delight the other guy *and* send him running. But when they part ways and go spinning into the sky in opposite directions, it can be a tragedy. This person who was your mirror takes off with your reflection. When you look for it after they've left, your gaze goes on and on.

Out there in the blackness the Aquarian constellation flexes his water jugs in the sea section of the southern sky, where the celestial dolphin, fish and whale also swim. His heavy yoke marks his shoulders with stars, Sadalmelik and Sadalsuud. There's also a star on his right knee called Skat. In Hebrew, *skat* means "He who goes and returns." You can sometimes see it in the fall in the northern hemisphere, glinting like a spinning mirror.

There's comfort in that.

Skat was in the sky the night I went to the Fleetwood Mac concert, the night I realized I was okay. I had bought a single ticket, almost on the floor, ten rows from the stage, $270 for a singular experience years after our end. It was easy to get a good seat as a solo purchaser—the secret of the authentic fan. Like Sam, who used to go to concerts on his own a lot—Peter Frampton and B.B. King and Carlos Santana. He never felt awkward, he said, was always just grateful to enjoy the music without owing anybody anything. But an unaccompanied concert was unique for me. I was worried about the music's power, that I might vaporize in the stands.

I took the risk on a mild Friday night in November. This was a massive world tour, and the crowd, thwarted in April when Stevie Nicks got the flu, was champing for this replacement show. I joined their river down from Union Station and came into Scotiabank Arena to find my seat. How extraordinary it was to be in such a grand stadium awaiting a certain spectacle without Sam and his focus on the stage, in darkness save a blue-lit drum set. I peered at it across my aging cohorts and let him tumble through my brain. *We'd be here,* I thought, and reached for my phone. His absence in this space, which we'd so passionately occupied together, was too big not to acknowledge, though I wrote him so seldom those days. "Alone at a Fleetwood Mac concert, wishing I could fold back time and have you beside me," I texted into his silence. But I was okay.

They opened with "The Chain," a recovered Nicks sashaying onto the stage, all black, velvet boots and alto voice, as familiar as a friend. "And if you don't love me now, you will never love me again," she asserted right off, and I let the lyrics lick at my insides. They played everything we wanted them to, "Second Hand News" and "Go Your Own Way" and "Gypsy." The audience swayed in dreamy unison, holding up their iPhones, remembering the stories the old songs stirred in them. Lots of them smoked weed in the stadium, for nostalgia's sake. When they did an encore tribute to Tom Petty, playing "Free Fallin'" in front of old photos of him with the band, everybody so young, lots of us wept. But I was okay.

Sam and I would've gone to this concert together. We would've smoked a joint in an alley outside and made our way into the great big theatre with the twenty-five-foot video-screen and the massive ring of ceiling lights. We would have shuffled off our coats into our seats and settled back into that throbbing display and loved it so much. But Sam hadn't been around for years. I smoked my own joint and shuffled into my own seat and settled into my own display. And I loved it on my own, even when they belted out "Landslide," as Sam had in that Málaga sunset with his family all that time before. Throughout this poignant song about change and time, Stevie Nicks fixed her gaze on me, so different from when I was on that Spanish patio and still had so much ahead. "Well, I've been 'fraid of changin'. 'Cause I've built my life around you," she told me, watching my tears. But I was okay.

In *The Interpretation of Dreams*, Sigmund Freud declares that nothing important had been written about dreams before he got to them, but lots of ancient dreamers would take exception. In fact, our dreamy ancestors had plenty of thoughts on the subject that they considered an other-world conduit through which wisdom and divination flowed. Lots of them sought an audience with these favours by way of incubation, making pilgrimages to holy places where they hoped sleeping on sacrificed animal skins would encourage prophetic night-time visits.

Most ancient cultures believed dreams originated outside the individual, sent by gods or demons and drenched in portent. In Christianity's earliest texts, martyrs and converts talk to God in their sleep. Buddha's mother, Queen Maya, dreamt of the four guardians of the world carrying her to a divine couch in the Himalayas where she's visited by the future Buddha as a white elephant clutching a lotus in his trunk. In a Hindu tale called the Mahabharata, the Kuru leader speaks of dreams he and his soldiers are having about a looming battle with the Pandavas. They see trumpeting elephants, weeping horses, and their enemy eating rice and butter atop piles of bones. All of this foretells the Kurus' defeat, the leader says. The message was clear: our dreams contain the future.

Not so fast, said Freud twenty-three hundred years later. Dreams are the product of our interior, not our exterior. He called the dream the *via regia* to the unconscious—the royal road. It is "the gracious fulfiller of wishes," a psychological structure "full of significance" for our roiling private lives. When we uncover its hidden message, Freud wrote, "we find ourselves standing in the light of a sudden discovery."

I've dreamt about Sam since he left, waking in the fine dust of him and knowing he's been by. "All the time," I wrote him once of our nighttime encounters, "our stories play out in my head." I've dreamt of us running through my neighbourhood to make a movie on time, smoking at a funeral, in a flooded house. Six years since I'd seen him I had a vivid dream that left its powder behind for such a long time. He had this huge presence. I could feel his hug so physically. I kissed his throat with such relief and his skin was as soft as ever. *I love you and miss you,* I said, and meant it so hard it transcended the sleep–wake divide. *Me too,* he said, looking at me. I woke up inside all this energy and loved it for as long as I could, treating my cells to him, grateful for every dissolving moment. "Love, if I weep it will not matter, / And if you laugh I shall not care," wrote Edna St. Vincent Millay in her poem "The Dream." "Foolish am I to think about it, / But it is good to feel you there."

But I've mostly forgotten my dreams by morning, their particulars as ephemeral as childhood. Indeed, if we believe the physiological evidence suggesting we dream for about a fifth of the time we're asleep, we forget the majority of our dreams. Mostly, says Kelly Bulkeley in *Dreaming in the World's Religions*, we remember the dreams that are packed with feeling.

I had the first of so many *after* dreams three weeks into heartbreak, so packed I had to tell him about it the next morning. "It was awfully, terribly, dreadfully real," I wrote. "When I woke up it was several seconds of such profound relief to know you were beside me, and that the pain was over at last." We were together again, watching *The Walking Dead* in a hotel room whose TV I'd hooked up to my laptop. He was on one bed and I was on the other, but he invited me to his and we lay together, me not daring to breathe, so grateful for the reprieve. Then Sam went down on his knees between the beds and I stroked his hair. He said it was time to end it, meaning my suffering. "It's enough now," he said, like he had to the airport people in New Orleans when they lost our luggage. When the dream ended and I saw we hadn't reunited after all, I was a zombie too—alive but not really.

It's the ancient idea, where dreams are magic, that most appeals to me. Imagining I'm receiving mystical insight about things my waking self doesn't know is reassuring. As it was for Odysseus's wife, Penelope, when she dreamt of the goddess Athena standing at her head urging, "Courage! Don't be overwhelmed by all your direst fears," and knew all would be well.

I've had the same dream for all my heartbreak. Its particulars differ, but there are two constants: we are together again and he will leave again. There's a desperation to these dreams, me tearing about in ecstasy for our recoupling, pursued by its ending, which always arrives. Once, it went off script, though, on an October night almost five years after he left, when the twilight star Arcturus was a forlorn ghost of the departed summer sun, and I dreamt of him again. It broke up into morning too quickly, but I'd noticed a message at the end that lingered. I found a pen in my bookcase and an index card, and wrote it down, the two words the dream Sam had said to the dream me from across a great distance: *Home soon. I* was *home,* I thought, as I tucked the card back into my bookcase. He'd be back. My dream had told me so, and it filled me with such peace.

There was also peace in my relationship with Tanya—*crazy* because she was a sibling of the man I craved ("Wait, *you're still friends with his sister?*" people would ask, incredulous) and *crazy* because it had evolved as a product of heartbreak. But heartbreak makes us humble and honest, its despair crowding propriety, and the human connections we make in it are profound. That's because we can be whatever other humans need us to be in its grace. Guides for travellers or a bridge to traverse the water, as the eighth-century Buddhist monk Shantideva prayed. As John Keats's sister was for Fanny Brawne, and Sam's sister was for me.

The eighteen-year-old Fanny Brawne became John Keats's muse soon after they met in the fall of 1818. The love letters he wrote her are emphatic and romantic, among the most famous ever written. "I could be martyr'd for my Religion," he told her in one of his earliest. "Love is my religion—I could die for that—I could die for you." Fanny Brawne quickly moved into Keats's cottage on the edge of an ancient heath under whose plum trees he wrote "Ode to a Nightingale." They saw each other every day and (probably) got engaged at Christmas. While none of Fanny Brawne's letters to Keats survive, her letters to his sister do.

Fanny Brawne and Fanny Keats began writing each other in September 1820, when the former was twenty and the latter was seventeen and both were saying goodbye to their beloved John Keats, who was leaving England for Italy in pursuit of a more curative climate for his tuberculosis. But before he left, he set the scene for a friendship that would outlive him. In Fanny Brawne's first note to the sister of the man she loved, penned five days after he departed, she tells her Keats suggested she write and that she's sorry this introduction is "a little stiff." But that fell away quickly as Keats's condition was grave, and the two women reached for each other in their sorrow.

"Oh my dear, he is very ill," Fanny Brawne confided in Fanny Keats before she knew her at all. "If I am to lose him I lose every thing." When John Keats died in Rome five months later, she wrote his young sister candidly of her grief: "I have not got over it and never shall," she said.

The pair of women were prolific in their correspondence for four years, the last three after John Keats had died. In 1937, Oxford University Press published thirty-one of their letters in *Letters of Fanny Brawne to Fanny Keats*. The world would never know of these two women, goes the foreword, "had it not been that the one loved a great poet and the other was the poet's sister." More than that, their intimate friendship might never have been had desperate measures not sealed it. "I felt so happy when he desired me to write to you while he was away," Fanny Brawne once wrote Fanny Keats. "I little thought how it would turn out."

Same thing for me and Tanya.

Before Sam left me, his sister, Tanya, was a minor character in my life. She was Sam's glamorous only sibling. Younger than me and beautiful. Cosmopolitan and stylish, skipping across Europe in international PR jobs, howling under a pink wig in an Asian nightclub in her social media posts, living the life. She and her boyfriend lived in Singapore and then Paris and I only ever saw her on Skype in Sam's apartment, over Christmas at their parents' or in perfunctory email exchanges. She signed her notes "T"; I signed mine "L." We talked about our kids and her brother, our biggest connections. A couple of years before Sam went away, Tanya and her family rented a cottage in Grand Bend for the same week we were there. "Can't wait to hang and chill and chat and swim and drink beer and BBQ and eat cotton candy and go to the drive-in," she emailed me in the spring. But it didn't play that way. The siblings fought on that holiday, and Tanya and I were on opposite sides, stiff as anything.

Then Sam left me and we instantly softened. I reached out to her from my wreckage, snotty and hoarse and wild with despair, hurling myself at her without cover, compelled by her proximity to the object of my yearning, which gave her super powers. Pretense is a luxury in the gallows and I, a brutal and inconsolable gargoyle to her poise and beauty, had none of it. I asked her to call me and closed my bedroom door to wait on the floor on the other side of my bed. I had a terrible cold that was just turning into pneumonia and had been crying for days. I was so miserable, always in my sweaty sheets, my sick body where Sam's had been. I had no voice at all when I begged Tanya, six hours ahead of my misery, to ask her brother to contact me. An ocean away, confronted with such a spectacle of despair, Tanya assured me she would help. "This must end," she said. "You deserve to live again."

After, when Sam didn't oblige either of us, we stayed in close touch. I wrote her rambling, wretched emails about my pain, blocks of text jammed with upper-case imploring and repeating questions *(Why, why, can you tell me why?)*. "The silence is killing me, Tanya," I wailed in one. "I think I'm dying here." I signed my notes with effusion: "So much love," I'd write. "Your presence in my life means so much."

She always wrote back. "I am here, darling," she would say. "You are not alone." She would tell me I wasn't dying, and over and over that I was whole and strong and blessed. She would say she wished I could fill the hole her brother had left with love for myself. "Don't waste all that you are on sorrow." Eventually we started talking on the phone, and saying *I love you* at the end—and I really did love her, this woman who'd so tenderly scooped me from her feet.

When she moved to Montreal, Tanya began visiting me in Toronto, including in April four years after her brother left. It was a Friday the thirteenth, cursed by King Philip IV when he arrested hundreds of Knights Templar on that day in 1307 and the Grand Master, facing a hot stake in front of Notre-Dame, cast a hex on it for the ages. But for me it was lucky, because I was getting a tattoo with my surprising consolation prize, whose treasured friendship, forged in fire, flourished, even in the ashes of the one that launched it.

The tattoo parlour, the Pearl Harbor Gift Shop, is an old-school standard in the city's hipster Kensington neighbourhood. Up two steps in a row of tall Victorians with painted fronts, the bright shop is outfitted with century-old general store cabinetry and a tin ceiling. The shelves, salvaged from a shuttered Toronto hat shop that had been seventy-five years old, are lined with World War II knick-knacks—china plates and plastic dolls. On the walls is ink inspiration for people filling in the paperwork at the desk: stencils of steer skulls and eagles and blindfolded maidens with cigarettes between their lips.

I had thought about this tattoo—my children's signatures, wrapped around my ankle—for a long while, but had always put it off. Leave it to my madcap friend Tanya to whirl into my city and declare that this was how we would spend our day, getting our first tattoos together. There was never any question.

We had no appointment and there were already customers splayed across the cots with needle-wielding artists bent over them when we came in that morning, so we put our names on a list and went out into the drizzle to get Tanya a coffee with butter in it. I went first when we returned, hiking up the right leg of my jeans and lying back on a vinyl table draped in a white sheet. Our tattoo artist was Franklin, whose portfolio showcased elaborate mushrooms, reptiles and swordfish. He wore a T-shirt hailing a Swedish grindcore band and a sleeve of intricate Maori tattoos that extended to the top of his blue rubber gloves. He adjusted the lamp above my ankle and got to work. The pain was insane, but Tanya just laughed and took photos of me gripping the bed. She was next, cool as a cucumber as Franklin poked needles in the shape of a symbol for home into the tender skin of her left forearm, chatting with him about his accent and smiling with her other arm behind her head in all my shots of her.

We were thrilled with our transformed selves. But the symbolism of that afternoon's efforts went beyond the designs we'd chosen for life. We'd gotten ink put in our skin together, Tanya and I, an unlikely pair in the wake of such tragedy, laughing like drains, never not knowing it made our friendship permanent too.

I wondered what Sam thought of his sister's tattoo when she presented her left arm to him after our transformative weekend in Toronto. I wondered if he asked her about *my* tattoo and got a picture in his head of my ankle. I wondered what other pictures he had. I had so many. They were my secrets, the way my babies were when I carried them inside. No one knew that Sam still clung to my nerve endings, even after all these years. No one knew about this craving, which spiked according to nothing in particular. Shimmering days when the sun was out and I could sniff one of our afternoons in the air, I'd think: everything would be perfect *if*. But it was the same on the shit days when I was grey and I'd think:

everything would be better *if.* Either way, he still made all the difference.

It's a conviction whose comfort addicted me. My muscles still sometimes jumped on Friday nights, that day saturated with six years' anticipation of him. Could be my whole system was still coiled, interpreting this stretch as nothing more catastrophic than a long gap between visits. Ours was a relationship of missing, after all.

Now there were six years of it, a lamentation whose ribbons trailed so long they rivalled a widow's robes, though I secretly knew mine were longer. For the widows, the dead have no agency; for me, the person who left still went to the gym every morning and checked Facebook and greeted a cat I'd never met, doubled down with every silent minute his commitment to erase me, though so much time had passed. We'd lost an airline and glaciers and so many trees inside it. We'd sustained one pandemic and played four Olympics, including one I spent puddled on my parents' couch, weeping and watching Russian bobsledders at sunrise. We'd read books and watched the world shift and formed points of view. And all with Sam in his place and me in mine. "Two roads diverged in a yellow wood," Robert Frost wrote. "And sorry I could not travel both." Me, too.

One summer afternoon when it was still common, our road was a boardwalk on Lake Ontario. It was the Saturday of a Toronto weekend and Sam and I were strolling along the water like lovers when we came upon a film crew beside a beach volleyball court with boom mics and Adirondack chairs. They were looking for couples they could interview about their relationships for a new Oprah Winfrey promo. I dragged Sam into the spotlight and said we'd love to chat. The TV crew shambled around in the sand behind us, adjusting reflectors on poles and blowing into microphones with furry muffs before announcing they were ready. Then the host introduced us and folksily asked if we'd share something about our partner that drove us crazy. Sam talked about how my closet was filled with clothes I'd forgotten I'd bought, still dangling with tags. I talked about how he couldn't help but take on the accent of whomever he was speaking with, that I worried the other guy might feel ridiculed. Then I laughed and told the producers that it was Sam's natural empathy that made him do it, and Sam said something about me having a natural empathy for shopping and this time everybody laughed. They thanked us and Sam and I picked up our stroll along the boardwalk, its diverging point still well in the distance. Behind us, the encounter we'd had with the film crew fluttered up above the lake and then away, reduced to its elements, just a moment.

It was still up there in the sky taking up the same space all the other moments did, years after the road below had split. And this enduring fact of us was, at last, the greatest comfort I'd discovered in the six years after Sam left. If we believe dead people live on so long as we still think of them, the same surely extends to people who've shuffled off a different kind of mortal coil. Six years after we ceased to be, it comforted me that we'd been. Six years after we walked it together, our road still bent and climbed in some existential yellow wood. That we were no longer on it almost didn't matter. Because once upon a time, we were.

13

Faith

These seven years have been a ride. Mostly unpleasant, so lonely. I have left my sorrow across all of them, in the spots I've sought refuge through the dark days. It is the map of my heartbreak. One freezing Saturday in the early weeks, I went to a bulk food store with my children and poked at hills of cornmeal and hulled millet and felt so bad. Across the snowy street was the music store where Sam would visit the guitars, and I remember looking out at it in free fall and wondering how I was going to get through with all these kids and responsibility. "Do not leave me in this abyss, where I cannot find you!" Emily Brontë wrote. "I cannot live without my life! I cannot live without my soul!"

When I passed the bulk store seven years after my grief began, the memory of it shocked me and I had to turn away. Part of every misery, said C.S. Lewis, is the misery's shadow: "the fact that you don't merely suffer but have to keep on thinking about the fact that you suffer." When I saw the shadows I left on these sites of mourning when I grieved inside them, I was shot back to the saddest thing: me, when I was as hopeless as could be. Such is the arc of heartbreak: feeling sorry first for the loss and then, by degree, for the person who suffered it.

The loss of Sam, who was my best friend, has been excruciatingly out of character. I can't bear losing people, and so take care not to. When I was in high school, my classmates voted me most likely to plan a reunion. When I did, twenty-five years later, it was easy because I'd stayed in touch with so many of them. My oldest friendships are as old as me. I stumble across my kids' father at neighbourhood fruit stores and leave our chummy exchanges feeling like we invented the best-case scenario for mitigating loss. When you love someone, you always love them.

"We all know that something is eternal," Thornton Wilder's narrator says in *Our Town*. "And it ain't houses and it ain't names, and it ain't earth and it ain't even the stars. . . . Everybody knows . . . that something is eternal and that something has to do with human beings. . . . There's something way down deep that's eternal about every human being."

Seven years out, I had the same conviction. That even all our vain preoccupations and lost hours and heartbreaks have value enough to guarantee their eternity. That our relationships aren't random. We're in each other's orbit for a reason— this time and all the ones before. That the dimes and licence plates *are* signs. That he *does* think of me when I think of him. Because if we don't believe that everything means something, we don't believe that anything means anything. Better to endorse the former and let it be an air mattress for this heavy life. Better to have faith.

When Sam went away, he took my floor with him and I just fell and fell. I plunged past everyone—impassive bystanders and well-wishers and fatalists—and none had a thing to offer. Just six years of nothing, all that luck and limerence disintegrating in the useless ether. I fell through the crazy where everything was in ebb: my sense of self, my worth, my assurances. I could be sure of nothing in this nosediving reality. Not the New Orleans afternoon when we dashed through the rain in Audubon Park. Not the bicycle ride up Mont Tremblant, which we did twice because I left my wallet behind. Not the idling white Toyota in the hotel parking lot.

Here, our shuttered relationship—which left no mark, no children, no cottage—was revised. In its place? The swamping possibility that he never cared a bit. That I'd misunderstood. *He never loved me; I was never special.* I was a weightless dunce with nothing to offer but a propensity for overblowing what was a mere trifle of a relationship and was in fact worthy of nothing—least of all eternity. And I had nowhere to land.

I had had to come up with something to rescue my children (who had been relieved of another intimate figure and the serenity that relationship lent to their mother's psyche) and the rest of my life now that it was only me. "No one saves us but ourselves," Buddha said. "No one can and no one may. We ourselves must walk the path." And then came the day I believed our resonant love affair had value, even though it had ended. That our ending did too. That everything did.

Truly, I have always been riddled with faith. I believe in so much. Goodness. Redemption. That we already have everything we need. And I believe that when you've lost your way, it's only a temporary condition. I believe that in part because of Sam, whose philosophies reassured mine on this front, though he became the very man to test them. Sam is a person who's experienced profound sadness and who's applied the same dedication to overcoming it that he applied to his music and his swimming and his grip on this idea that if you ignore someone long enough, they forget. He understands the importance of climbing on top of grief, of dominating it, no matter how high the pile. He shared his tips for this mastery with me, well-thumbed concepts he kept behind his ribs. "You're on your own team," he would tell me, when I was tearing myself down. *Why would you fight your own team?* He'd say, "Don't catastrophize," to stop my anxious snowballs when I'd set them off from a hilltop. But the best were the all-purpose dictums he used as planks for the floors he built under my plummeting dread. "It will find its way," he'd say when I'd lost it. "Everything will find its way."

I always believed him, and it always has. My children's aberrance. My mother's cancer. All the times I've panicked in this lucky life. I am the person who uncovers her lost keys, even when they're in a Niagara Falls Target or the sand at the beach during Canada Day fireworks. I drop my phone in the hot tub and leave my bike unlocked when I go into a store. Everything has always found its way. It has, I think, because I've always known it would.

"I will not doubt, though all my ships at sea / Come drifting home with broken masts and sails," writes Ella Wheeler Wilcox, a free-thinking American poet from the turn of the twentieth century. I needed to believe in my own seaworthiness, like Henry Ford did with the V8 engine, and Roger Bannister when everyone told him his lungs would explode. He broke the four-minute mile because he believed in something else.

It took a while for me to find and apply this faith to managing my heartbreak—but I got there.

"We were destined," I wrote Sam once, after he'd gone. "From our fierce passion on the dance floor we had found each other. And on some plane of existence out there, the universe preserves our union. We are always, as much as you drew to a close the daily rituals and accumulation of shared experiences. In the heavens, between the stars, we still exist. Laughing like idiots and watching our teams and kissing till we're weak in the knees. Always, always, Sam. There will never be another us."

I still believe it, after all these years. That we meant something and not just for a minute. Our passionate story, which still flaps without resolution in the breezeway between Canada's two biggest cities, is crammed with value: gratitude and grace and certitude. My enduring heartbreak is proof. If the universe hadn't assigned it value, why would my chest still hurt? Our memory sees to it that we haul our energy around forever. So we will always be. And this eternity, which you can take shelter inside, is our value.

It thrilled me to have found a way to package my pain.

Now all that grief had a tributary, flowing to a precious place. "Recognizing the necessity for suffering I have tried to make of it a virtue," Martin Luther King Jr. said. "I have lived these past few years with the conviction that unearned suffering is redemptive." It has taken a long time to create a world that lets me be okay. Faith is what finally broke my fall.

Still, my faith left room for yearning, which, seven years since I'd seen him, was panning out to be a constant. I missed Sam as much then as when I wept in the car outside the trampoline gym or hung the fishing-line wish up in the art gallery. I missed our nighttime parties and New Orleans antics and laughter. We made each other laugh for six years—you don't get over that deficit fast or maybe not ever. I missed our music and anticipation and how our love for each other climaxed when our bodies did. I missed his heart, which he'd removed from my reach.

I missed his texts saying his plane had landed. I missed talking about myself like you can with a lover. I missed his long fingers and weird lobeless ears. I missed his secret notes. "All the things that make you the lovely rare being you are remind me there is profound goodness in this world," Sam wrote in one, back when he still wrote. "You mean everything to me."

One winter in the middle of our relationship, we took a trip to Cuba, a week away from snow and duty. The resort was simple, but did the job; the beach was the thing. And what lapped against it. We took a bus to a scuba launch in Havana a couple of days in. Sam's hair was at its longest that trip, curling over his wooden beach necklace with the bravado of a young Fidel, and we couldn't keep our hands off each other in our back-row seat, sending other passengers' eyes to distractions. They unloaded us without ceremony at the scuba launch and we sat at picnic tables in our wetsuits until someone thought to organize our groups. The instruction we got in the swimming pool was equally casual and then it was thirty open-water metres deep and—impossibly—breathing with our lungs.

Not surprisingly, the instructor had failed to inform us that we'd be going through a curving, tight cave, whose fifteen-metre length might have been two hundred for all I knew going into it with a tank on my back. I was terrified, and Sam knew it. *I've got you,* said his eyes behind his mask, his arms sculling. And I, near paralyzed with claustrophobic fear, never doubted it. After we surfaced and returned to the bus, Sam was lit up with pride. His praise of me and what I'd overcome in the Atlantic was emphatic and true. *I missed that.*

I missed his presence, sure as gravity and my children, which kept me anchored to the floor. In *Jane Eyre*, Rochester tells Jane, "I have a strange feeling with regard to you: as if I had a string somewhere under my left ribs, tightly knotted to a similar string in you." I had the same feeling about Sam. Seven years out, he still swam into my consciousness every morning, I still conjured him through every day.

It shocked me to still be conjuring after all these years. It shocked me to feel what I did about this man who left me and ignored my pleas for a response, even though I'd told him I was broken, even though it had been so long. I found the bottle of candy "pick-me-up pills" my little girl had made me in the throes of Sam's leave-taking and remembered the tremendous pain that had prompted this act of childish concern. And I realized it was still there, just flattened out at the bottom of my soul.

I felt silly still being this much attached, still crying at the park. I was embarrassed to remember the secret message I wrote on the back of a guinea pig photo I once sent Sam's nephew, before sealing it in a frame. "For Oscar, whose uncle used to love me," I wrote, and then wept to imagine its infiltration into Sam's world. Sometimes I'd forget that he was just ignoring me and not dead, and sense he was communicating with me supernaturally.

How insane, my brain would go. But it couldn't be helped. This was my loss. This was the brick in my gut. We all have bricks; this was only mine. This had been part of my being okay—recognizing how unremarkable I was. My story was quite usual: single mom gets dumped by younger, childless man, sustains a broken heart. Still, he was not immune to discomfort. Sam, I believed, was holding his ground for reasons that were important to him. I knew he didn't feel good about having caused me pain. That he had faith in his enduring choice to snub me was part of *my* faith; that he wasn't hurting me lightly; that he, too, was guided by fervour.

I wonder if I'm his lapsed and lamented friend Adrian once again, if Sam's made more wistful declarations about our divide and about *one day* being the right one to remember me. And I wonder how he felt when he found out Adrian died before their day arrived. Surely it heightened the ticking passage of another mortal summer, which bloomed and withered in silence.

I sometimes see Sam in his sister's Facebook photos but only linger a moment. Just long enough to take him in, to note his greying temples, his public smile, his beautiful bones. And then I have to move off; I can't stay on him long. I never return to those photos, either—versions of him that have nothing to do with me. Or to the last email he sent, the day after my birthday "to spare the day," when he said it was over, that he couldn't disappoint me anymore, that we'd been in trouble since the summer. I only ever read that once; who wants to keep watching the blade fall?

It's like *The Tree of Life*, Terrence Malick's epic contemplation of human existence, and the final scene on the honeyed beach, where everyone we've loved comes together. I could only ever watch it once; it's too poignant to imagine, the idea of people finding each other at last but in another realm because they didn't hit the mark in this one. To watch it again would be to remember the magnitude of my loss.

Just the same, many people are enraged to learn I still think of this man who left me so resolutely all that time ago. They screw up their faces and retreat from the concept. *Imagine holding on to those feelings still,* they say with their disgusted noses.

Imagine not.

When you love someone, you always do.

"I tried to pretend that my love for you was dead, though I could only do so by pretending myself that my heart was dead," T.S. Eliot, who knew about faith, wrote to the American schoolteacher Emily Hale in a letter she kept locked in a passionate collection until both of them were gone.

That's a lesson heartbreak taught me, never to assume we're the same. Not our sympathies, not our values, not our sorrows. "I measure every grief I meet with narrow, probing eyes," Emily Dickinson wrote. "I wonder if it weighs like mine or has an easier size." Once, I published an essay about heartbreak in a newspaper and it drew so many furious responses from readers who wanted to punish me for the stickiness of my focus on a guy who felt otherwise. The restrained ones urged me to find my pride; the infuriated ones called me a loser. One guy said he'd have left me too. Most pronounced my long suffering a weakness, leaning the weight of their disappointment against me hard.

These are the people who have Jack Kerouac's advice, *accept loss forever*, tucked into their mirrors. These are the stoics who heave their broken hearts overboard and call it success when they sink like stones. I think about them congratulating themselves for drowning something that once lifted them into the air and wonder how we could ever know each other's worlds. And—all these years on and the tskers be damned—I don't feel lesser for still being smashed up; I feel natural. It was a massive relationship; of course it left a massive absence behind.

And I still have hope that he might one day feel inclined to reach out and restore a modicum of my dignity with his acknowledgement. Every day might still be the one he texts or emails, bent with capitulation, sorry at last, in the downsweep of all these wasted years. Every day might be the one he ties off the loose threads. Or tells me why. Stops the clock on this enduring tragedy. *Just for a moment let's be happy. It goes so fast. We don't have time to look at one another.*

"Everyone has three lives: a public life, a private life and a secret life," said Gabriel García Márquez. My conviction that my path will intersect with his again is the atmosphere of my secret life, another strand of the faith that sustains me. *It would've by now,* cluck the people I allow in on the lunacy, but I don't agree. Things that happen are always preceded by stretches of time during which they *didn't* happen. I believe it because of this: How could I *not?* We were so big. *We are both still here.* I believe it because my dreams still bulge with *saudade*, the Portuguese concept of missing, which doubles as the ecstasy that grips you upon a reunion. I believe it because of *Love in the Time of Cholera*, and the faith Florentino Ariza had that he loves Fermina Daza with good reason. He is patient for fifty-one years, nine months and four days, and his faith is borne out on a river cruise under the yellow flag of cholera, which denies this renewed couple port forever. And so their love is eternal after all.

Kindred souls can take many forms; seems to me one should exhaust the lot, given how seldom they appear in a short life. My faith extends to creative reimagination of how two people who were lovers before can still know each other after. "There are more things in heaven and earth," Hamlet upbraids Horatio, "than are dreamt of in your philosophy."

Tanya visited me one hot July weekend when her brother had been gone for more than five years and we decided we'd spend the Saturday afternoon getting our fortunes read. Our psychic, recommended by my friend Alexandra, plied his trade from his seventh-floor studio apartment in a classic Toronto building in a tony neighbourhood. We Ubered there and I went shopping on Bloor while Tanya took the first hour-long appointment. We'd agreed we wouldn't tell the guy anything about ourselves, and when Tanya came out and I went in, we did the exchange wordlessly.

The psychic, who had three first names but went by Starhunter, welcomed me and asked me to shuffle a deck of cards while he "ran to the restroom." He had a moustache out of '70s porn and a nasal voice that he pitched from the bathroom when he yelled: "Oh, I do estates and antiques, that's why all that shit's around." I sat in a William IV chair at a glossy mahogany table whose legs were like lions' paws and took the cards into my hands. The table was strewn with tchotchkes: a silver chafing dish, a porcelain teapot strung with blue flowers, a ceramic beagle on his haunches. On the walls was a gold-framed gallery: antique paintings of dogs and solemn cherubs and collared visitors from another era whose eyes were filled with warning. Beneath them, sideboards bowed under hurricane lamps and vases and a china candy dish shaped like a curly-horned ram. I passed the cards between my hands while, under the table, a one-eyed Pomeranian named Chloe licked my bare calf like it was her part in the contract. "Sorry about her," Starhunter apologized when he returned to the room, but I didn't mind.

I laid out sixteen cards, so worn they felt like skin, one on top of the other, face down as instructed. Starhunter flicked his eyes across my spread and declared, "You've got a lot going on here in terms of travel, holy shit," before even taking his seat. He was tall, with light eyes under animated brows, a receding hairline and an extravagant way. I needed to take care about getting into vehicles with people under any kind of influence, he said, his eyebrows leaping and diving. And to expect issues with my shoulder that I had to respect—"Don't be a hot dog," he said. He told me there was going to be an island in my future, and that I would eventually split my time between it and Toronto. "It's a little bit too good to be true," he marvelled, and encouraged me to accept all invitations off the mainland. "It could be any island," he said. The Caribbean. Georgian Bay. And then he said, "Maybe Montreal," just as Chloe's tongue started up again and my whole body jumped.

Also good, Starhunter said, was the transformation that loomed on my horizon. Everybody has these, he said, but mine was a standout for the conclusion it featured. "You have acceptance and you are moving on," he said. "All of this fear, worry, et cetera, is winding down. There is forgiveness ahead."

For the next spread Starhunter asked if I had any questions for him, and I couldn't resist. As much as I feared hearing an answer that would crush my bones to dust, my brain told my mouth to form the words and my lips parted to let them out: *What about Sam?* I asked in a little voice, little to keep a lid on the detonation. He was a man I loved who had left me and never said another word, I told Starhunter, and . . . I was curious: Would our paths ever cross again?

You'd better believe it, Starhunter told me straight up, and my bones went hard. *They always have*, he said. Ours was a karmic relationship, the kind you see with people who find each other across lifetimes. He said my connection with Sam went back a century to past lives in Europe, and that if we ever did our DNA, we'd discover we were related.

"I've very rarely seen a sense of connection like this," he announced down his nose, and then dropped his volume and said he didn't want to upset me, but there was a woman he'd once read who was very connected to her ex-lover. She found out he was dying and returned to him for the last five months of his life in Vancouver. "They resolved everything," Starhunter said, his eyebrows soaring. "It was still there, all the love they felt."

I prattled giddily in response to this fantastic story, desperate not to have him retract a word, wanting him to wrap it up so I could go away and think back on it. But Starhunter interjected to say again how our connection, the one linking me and Sam, was just as potent. "This is unresolved," he said into my eyes, barely looking at the cards between us. "There are so many things unfinished in your link with him. It's not over, your connection. It is not over."

I think so too. Because I'm a writer, and believe everything gets a satisfying ending. Our storyline's still bloated with expectation, awaiting the magic-hour final shot on that eternal beach, that choleric boat ride under an eternal yellow flag.

And if I'm not Florentino Ariza but Miss Havisham, dead in a wedding gown after a lifetime of faith, I'll still be improved for having carried it so long. Better to believe his long-ago declaration about the permanence of the place I'd made in his heart than the opposite: that I've dissolved into vapour. So long as I don't know which, I'll presume the former. Which gets me an easier life.

What if at the end of it all, there is nothing? a character called Me asks in Richard Wagamese's *Embers*. "Then we still come out better people," the old woman answers. "Can you think of a better way to live than in gratitude? Can you think of a better way to be than to be kind, loving, compassionate, respectful, courageous, truthful and forgiving? Even if we're wrong, can you think of a better way to breathe than through all that?"

Epilogue

Partway through a pandemic, I returned to Montreal. I had to drive my youngest to a redstone near Atwater Market where she would study languages from a bedroom facing the street. When she'd announced her intention to go to McGill, I'd felt so sad. Her presence there would tear off the scab I'd nurtured so attentively. I'd ignored that city for so long and now all the pieces of my heart might meet on Sainte-Catherine.

That I would *never* go to Montreal again I was certain; that much of my life I could control. Why invite trouble? So I told my daughter I wouldn't visit her at McGill, not even to get her set up, and insisted she let me off the hook. *I will see you when you come home,* I said, cold as anything.

But then came moving day and my daughter kissing her dog goodbye and getting into the car with her sister and a metric ton of stuff—and, behind the steering wheel, her mother, who'd realized she had no choice. It had been an extraordinary summer and I had spent it enacting a transformation in my brain. I loved my girl, I realized, more than being stuck.

So my daughters and I squeezed ourselves between the pillows and pans and set off on a five-hour drive to the place I *would never visit again* with no line of vision in the rear-view mirror. We bought an audiobook subscription and downloaded the first *Harry Potter* and listened when the Toronto stations started to fuzz. We played the alphabet game and sang musical theatre numbers, all the while closing in on this damnable destination. But I was forward-facing and thickened by 2,500 days of meditation.

It could be I was even at peace. If I didn't know precisely why he'd left, I felt sure now that *he had to*, that he wouldn't have *unless he did*. And that was a lot. I also knew why he kept silent, or at least had a plausible theory. It fed his sense of self; it gave him definition. I don't know him anymore, but when I did, Sam was a man of conviction so fierce it sometimes exceeded common sense. I believe he keeps his mouth shut because he thinks, if he opens it, his soul will pour out and he'll be left empty. Me, I open my mouth all the time, still talking to him when I feel stirred to. It feeds *my* sense of self, gives *me* definition. We're just different people is all; we take different approaches to endings and things.

Once, Sam told me that his friend Phil, just out of a long marriage, was buying a house with his new girlfriend, and he clucked at how foolish Phil was being. It's too soon, he'd said, he's just going to repeat his mistakes. It really rankled Sam's sensible soul. But I told him, *Who cares? It's what he wants. Let the chips fall.*

"I wish you could stop talking yourself out of me," I wrote him in that long-ago McDonald's letter. "What if I crash my van into a guardrail tomorrow and die in a fiery instant? Would you love your next partner with the abandon of someone who's learned that all the prudence in the world is no match for the heart?"

Certainly I had learned this, and I packed its lesson into the Honda with my daughters and *Harry Potter* on that late summer day we gained on an impossible scenario that provoked phenomenological fascination: the possibility of seeing the impossible through.

I grew concerned at the border. Now the road signs and licence plates were French and that was a blow. I remembered how exalted they used to make me feel. Part of a private club. I'd come home from my Montreal weekends and hold court with girlfriends about my exotic other life with my lover in Montreal where everything was so *French*.

But it was more than the signs and cars that spiked my senses now we were in Quebec. The light was different; there was something fantastic inside it. I let it fill me fearlessly, and we climbed onto the Autoroute 20, where I saw stores and street names that had been part of my movie. *He's here*, I thought, and started looking in the windows of the cars we passed. We crossed over the airport and train station, the sunset flaring the windshields of all the traffic stuck in construction, and the memories roared: Sam and I starting or ending a weekend, filled with elation or melancholy, always an extreme, always with music.

I wonder what he thinks when his eyes catch on our landmarks now. I wonder what he does when he passes the train station or watches a plane take off. I wonder if he even reads my emails and texts, the river I've sent over the months and years, and I wonder how they make him feel. If he lets my emotion reach him or he's built a dam. All these years since I knew this man so well; now I wonder who he is. Amazing how life goes.

I'd been in Montreal a few hours when I left my daughters to visit Tanya. That had always been part of the plan for this excursion. But driving through Sam's neighbourhood had not—I'd somehow imagined reaching his sister's house from the other direction. But suddenly there was *our* grocery store and the roads we would cross. The dépanneur and massage parlour across the street. I saw Amir, where we'd get shish taouk on Friday nights. The strip club and sports bar that shared a parking lot. The diner where we'd eat Saturday breakfast: bacon and eggs, no beans, extra fruit. My head spun, taking in the sights, this source of long-ago pleasure and that, all of them survivors while I had perished. It was awful, this tour. Out there on Sherbrooke Street, dodging our ghosts, enduring our mortal memory, it occurred to me that I might just expire, the victim of crushing emotion.

But by then I was committed to this perilous odyssey, and so drove right up to his apartment and stopped outside. Stared in. Couldn't believe my eyes. There we were, a lifetime ago, bounding those concrete steps like ballers, owning the world. I had not seen his apartment since the last time I'd alighted from it, on my last visit, two weeks before he left me in Toronto, likely hauling bags and gloom, bound for home, dumb to the day's significance.

But now, all these years later, I was parked outside this museum of my youth and ecstasies, looking at the scene hard. The red brick and hedges and brightly lit foyer. And me inside its memories, as persuasive as the mailboxes. I mourned the loveliness of that ignorant youth, but knew I was her superior. What a thing to overlay my latest version on something so perfectly preserved, and to see in the register all these new shadows and lights.

I pulled away at last, terrified and excited by the possibility of his backlit appearance at those glass doors. After, when he didn't appear and I'd visited Tanya and returned to my daughter's new apartment, we went to the Saint-Henri supermarket, my girls and I, an unexceptional errand in such exceptional circumstances, and I kept my head up in case a familiar face passed, my heart hammering harder down every aisle. But I knew it was *our* supermarket now, mine and my daughters', including my eldest, who would move there a week later—*our* city.

Everything would be repainted.

After all, so much of me already had been. When he left, I'd had children who lived in my house; now I have adults who live in their own, including two in Montreal, whom he might meet at a park and make good on an offer. When he left, he messaged all my kids to say he would miss them. "You guys can come to me anytime in your life," he'd said. I remember how these notes stung me, how I wished he'd extended the same access to me.

But now I was repainting. I was stroking new colours across the lot of it, till every place was redone.

Halfway home and trailing pigment, my daughter and I pulled off the highway for dinner, and I was shocked to discover myself outside the Toronto–Montreal midpoint motel where Sam and I had had our first date. *It was here,* I told my daughter, slowing in the parking lot where he'd walked toward me, one hand on my open trunk, my face split in a smile. I saw the square of asphalt that had braced our launch. I drove around the back to our room, where we'd put our wine bottles to chill outside in the November air. The door was open wide and a guy in a ten-gallon hat was, strangely, sitting in the threshold we'd crossed that first night, drinking a beer. Next, I cruised past the chicken joint across the street where we'd hobbled, drunk with discovery, from our maiden hotel bed. I peered into the window and found us there eating our first meal together, amazed by each other.

Further into the same pandemic, I returned to Montreal to pick up my youngest daughter and bring her home, and this was a trip that proved dangerous and revealing. The drive from Toronto was endless, my tires solo-spinning across the highway toward a place that used to thrill me, and all the while a clot was forming in my leg and travelling in my blood to my brain. Then, as I got under Montreal's sky and let it infect my emotions with sorrow and memory, intense waves of dizziness washed over me and I lost control of my left side. I was with my daughter by then and she drove me to the hospital. I had had a stroke in Montreal, the doctors said. And when they looked closer, they discovered why this blood clot had been able to surge from the bottom of my body to the top in that infected city, how it had navigated the wall between my left and right atria. There was a hole in my heart, they told me, peering at images captured inside an MRI hull and then wheeling around to report their conclusion: my heart was broken, they said. This pounding return to ground zero had exposed it.

There was a hospital stay, and a period of mild alarm while my family digested the news. But at last I drove off, back toward Toronto with my daughter, leaving behind a new tragedy and an old city I'd adored and sworn off and repainted.

My love story had been with Montreal as much as with Sam, and I'd held that town—for a half-dozen years a site of such reliable, exotic pleasure—accountable for my ordeal, to some extent, like she could have made a case to the man who dismissed me. But now I saw she was no more culpable than the rest of us.

Narrative therapy, developed in the 1980s by Michael White and David Epston, draws on the work of French philosophers Jacques Derrida and Michel Foucault in its rejection of an "objective reality." Our self-narrative helps us organize and maintain our own realities, and if we subscribe to an adverse one, White and Epston theorized, it could have a profoundly negative impact on our quality of life. But by telling ourselves a different, more positive story—which we're free to in the absence of a universal truth—we can rewrite our narrative with ourselves as hero, not victim. Also known as "re-authoring" or "re-storying," this branch of therapy capitalizes on humans' fondness for identity-asserting storytelling with an edit that renders the story more pleasing. More than "thinking posi-tive," this is a specific technique for people to develop life-affirming stories.

Eight years out, I've told a lot of stories of my heartbreak. As an inevitability, for example. A relief, even, for its salvation from potentially monotonous or bitter years together. In my rewritten narrative, the six years we had are a gift and I'm grateful I got them. Where I used to choose "to never have loved" over "to have loved and lost," now I know it's better to have had him than not. So six years was all we got. Some relationships get fifteen or forty-four before busting up, often in resentment or pain. I got six—you get what you get. And there are other measures than time for assessing a love.

Besides, what if it's not the love but *the longing for it* that's the thing? That's the question my story, with its deficits rewrit-ten as gains, would pose. What if, as María Elena said in *Vicky Cristina Barcelona*, "only unfulfilled love can be romantic"? So long as the idea's an aspiration, the fact of its unfeasibility doesn't figure. "As a climax is reached, it turns immediately into an anti-climax," Semir Zeki, a British neurobiologist keen on the neural correlates of love, said in 2009. "My love dies when I'm together with you, and comes to life when we separate," classical Arabic love poet Jamil Buthayna wrote, as referenced by German orientalist Hellmut Ritter in *The Ocean of the Soul*. Ritter also quotes Moroccan Sufi Abd al Aziz al-Dabbagh, who wrote of Majnun berating his coveted lover Layla when she appears before him thus: "Be gone from me! Love for you so engages me that I have no time for you!"

In my rewritten narrative, this side of the zenith, where

unrequited love's eternal climb keeps it immaculate and its unattainability is its pounding attraction, is the better one to be on. Here, possible years of grinding irritation and disappointment are swapped for an experience that expanded me—an experience that's as emotionally intense as a relationship, in point of fact, so meets my preference for a high-frequency life. An experience that left a beautiful oasis of thought behind: this pristine preoccupation with a man whose enduring memory enriches me still. In this iteration, Sam is unsullied by slights and irritations, preserved in the dream catcher he got me after Cuba.

So many nights I sit in the boozy company of candlelit peers decrying the *hopelessness of it all* and think of Sam, whose only appearance these eight years has been in my spotless memory—and let it feed me. Here, the rigid *reminiscence* of an extraordinary relationship is more rewarding than its potentially sagging *reality*. Love that's unrequited is still love, if you adjust the lighting a little. Could be this stage of heartbreak—a drifting notion in a perfect sky, thrillingly outside the humdrum, its players always having the time of their lives—is the ultimate stage.

One out of two ain't bad.

Eight years since we ended and I still believe it was the real thing, that what we had was fairy-dusted and that we were lucky. It was a singular experience. *Sui generis.* I've only ever known it with him. It didn't evolve, people used to cluck at our perpetually long-distance arrangement. But our relationship started with intense romance and stayed there. Why would we want it to evolve? The stage after intense romance is not celebrated for its ascent.

So we broke, still way up there in the clouds. But now, when I tell myself this story, it's with a revised bias. "Everyone forgets that Icarus also flew," Jack Gilbert writes in "Failing and Flying," a poem with a different take on a relationship's demise. "I believe Icarus was not failing as he fell, / but just coming to the end of his triumph." It's simply a question of "re-authoring" it. Now, when I spend time with Sam in my head, wandering among our memories, wondering at the current version of him, marvelling at the miracle of my ordeal, it satisfies me some, makes the story of my heartbreak a little easier to tell.

Author's Note

There are a couple of areas of indulgence I'd like to beg of *Heartbroken* readers. They are special considerations for a handful of choices I've made in my writing. But they are the thin exceptions to a meticulously researched and scrupulously accurate project. The fat bulk of this book asks nothing of its reader but engagement.

Heartbroken employs a hybrid style, with memoir as the ribbon that spools my contemplation of the characteristics and considerations of the mortal tragedy of heartbreak, and elevated research as the fabric. The personal threads of this book are sewn into a wide range of material that draws deeply from academic sources: social science. Psychology and physiology. History and philosophy. There is a profusion of literary allusion, wherein my fondness for poetry gets play. And through it all: rigorous investigation.

But density of research needn't translate into density of presentation. So while I stitched it into the textile, let it thicken the weave, my aim was always to keep the material pretty.

Which brings us to the first indulgence. Frequently, when I draw conclusions in my reflections on the psychological implications of rejection, say, or on the biological underpinnings of romantic love, I draw them from published scientific material. But including the full gamut of this material's cited mention—the study title, lead author's name, journal of record and explanation of research context—would be cumbersome. That level of detail, inevitably presented as inelegant bullets of official data, would interrupt the narrative smoothness I have worked to cultivate in this sometimes erudite account of an emotional subject. It would do so both for its volume and for the inherent clunkiness of its convention.

And so, while my sources are always attributed and information always verified, I have mostly chosen to snip the threads of scholarly citations rather than leave their trails everywhere. And I have employed various versions of "many scientists say" and "lots of studies have found" to convey consensus on facts so widely accepted that citing one source would unintentionally devalue others.

With that choice comes an application to the reader for a certain amount of faith. Because while the prose is not crowded with the specifics of my investigative discoveries, I hope the fact of them is implicit. I am a journalist and always have been. My lifelong professional interest has long been trained on thorough and accurate reporting; this commitment follows through to this book. And so I ask for the reader's confidence in my assiduous research in exchange for what I hope is the pleasure of an economy of words.

And while I'm making one application for special consideration, here is another, this for the vicissitudes of that most unreliable of human faculties: memory. Let me say that I have, as much as possible, included original source material in the memoir pieces of *Heartbroken*: letters, emails, inscriptions in books, texts, social media conversations and a sad string of greeting cards that passed between Sam and me, his erstwhile love, over the course of our six years together. And so I have quoted Sam only when the words came from his own mouth, and never imagined a conversation or guessed at a typical thing he might say. I have not re-created any dialogue (except briefly, on a handful of occasions when things said were pointed and memorable) or taken any creative liberties with the scenes I describe. I have not altered any details of the characters of my story. The encounter with the psychic was recorded.

I also should say that my memoir research—and my confidence therein—was much fortified by my access to the modern memoirist's most useful tool, which is Street View, a Google Maps feature that offered me 360-degree panoramic street-level views of Montreal, New Orleans, Mijas, Barcelona, Amsterdam. Thanks to this innovation, I was able to wander the neighbourhoods of these cities carefully, marking the whitewashed courtyard where we ate our anniversary meal in Málaga, the glowing purple windows of Amsterdam's De Wallen, the snow-stacked balconies of my beloved Montreal. It's a tool that enhanced not only the veracity of my material but the emotional immediacy with which I was able to present it.

I thought long and hard about whether to change the name of the man at the heart of this book. Certainly I wrote the entire manuscript using his real name; otherwise, I wouldn't have the proximity that was so critical to describing the emotions of our interactions. I only ever intended to use his first name in publication, and thought for a long time that would be okay, that it would extend him anonymity enough. And I liked the authenticity of everybody appearing in their true character—again, an instinctive by-product of journalistic rigour that always seeks in-the-eye attribution.

But I eventually balked and assigned him a pseudonym. It makes me sad to see this person I knew so well and love so deeply represented by this random name, which isn't him at all. But it is always the memoirist's peace to seek regarding stories she writes about other people that intersect with her own. And this is what I eventually landed on for my peace. This is *my* book, after all, not his. I guess he can use his real name if he wants to write one too.

But the rest of the memoir section is dredged from the deepest recesses of my grey matter. While I have described my scenes only with detail about which I feel confident, I know that confidence is not invincible. I worry a little, for example, about my descriptions of our time in New Orleans. We visited that city many times, and there's every possibility I've conflated some aspects of the experiences. Did I eat jambalaya at the Gumbo Shop on the first visit there or the third? Same thing with Mont-Tremblant, where we went so often. I simply can't say for certain on which of our visits we encountered the fawns by the beach or had poutine in the village. But it was during one of them—I hope that's enough.

Still, I bristle at even that concession. As I do when I read Author's Notes seeking readers' buy-in on composite characters or imagined conversations a writer has taken the liberty of creating for convenience, no matter the vigour of their reassurance that their inventions are *accurate enough*. It is my sincere desire, always, to be as true with my information as I possibly can be. I trust that the reader, having allowed me these minor literary indulgences, will take me at my word.

Acknowledgements

It feels like I've been working on this book for so long that the story of my heartbreak exceeds the story of my romance, which I suppose it does. Which I suppose is the point. I have lots of people to thank for *Heartbroken*'s existence. It started at the University of King's College, under the auspices of an MFA in creative nonfiction and the guidance of so many smart, sentient mentors and fellow writers and administrators. My time in Halifax with this powerful crew was profound and foundational—I wish to express huge and grateful thanks to these invested souls for helping me find my voice and trust the value of my story. And at least as much gratitude to my dear family, who have always been there, especially my steadfast parents and my four extraordinary children, Kenya, Malindi, Finn and Kaikoura. And thanks to my friends, who endured my heartbreak twice—in real time and in its retelling. You guys are pretty fantastic and I am lucky to have you in my life. I am lucky, too, for the professionals with whom I make a literary team, including my tack-sharp agents, Kathryn Willms and Sam Hiyate, and my brilliant, sympathetic editor, Deirdre Molina. Finally, I feel I should thank my erstwhile love, as unorthodox as that may seem. Without him, after all, I wouldn't have known the ecstasy *or* the agony, and so wouldn't have had my humanity expanded in either direction—or have had the opportunity to write about it. I miss you so much.

Permissions Credits

Grateful acknowledgement is made for permission to reprint from the following:

David Whyte, *Heartbreak*, from *Consolations*. © 2014, David Whyte. Excerpt reprinted with permission from Many Rivers Press, Langley, WA. www.davidwhyte.com

Patti Smith, from *Just Kids*. © 2010, Patti Smith. Excerpt reprinted with permission from HarperCollins Publishers, New York.

Edna St. Vincent Millay, excerpt from "Dirge Without Music" from Collected Poems. Copyright 1928, © 1955 by Edna St. Vincent Millay and Norma Millay Ellis. Reprinted with the permission of The Permissions Company, LLC on behalf of Holly Peppe, Literary Executor, The Edna St. Vincent Millay Society. www.millay.org.

"River"; Words and Music by Joni Mitchell; Copyright © 1971 Crazy Crow Music; Copyright Renewed; All Rights Administered by Reservoir Media Management, Inc.; All Rights Reserved; Used by Permission; Reprinted by Permission of Hal Leonard LLC.

LAURA PRATT is a long-time journalist, writer and editor. She writes for Canadian magazines, and edits books. Her first memoir is called *The Fleeting Years*. She lives in Toronto with whichever of her kids and dogs she can corral to join her. She's a graduate of the University of King's College's creative nonfiction MFA. She won an honourable mention in *Prairie Fire*'s CNF contest and was shortlisted for *Fiddlehead*'s CNF contest. She has served as a judge at the National Magazine Awards for several years.

www.laurapratt.ca
@LauraPratt33